ALSO BY MELODY BEATTIE

Gratitude

The Grief Club

52 Weeks of Conscious Contact

The Language of Letting Go Journal

Choices

More Language of Letting Go

Playing It by Heart

Finding Your Way Home

Stop Being Mean to Yourself

Journey to the Heart

Lessons of Love

Codependents' Guide to the Twelve Steps

The Language of Letting Go

Beyond Codependency

Codependent No More

The New Codependency

HELP AND GUIDANCE FOR TODAY'S GENERATION

Melody Beattie

SIMON & SCHUSTER PAPERBACKS
New York   London   Toronto   Sydney

The names and details about some individuals have been changed.

Simon & Schuster Paperbacks
1230 Avenue of the Americas
New York, NY 10020

First Simon & Schuster trade paperback edition January 2010

SIMON & SCHUSTER PAPERBACKS and colophon are registered trademarks
of Simon & Schuster, Inc.

For information about special discounts for bulk purchases,
please contact Simon & Schuster Special Sales at 1-866-506-1949
or business@simonandschuster.com.

The Simon & Schuster Speakers Bureau can bring authors to your live event.
For more information or to book an event, contact the Simon & Schuster
Speakers Bureau at 1-866-248-3049 or visit our website at
www.simonspeakers.com.

Designed by C. Linda Dingler

Manufactured in the United States of America

10   9   8   7   6   5   4   3   2   1

The Library of Congress has cataloged the hardcover edition as follows:

Beattie, Melody.
    The new codependency : help and guidance for today's generation /
Melody Beattie.
        p.   cm.
    1. Codependency.   2. Self-care, Health.   I. Title.
RC569.5.C63B436 2009
616.86'9—dc22   2008042271

ISBN 978-1-4391-0192-6
ISBN 978-1-4391-0214-5 (pbk)
ISBN 978-1-4391-1769-9 (ebook)

ACKNOWLEDGMENTS

Thanks to God, who keeps me writing;
Thanks to my mom, who in her passing helped us both
discover love for each other;
and
A special thanks to Jim and Pam Lee—
my brother and sister-in-law—
who stepped in and made it possible for me
to write this book. I finally found my brother.

FOR

- People affected by someone's alcoholism, addiction, illness, compulsions, hurtful or irresponsible behaviors, including anger management issues, rage, and abuse;
- Double Winners—Alcoholics or Addicts with codependency underneath—especially those addicts and alcoholics who need to forgive themselves for having this disease;
- People legitimately caretaking anyone—parent, child, or ill spouse—who need to remember to take care of themselves, too;
- Adult and Teenage Children of Alcoholics, Addicts, and parents whose problem affected (and still affects) us;
- People codependent on codependents;
- Classic codependents who want more information, peace, and power and are ready for an upgrade to *Codependent No More;*
- Men, women, and children who have been sexually, physically, or emotionally abused;
- People who turned an idea (codependency recovery) intended to free us into another set of repressive, fundamentalist rules;

- People who need to attend meetings all their lives. For them, codependency can be fatal. As one woman said, "I'll die if I stop attending groups. That's how badly codependency affects me."
- People who need to go to groups for a while;
- People who hate the word *codependency* and don't need to go to groups or therapy at all;
- People affected by mutated codependency—survival behaviors that have adapted to the changing world. It's easier to take antidepressants and antianxiety drugs to mask codependency's emotions and depression than it is to deal with feelings and get to the core of the problem, but it won't bring us what we're seeking.
- The New Codependents—people who need help taking care of themselves in a changed world whether they choose to identify as codependent or not;
- The new me. I dedicated *Codependent No More* to me because healing from it saved my life, but I still felt alone. After twenty years of learning to set limits and take care of myself, I know that Oneness isn't a cliché. It's a codependent illusion. It's impossible to be alone when we know how connected we are to God, other people, and Life. That's why *this* book is dedicated to "Us."

CONTENTS

SECTION THREE
Making a Conscious Connection with Yourself

SECTION FOUR
Catch and Release: It's Only a Feeling

SECTION FIVE

Troubleshooting Guide

The New Codependency

Crossing Lines and Getting Back over Them Again

1 • Taking Care of Ourselves

I know what it's like to lose yourself so badly that you don't know if there's a *you* or ever was one. I spent thirty years not knowing what boundaries were and another ten learning to set them. I gave until I was depleted and needed someone to take care of me. I threatened, begged, hinted, and manipulated to get what I wanted. I was convinced that I knew what was best for other people. I got so busy teaching them their lessons that I forgot to learn mine.

Within minutes of meeting a man, I was sure I'd met my soul mate. A few hours later, I'd fantasize about the wedding. That's how it happened on television. Isn't that how it happened in life? I'd spend two years trying to get into a relationship, and the next five trapped, clawing my way out. I obsessed until my head ached. Literally, it hurt. I didn't know what feelings were. Whenever I said I felt something, people said, "Don't feel that!"

Like millions of other women and men, I was victimized as a child. Instead of holding the perpetrators responsible, I blamed myself. *There's something wrong with me,* I thought. I didn't see the bad things that happened to me happening to anyone else. Feeling like we caused the problem is a legitimate stage of grief. Feeling ashamed is normal when we've been abused. Blaming ourselves is a survival skill. It helps us feel in control when life doesn't make sense and being abused doesn't make any sense at all.

Besides, aren't women supposed to suffer? We sacrifice ourselves. I became a martyr. I thought taking care of other people was my job. If I took care of them, I hoped they'd return the favor and take care of me. But that didn't happen. People expected me to take care of them once I started that pattern. There were many reasons I didn't take care of myself. The word *no* wasn't in my vocabulary. Good people were selfless. Loving myself was out of the question. Selfish! But the biggest reason I didn't take care of myself is that I didn't know how to.

Many of us didn't (or don't) know about self-care. It wasn't written about in books or talked about in school. We get user manuals for simple products, but we don't get a handbook for life. We stumble through complex situations, figuring things out for ourselves. Controlling and taking care of others—the entire package of codependent behaviors—become survival tools, living skills that we think will keep us safe. Then one day these behaviors turn on us. Our relationships and lives stop working and we don't know why. By then these survival behaviors are habits. They're all we know how to do.

If I had the years back I spent worrying about how the things I couldn't control were going to turn out, I'd have a third of my life to live over. That would be a life in which I wouldn't feel responsible for everyone or feel guilty all the time. I wouldn't waste energy controlling, enabling, and obsessively rescuing people—the "helpful" things codependents do that don't really help. I'd let people take care of their responsibilities and I'd take care of mine. I wouldn't let people hurt me. I'd set boundaries—say *no*. I wouldn't do only what other people wanted me to do; I'd do what I wanted, too. This time my giving would come from my heart, and my helping would actually help. I wouldn't judge everything that happened as wrong, including what I did, said, thought, and felt. I'd let life unfold, people be who they are, and I'd let myself be me. This time, I'd have the courage to experience true love.

I'd trust my intuition. If something didn't feel right, I'd know it probably wasn't. If I felt sad, I'd cry. If I felt angry, I'd feel that. I wouldn't ignore emotions until I imploded in illness or exploded in rage. I'd get out of my head and into my heart. I'd deal with my and others' feelings without all the drama; as much as possible I'd handle uncomfortable situations with diplomacy and tact. I wouldn't feel obligated and trapped. I'd know I had choices— whether that means choosing attitude, gratitude, meditation, or prayer. Instead of protecting myself with fierce independence, I'd ask for help. I wouldn't be controlled by people and external events. My control center would be where it belongs—in me. I wouldn't let other people's approval determine whether or not I approved of myself. I'd be energized by nature, God, and Life. I wouldn't drain other people, and I wouldn't let them drain me so much that my battery would die.

My relationships would be equal ones. I'd share power instead of one of us controlling and the other being controlled. I wouldn't have to create chaos to feel alive; I'd know I'm real. As one friend reminds me, instead of running headfirst into trouble, I'd go around it whenever I could (without resorting to denial). I know the value of peace. I'd create beauty, be of service, and have fun. I'd live and love at the same time. I'd admit my mistakes. But I'd also appreciate what I did well and let myself enjoy success.

This time I'd know what it means to love and take care of myself.

2 • How to Use This Handbook

To prepare for writing this handbook, I reread books I wrote years ago: *Codependent No More* (1985–86), *Beyond Codependency* (1988–89), *The Language of Letting Go* (1990), and *The Codependents' Guide to the Twelve Steps* (1990). I was surprised by how much I have changed. I barely recognized who I am now compared to who I was back then.

When I first wrote about codependency, I couldn't get the word past my computer's spell-checker. Most of the world didn't recognize the word yet either. For a book originally rejected by twenty publishers ("Nice idea," they said, "but there aren't enough codependents to make publishing the manuscript worthwhile"), *Codependent No More*—strictly by word of mouth—became a best-seller. It hit the lists and is still a backlist best-seller. My Beverly Hills internist read it as part of his medical training. It's part of many school and college curriculums. Therapists recommend it to patients. Thousands of people give it to family and friends. It's read in treatment centers, recovery groups, and by people around the world searching for how to make the pain from self-neglect stop. The subject of codependency and how to recover from it struck a universal nerve.

Naming that pain was like discovering fire—a fire that people still discover each month as thousands begin the journey we started back then.

"We're part of a groundswell movement that's come into its own time," I wrote in *Beyond Codependency*. "Media and public attention may subside. But recovery from codependency is more than a fad. We started the journey of self-care and self-love. We're not stopping now."

Those words were prophetic. Concepts such as letting go, detachment, setting boundaries, and self-care mainstreamed. They worked their way into the culture. Ideas previously unknown or talked about only by small groups of recovering people are now discussed almost anywhere, from coffee shops to TV. Ideas that originated with the codependency recovery movement are now how millions of people—whether or not they're in recovery—live.

Four of the fourteen books I've written are devoted to codependency. I didn't think I'd ever say this, but those four aren't enough. I'm writing this book to clarify confusion, discuss new information, write about how codependency has mutated, address new support options, and remind us about what we learned.

Although I've changed significantly since writing *Codependent No More*, I still step in codependent puddles. I might get hooked into someone's stuff, let their problems control me, over-engage, or start reacting instead of taking right action. I'll let family conditioning affect me, neglect to set boundaries, or shut down emotionally. There are times I have to slam on the brakes, STOP, and remember to take care of myself. I don't sink in quicksand like I used to, but sometimes I revert to survival mode. That's yesterday's news.

I don't call that *relapsing*. Caring about people we love, feeling victimized when we're betrayed, giving our all to people we love, or wanting to control people because we're watching them destroy themselves and hurt us doesn't mean we're sick. These are natural reactions. Codependency is about normal behaviors taken too far. It's about crossing lines.

This book is written for beginners and those further down the taking-care-of-themselves road. It offers practical help for people recovering from chemical dependency when they bottom out from codependency, usually after being sober anywhere from seven to ten years. The seven-year mark for recovering alcoholics and addicts is a widely accepted but unofficial recovery rule of thumb. After people stop drinking, they discover there are many things other than alcohol and drugs that they can't control, a rite of passage that could be dubbed "the Second Great Surrender." We let go of all illusions of control.

I also wrote this book for people who want to learn more about behaviors such as setting boundaries or dealing with feelings, but who don't want or need to go to treatment, therapy, or attend recovery groups. You don't have to label yourself codependent and embark on a grand transformation to benefit from this book. Instead you can learn about specific behaviors that will help you take better care of yourself. This book complements my other writing, but the material in here is fresh. This is an upgrade, building on and enhancing the work I did before, like when Windows evolved from DOS. This book can be used with my other books or by itself.

The material is divided into sections, the sections into chunks. It's structured like a shopping mall directory. Locate the spot that says YOU ARE HERE and you'll see how to get where you're going next. Section Two—Breaking Free from the Control Trap and Getting Some Grace—offers alternatives to codependent behaviors. Section Three—Making a Conscious Connection with Yourself—will help you create an emotional profile. Section Four, Catch and Release—It's Only a Feeling, is about maintaining emotional health. Section Five is a trouble-shooting guide, offering suggestions about what to do when specific aggravating situations occur. At the end of the book, you'll find an easy way to locate almost any kind of assistance available. But by the time you finish this book, I hope you'll know that Life will bring you what you need.

You won't find a long list of dos and don'ts. It's not my job to tell you what to do. Self-love means trusting ourselves, not following someone else's rules. Although this is categorized as a self-help book, the "how-to" is in *you*.

Beginners can use the information and activities to go deeper into problem areas. It may help speed the learning curve, but growth has its own timetable. For others, sometimes a reminder is all we need, but there's still not always a quick fix. *Gray areas* and *being between a rock and a hard place* are more than clichés. They're real situations in people's lives. "My life hasn't been as seamless as it looks," a woman who is strong and admired by many said. Most of us find ourselves in tricky situations—those where the only way out is through. These situations can be confusing. We can't identify what's going on, so we don't know what to do. Sometimes the answer isn't doing something; it's letting ourselves.

Section Three consists of quizzes. This is a new addition to my previous work. It does more than break codependency down into behaviors and isolate what's causing the problem; it helps us look closely at the emotions underneath what we do. As a bonus, most of the quiz statements double as affirmations. A light will come on; you may get the answer you need just by taking a test. The book becomes part of the change process itself. Sometimes one moment of awareness does more than months of hard work. Identifying resistance or releasing a feeling can be all we need to set the healing process in motion. That's what happened to me. After years of denial, I finally felt safe enough to feel one feeling. In an instant, I immediately came into balance and started taking care of myself. Take the quizzes often—regularly and when you're stuck. You'll get different messages at different times, depending on what you need.

Once we relax and surrender, taking care of ourselves can become fun. But self-care is a full-time job. Sometimes it's hard work. Healing can dredge up painful memories, like cleaning an old wound. We may get turned upside down while our lives rearrange. Or we may need to start over again. Change can be uncomfortable, but so is staying the same. Sometimes we lose the people we love most. Life has its moments, and some of them hurt. But self-care still feels better than neglecting ourselves. Instead of calling this a workbook, how about thinking of it as an owner's manual for you and Life.

3 · What Codependency Is and Isn't

An acquaintance explained how much he enjoys being a husband and father. "I suppose that makes me codependent," he said, apologetically.

"No," I said. "It means you like being married."

When it comes to codependency, some people are confused.

They may associate codependency with rabbit-boiling *Fatal Attraction* behavior. Or they confuse codependency with psychosis, borderline personality, or obsessive-compulsive disorder. Some people think codependency doesn't have anything to do with them because nobody in their family drinks or they're not being abused. Or they think recovering from codependency or adult children of alcoholic issues means they get to blame their parents for everything they (the children) do.

Recovery isn't about pointing fingers; it's about taking responsibility for ourselves.

Some people call codependency a sign of the Me generation, another excuse for selfish people to continue putting themselves first. Some people believe (incorrectly) that recovering from codependency means they have to get a divorce. Or they're afraid that codependency recovery behaviors will conflict with their religious beliefs. Others think detachment means becoming cold and uncaring. Those are misconceptions that don't come close to what being healthy and functional means. Or, like my friend, people mistakenly believe codependency means enjoying marriage, which couldn't be further from the truth.

I understand the confusion. I devoted an entire chapter to defining codependency in *Codependent No More* and classifying it is still challenging. People often define it by the behaviors they engage in. "Codependency is being a caretaker." "It means being married to an alcoholic." "I cling to people, glob onto them." "I walk into a room and am immediately attracted to the sickest person in it." While these can signal codependency, they are only part of what codependency is. It's not so much what we do as why we're doing it.

In *Codependent No More*, I defined a codependent person as "one who has let another person's behavior affect him or her, and who is obsessed with controlling that person's behavior." But codependency is still about more than that (although controlling and obsessing are good places to start).

Years after writing *Codependent No More*, I was haunted by the fear that loving myself would make me lazy and self-indulgent. It took a long time to know that appreciating myself is motivating.

"It's not what we don't know that hurts us," people say. "It's what we believe is true that isn't that does the damage."

There's a difference between loving someone and being trapped in a miserable marriage. There's a difference between giving to get someone to like us, which leaves us resentful, and giving from heartfelt generosity. There's a difference between enabling someone to drink and nurturing people we love, between narcissism and self-love, and between self-centeredness and staying centered in ourselves.

While alcoholism in the family can help create codependency, it isn't essential. Some people call codependency a disease. But how do we know whether it's a disease or a problem? Does it help to call ourselves sick when we already suffer from low self worth? The behaviors associated with codependency make perfect sense if we look closely enough. It's understandable that we would confuse control with love when control is all we've known. It makes sense that we think controlling will keep us safe because it did—for a while. All codependent behaviors make sense if traced to their origins.

The behaviors associated with codependency—from controlling to caretaking—are behaviors that saved our lives when we didn't know what else to do. In most situations, whether alcoholism was involved or not, codependent behaviors are what anyone might do if he or she had walked for five or ten years in our shoes.

It's natural to hurt when we lose our marriage or to go crazy when we discover our daughter smokes crack. Many codependent behaviors—such as worrying or controlling—are what ordinary people do from time to time. But we get into trouble when these become behaviors we can't stop.

Codependency is normal behavior, plus. There are times we do too much, care too much, feel too little, or overly engage. We forget where the other person's responsibilities begin and our responsibilities stop. Or we get busy and have so much to do that we neglect ourselves.

Codependents may be smothering, clinging, and needy (they kill us with kindness and try to please us until we can't stand them). But on the brighter side, once they work through these issues, they can become outstanding people. Many use their experiences to become successful entrepreneurs. Studies show that people who grow up in troubled families handle stress significantly better than others; they keep going when people around them who had it easier fold.

Some professionals call people with codependency issues "overachievers," but that's demeaning. "They're super-achievers," one therapist said. That's kinder and more appropriate. Solving problems and possessing endurance (two positive codependency traits) are second nature to people who have already been through so much.

When we start taking care of ourselves, the deficits from our pasts transform into assets. Many people with codependency issues are loyal and dedicated. They get the job done. They obsess, but they also persevere. They want to help, and once they learn to help themselves, they usually do. Many become leaders, people who change our world.

Codependency is about crossing lines. How can we tell if what we're doing is codependent? When we cross the line into the Codependent Zone, we've usually got an ulterior motive for what we do, and what we're doing hurts. It doesn't work. This handbook will help us get back into our lives. Then we can choose behaviors that work for us.

It's easier to see what other people are doing than it is to see ourselves. That's a human trait and codependent behavior. Because codependent behaviors protected us, letting go of them can feel frightening at first. Are you willing to feel uncomfortable for a while?

4 • The New Codependency

"I was able to go to ninety meetings in ninety days when I began recovery. Now that's impossible," a woman wrote to me. "Many meetings have disbanded. Is codependency recovery disappearing?"

"Just the opposite," I replied. "In the beginning, we had Al-Anon groups [for people affected by a loved one's drinking]; ACOA [Adult Children of Alcoholics], and Co-DA [Codependents Anonymous meetings]. Now we can find support groups for caregivers of people with almost every problem—not just for the person who has the problem and not only when the other person's problem is a compulsive or addictive disorder. There are groups for people who love someone with cancer, Alzheimer's, spinal cord injuries, brain trauma. There are support groups for people with almost every problem we can name and the people who love and take care of them."

We even have Double Winner groups now, where people can work on addiction and codependency issues at the same meeting— something unheard of when Twelve-Step Groups began. We still have ACOA, Al-Anon, and Co-DA. We have Twelve-Step groups for people affected by many addictions from gambling to Debtors Anonymous to love and sex addiction.

People don't need to go through any situation alone, no matter what they face. Neither do the people who love them. People can even go on the Internet and attend a support group without leaving their homes. If we love someone with a problem, it's culturally accepted that we have a problem, too.

Codependency hasn't disappeared. It's wearing new faces and using different names.

Codependency has mutated in other ways. The first generation of recovering codependents had parents who endured the Great Depression, fought in World War I or II, or suffered horribly from the Holocaust. Many situations affected the parents of this first generation. Information about the problem wasn't in the consciousness yet; we didn't have a name for the problem or a solution. These first-generation codependents had martyrdom and deprivation embedded in their DNA. Their parents had been through a lot. But many second-generation codependents, born in the seventies or eighties, have parents who wanted to make sure their children had everything they (the parents) didn't get. Many second generation codependents are taking it a step further, attempting to protect their children from every problem and emotion. This creates codependents with the opposite of deprivation—a sense of over-entitlement, over-protection, and inflated self-esteem that often crosses the line into narcissism. They expect life to be easier than it is; they want everything done for them no matter how they behave. Then they become depressed and confused when they don't get what they believe they deserve. Although first, second, and third generation codependents have many traits in common, and not all new codependents have been coddled (many are still horribly abused), the new codependents are a different breed from the classic ones.

The New Codependency has changed, too.

Since codependent behaviors mainstreamed into the culture, many people have learned to be codependent under the radar. They understand that certain behaviors aren't appropriate or therapeutically correct so they hide what they're doing. It's easy to disguise obsessing now. People don't have to sit at home staring at the phone, waiting for him or her to call like codependents used to do. Instead of detaching, the new codependents leave the house, bringing their cell phones and obsessions with them. It's also easier now to mask the anxiety, grief, and depression that accompany codependency by taking medications that weren't around when codependency recovery began. While using medication is a personal choice, it's important not to take prescriptions to endure miserable situations or lose touch with who we are and what we need.

Codependency survival behaviors and the need to change them haven't disappeared. Ideas recycle every twenty, thirty, or hundred years. Codependency recovery is coming around again stronger than before. Young people are flooding Al-Anon meetings, and older people are attending groups to understand healthy caregiving. They're learning to take care of themselves, not just other people.

Culturally, scientifically, and spiritually we accept that we're not isolated beings or individuals functioning independently in the world. What affects one person also affects that person's loved ones, family members, coworkers, and friends. The Butterfly effect, a contemporary theory related to the work of Edward Lorenz and more recently popularized by the writer Ray Bradbury, illustrates this idea. It's a romantic theory about cause and effect that poses the question: If enough butterflies flapped their wings in one part of the world, could that flapping influence (along with other conditions) a tornado—or at least a draft—on the other side of the planet? It's similar to the domino theory—place the dominos in a row, push the first one, and watch the whole row topple.

What we do matters. Our behaviors, beliefs, and actions affect the people around us, just as our behavior and beliefs have been influenced by others—including ancestors we haven't met.

Choosing our actions instead of reacting can change the course of history or at least the course of our lives. Most professionals agree that detaching in love from an alcoholic creates an environment more conducive to that person becoming sober than nagging, screaming, and beating our chest in martyrdom.

James Redfield (*The Celestine Prophecy*) and Eckhart Tolle (*The Power of Now*) describe codependency recovery as one small but essential part of a paradigm shift. Initially when I heard people talk about a *paradigm shift*, I'd nod my head and agree. But I didn't have a clue what a paradigm was or what it meant when it moved. All I knew is that I had finally learned what it meant to take care of me. Years later, I learned a paradigm shift is *a different way of seeing ourselves and the world*.

Since I wrote *Codependent No More*, the way we see ourselves and the world has evolved. Teenagers know about boundaries and limits; five-year-old children talk about feelings. Not being abused is talked about by seventy-year-old women and men and by children in elementary school. That doesn't mean we're all taking care of ourselves. Far from it. That's an ideal. But we're learning more about loving ourselves.

We've gone through a paradigm shift about what it means to love other people, too. Just as we're instructed in an airplane (in the event of low cabin pressure) to put on our oxygen mask first before helping others, we know that taking care of ourselves helps us love people better. Taking care of ourselves isn't selfish—unless we cross the line and don't care about others at all. That's as un-healthy as helping too much.

Whether we're first-, second-, third-, or fourth-generation codependents, codependency isn't "one size fits all." Each of us needs to discover how codependency has affected us and what be-haviors we're doing that hurt.

5 • Letting Go of Stigma from the Label

At first the word *codependency* was a godsend. Hallelujah! We weren't crazy; we were codependent. The word and all it meant brought a sigh of relief to millions. "Now there's a stigma attached to identifying ourselves as codependent," a social worker said. I agree. There's more stigma attached to identifying as a codepen-dent than to saying we're an addict. We don't need to be embar-rassed or ashamed of any problem we have. But being clingy and needy just isn't attractive.

"Can I help you, ma'am?"

"Why, yes. I'm looking for something to make me stop control-ling, obsessing about, and stalking my ex-boyfriend. I drive by his house almost every evening. I call him when I get home. If he an-swers, I hang up. It's been years since our relationship ended. But you can't snap your fingers and make how you feel about someone disappear.

"It's not only that. People walk over me so much I have foot-prints on my face. I'm tired of being a victim, but I don't know how to stop. Besides I heard those codependency groups sit around blaming their parents. My childhood wasn't *that* bad. I don't even know any alcoholics, and I'd never let anyone hit me. I'm indepen-dent and have a good job, but I can't function unless I'm in love. The problem is, I don't have a life. Unless I'm taking care of someone, I don't know who I am. I get angry when people tell me to take care of myself. I take care of everyone. Isn't that enough? Would you happen to have a book for someone like that in stock?"

Codependency isn't a romantic problem. But the denial, obsession with what we lost, guilt, bargaining, controlling, anger, and sadness—if we look closely enough we'll see how similar codependency is to grief. Most people with codependency issues have lost a lot. We may not be aware of how much we have lost if we lost something we never had—like feeling safe, protected, and loved. All we know is that we feel incomplete. We cling to anyone we can, hoping we'll find our missing pieces in them.

"How do you feel about identifying yourself as a codependent?" I asked someone new to Al-Anon.

"It's repulsive and I hate it," she said, referring to the word *codependent.*

Be gentle with yourself. You're not psychotic. You're on the path to healing. I don't know your story, but if you look at yourself with eyes of love, you'll see that what you do makes perfect sense. If you've crossed the line into the Codependent Zone, the good news is you don't have to take on the stigma. You don't have to call yourself a codependent to stop doing behaviors that don't work.

Whether you like the word *codependent* or not, stopping the pain from it feels good.

I heard a powerful businesswoman describe her busy life. "Each week I take half an hour to do something to take care of myself," she proudly said.

Half an hour? I thought. *That's barely enough time to get started before it's time to stop.* Self-care runs deeper than that. Loving and taking care of ourselves are undercurrents in our lives.

It's safe to surrender control. We don't have to make anything happen, no matter what we're taught or believe. We're not alone, separate from people and God. We're one with Life and everyone and everything in it, but not in the clingy codependent way. Take a deep breath. Look around. When you let go of fear and the need to control, you'll experience how mysterious, sacred, and interesting Life can be.

If I had to reduce this book to five pages, I'd write about awareness, caretaking, control, letting go, gratitude, acceptance, surrender, boundaries, feelings, dropping the victim role forever, and how to love ourselves. If I had to reduce this book to four words, I'd write: Be who you are. If I had to shrink it even further, I'd use two words penned by the ancient sages: Know yourself.

Breaking Free from the Control Trap and Getting Some Grace

1 • The Evolving Art of Self-Care

WHO'S TEACHING US WHAT?

A woman told me about her son, now a healthy, grown man. He spent most of his teenage years addicted to drugs. He overdosed and almost died several times. "In the beginning, I went crazy reacting to him. I gave him so much to rebel against that he'd probably be dead if I hadn't learned to detach," she said. "He was my teacher about letting go."

This woman had learned to see painful situations—the ones we don't ask for, expect, or want—differently. We can look at the people hurting us as *teachers* or as *enemies*. The most painful circumstances can become important parts of our destiny, or we can call them mistakes.

I learned about letting go when I unknowingly married an alcoholic. For seven years, I drove myself and everyone around me crazy obsessing about and trying to control my husband's drinking. After wearing myself out trying to make the situation be

19

anything other than what it was, I realized the lesson wasn't about changing him. It was surrendering to who I am and what was.

My husband's drinking didn't create my codependency. I'd been doing the behaviors his drinking triggered—controlling, taking care of others and neglecting myself, repressing emotions, feeling victimized—most of my life. His drinking just made these behaviors worse. I couldn't hide from myself anymore. This experience was the first course in getting my Codependency Degree.

I naïvely thought that to solve this problem I'd have to let go, detach, and surrender once. Little did I know I'd be practicing these behaviors the rest of my life. I was only beginning to see how many things I couldn't control, and how whatever I tried to control, controlled me. As I learned more, I wanted to write a book about codependency. I wanted to make information available to people like me—people who couldn't stop what we were doing because we didn't have a clue what we were doing wrong. I hoped that by understanding codependency, we could eliminate the pain it caused. But that's not how Life works.

Reading about a problem is like reading a travel guide. We find suggestions about what to see, what to avoid, and other tips. But reading the book is different from taking the trip. That's also how it is with growth. Information is essential. Change is experiential.

We can have stacks of information about setting boundaries, but it still takes those confusing, hurtful situations to help us understand our limits. Reading encyclopedias about caretaking and control won't substitute for a drug-addicted son or an alcoholic wife teaching us about surrendering or letting go.

We don't learn about taking care of ourselves the way we learn math. Although information is useful and sometimes critical, self-care isn't only an intellectual process. It's our experiences that change us. In *The Tao of Pooh*, author Benjamin Hoff combines the characters from Winnie the Pooh with Buddhism. He wrote brilliantly simple stories about how Pooh, Piglet, and the rest of that group stumbled through life. They'd fall into a hole, and then learn something from it. They learned something from each experience they had. Somehow Life worked out in the end. That's how we grow. Life unfolds, naturally and organically, presenting us with situations that allow us to learn. We don't control the process. It changes us.

It's easy to let the words "Take care of yourself and stop being a victim" roll off our tongues when people talk about their pain. But exactly how to take care of ourselves can be confusing, whether we're just beginning self-care or we've been doing it for years. Just when we think we have Life down pat, it shifts 180 degrees. What we did last year might not work today. Maybe we're meant to do something else. What we need to do today can be the opposite of what we did in a similar situation last week. Confronting someone might be ideal in one situation but inappropriate in another. Taking care of ourselves can't be reduced to a list of rules. Don't let anyone tell you it can.

Self-care is a constantly changing, evolving art. It requires awareness, presence, self-love, and authentic interaction each moment with Life. We have common problems: a chemically dependent child; an alcoholic parent; a series of disastrous relationships; betrayal by people we trust; exhaustion from taking care of a sick or dying parent or spouse. But we're each unique. To borrow a phrase from a friend: *No two moments in time are alike.* Neither are any two people. The basic self-care behaviors are the same, but exactly how and when to apply them can be different, depending on each situation.

Exactly what you need to do to take care of yourself is your decision. You're the guru. Your answers are between you and your Higher Power. I'm a tour guide—suggesting options, saying "Look at that" or "Watch out." Your behaviors are your choice. My job is to remind you that you can trust your Source, and you can take care of yourself no matter what you're going through.

This book offers a different spin on the saying "When the student is ready, the teacher appears." Your teachers are the people and circumstances already there, usually the experiences that hurt and the people we want to change. Some teachers are obvious—counselors, therapists, sponsors—but many aren't so easy to spot.

"What's next?" a literary agent asked after *Codependent No More* came out.

I couldn't answer because I didn't know. Decades later, I understood. That wasn't a question. It's a Zen riddle. *What's next* is whatever Life is teaching us, and it's not next—it's always now.

Can you see that person driving you crazy or that painful circumstance in a new light—as a teacher or class helping you get your master's or Ph.D.—instead of writing it off as another mistake or victimization?

What's that sound? Is it a bell ringing, announcing that class is about to begin? I don't know what you're learning, but you'll know soon. Do what you can to solve the problem, but don't get sucked into trying to control something that you can't. On the other hand, don't worry. If you do try to control, there'll be a lesson there, too. I'm not going to tell you, *Live one day at a time.* We can constantly live today waiting for tomorrow to come and still miss all today's moments—one day at a time. This new way of life is like breathing. We can't ever get ahead. We only get breath—and Grace—for the moment we're in now.

✑ ACTIVITIES

1. Identify your teacher(s) and some lessons you've learned. How did you feel at first? When did you realize that life was transforming you? How did it feel when you surrendered to the "class"? Are you learning something now? Can you identify who your teachers are? Don't worry if you don't know what you're learning. It's okay if you don't know. We often learn best when we're caught off guard.

2. Practice gratitude. Expressing gratitude is a powerful practice. It transforms (or helps neutralize) painful events. That doesn't mean saying "thank you" only for receiving something good, although that's part of it. This activity is about practicing gratitude for everything, as is. Some situations may be too much to express gratitude for or accept all at once (or maybe ever). But we can turn almost any experience around by practicing gratitude for what we experience or feel each moment, especially the moments we don't like. If we're grateful for what we label good, we'll only be grateful a few times each week. Please don't twist yourself into a pretzel trying to intellectualize how something may "work out for good" so you can be grateful for that. That's trying to predict how Life will evolve.

Each morning (or as soon as possible), write the top ten feelings or events bothering, upsetting, or confusing you. Write that you're grateful for those feelings or events—even if you're not. Write your gratitude list in a notebook, send yourself an email, or write a letter to God. Include gratitude for what you enjoy, the blessings, the good experiences, too. It's important to say thank you for our gifts. But you also have to fake, force, and will gratitude—write "I AM grateful for: _____," whether you're grateful or not. It's not lying. It's a spiritual practice and acting as if.

Be as honest as you can about how you feel. You can write, *Today I am grateful for: the way my true friends uphold and love me; the emptiness inside; feeling like a failure; someone I love betraying me; someone I trusted lying about me; or friends gossiping about me behind my back.* Write ten things—good, bad, and in-between—that are in the forefront of your mind. Instead of feeling lost, numb, or confused, we'll become conscious, aware, and alive. If you're going through a tragedy, I'm not suggesting you practice gratitude for that. You're in deep grief and right now you're learning something else.

This exercise helps us understand that each moment is perfect, as it is. Awareness leads to acceptance. Acceptance takes us to surrender. Surrender brings power and peace.

2 • Boundaries

WHEN:

- we're done saying "yes" when we mean "no";
- hurtful, disrespectful behavior must stop;
- we're ready to say how we feel, whether people want to hear it or not;
- we're willing to part ways unless we have equal rights in relationships that became one-way streets;
- we're ready to let people feel awkward by reminding them they didn't pay back money they borrowed instead of us feeling awkward when we didn't do anything wrong;
- we can't stand what's happening;
- we're done letting someone drive us crazy;
- the pain of living without someone is less than the pain caused by living with the person;
- we'll go to court instead of allowing injustice to occur;
- we want to stop doing something but people want us to continue, or we want to start (or continue) doing something, but people don't want us to do that;

It's boundary-setting time.

When I'd say, "I wish I could buy boxes of boundaries—I'd take four," in my talks after writing *Codependent No More*, people laughed and cheered. The word *boundaries* as it applies to personal limits was only now entering our vocabularies. I didn't know much about boundaries yet. Many people didn't either.

Boundaries aren't something we just "get." They come from inside of us as honest expressions of who we are. At first setting limits is hard, but it becomes easier with practice and time. We open our mouths and say what we mean instead of saying what we think people want to hear.

Boundaries are the limits of love.

TO SET BOUNDARIES, SAY:
- what we'll do if people don't stop treating us a particular way;
- what people can or can't do to or around us—in our space;
- how far we'll go for someone;
- how far other people can go with us;
- what we will and won't tolerate;
- "yes" when we mean it;
- "no" when that's our answer;
- "maybe" when we're unsure;
- what we will or won't do if people don't respect the boundaries we set.

Boundaries come from speaking our truth.

BOUNDARIES REQUIRE:
- self-awareness,
- self-love,
- honest communication,

- saying the hard stuff,
- aligning with or stepping into our power.

Limits can make or break relationships. They aren't only about how people treat us: boundaries are about how we treat them.

HAVING GOOD BOUNDARIES WITH PEOPLE INCLUDES:
- respecting their rights, privacy, and personal business;
- asking, not expecting, assuming, demanding, or insisting;
- doing what we say we will, and saying when plans change;
- asking if it's a good time to talk when we call;
- not arriving unannounced unless both parties agree that's okay;
- not borrowing without asking;
- paying debts on time;
- telling the truth;
- being nonjudgmental;
- not confronting, accusing, or intervening without checking facts;
- not pushing our beliefs on others;
- not feeling entitled to taking what others have by manipulation;
- calling at normal hours unless it's a true emergency and not drama;
- not talking about others behind their backs;
- not assuming we know the facts unless we do;
- not pestering, calling too often, or asking for inappropriate favors.

When we're uncertain what someone's boundaries are, ask!

✍ ACTIVITIES

1. Get a notebook. Or use a journal or word processing file in your computer—a safe, private place you can devote to writing about boundaries. You'll use it for answering questions and other boundary activities, too.

2. Respect others' boundaries. Has anyone had to set a boundary with you? How did you feel? Are you able to let people tell you their boundaries without becoming defensive or embarrassed? Practice staying calm when people set boundaries with you. Say something like, "Thank you for telling me about your boundary; I'll do my best to respect it." Or talk using normal words instead of recovery jargon. If you feel yourself becoming angry or defensive, it might be best to calmly excuse yourself and wait until you've dealt with your feelings before discussing the situation further. (This could save you from having to make amends later.)

3. Accept "No" as an answer. How do you react when someone says "No"? If you find yourself reacting strongly to "No," chances are you weren't asking—you were demanding or expecting. Prepare to respond peacefully no matter what answer you get. If that's difficult, study control in this book and the chapter about control in *Codependent No More*.

BARRIERS TO SETTING BOUNDARIES

- **Repressing old emotions.** When we stop denying how we feel about something that happened, that we didn't like or that hurt us, we'll know how we feel if it happens again.
- **Not knowing our feelings.** Emotional awareness is key to boundaries. We can't set limits unless we know how we feel.

- **Dependency on people.** If we're not afraid of being abandoned, we won't tolerate bad treatment to keep people from leaving.

- **Having our boundaries violated as children.** When we see our pasts clearly, inappropriate or unhealthy behaviors will no longer appear "normal." We'll trust the part of us that says *this isn't right* or *something's wrong.*

- **Abuse.** Repairing the damage from abuse heals our boundaries and our hearts. We'll know love doesn't equal being hurt, controlled, or abused. We deserve love and kindness from others and ourselves.

- **Not understanding limits.** We need to know what our rights are in order to get them. We need to understand boundaries in order to set them.

- **Poor parental role modeling.** We can stop unconsciously repeating destructive family traditions when we understand what really happened. Then we can let go of being victims when we deal with our feelings and achieve true forgiveness.

- **Low self-esteem.** When we love and appreciate ourselves, we'll give and receive respectful treatment.

- **Poor communication skills.** When we can open our mouths and speak our truths freely, we'll be able to tell people our limits.

- **Shame.** If it's okay to be who we are, our limits will be okay, too.

- **People-pleasing.** Stop pleasing others so that we can please ourselves.

- **Codependent caretaking.** Setting boundaries means we stop taking care of others and start taking care of ourselves. Often we can't do both (set boundaries and take care of people's feelings) at the same time.

As we practice self-care, we'll let go of these barriers and our boundaries will improve.

QUESTIONS

🖎 Which of the above barriers are problems for you? As you work on the above, check them off in your boundary book.

🖎 If you could say anything and it wouldn't be wrong, what would you say and to whom? That's the boundary you need to set.

🖎 Are you medicating or denying feelings to tolerate something that doesn't feel good? Were you abused but haven't dealt with it yet? If you answered yes to either part of this question, be sure to read and do the activities in Sections Three and Four of this book.

Boundaries for Beginners

I didn't think I would ever reach my limits with my husband. Neither did he. When we married, I thought he was a recovering alcoholic, but he'd been binge drinking since before we met. By the time I found out, we had two children in diapers.

One day he asked if I minded if he went with a friend to Las Vegas. After seven years of marriage, we hadn't been on a honeymoon or vacation. We were up to our eyeballs in debt. Did I mind? Yes! But a codependent couldn't say such things.

"Go ahead," I said. "Just promise one thing."

"What?"

"That you won't drink," I said. "If you do, the marriage is over."

He promised, then off he went. It would almost be funny if I hadn't believed him.

We planned on hosting a party to celebrate a neighbor's graduation from nursing school at our house that weekend, but he said he'd be home to help. Soon after he left, I got a gut feeling: He was drinking. We know the truth even when people lie to us or when we lie to ourselves. The party was Sunday. He said he'd be home Friday. It was Saturday. He wasn't home yet. He stopped taking my calls days ago. I was obsessed. Instead of preparing for Sunday's party, at 2:00 Saturday afternoon I started dialing his hotel over and over. *If he'd answer the phone, I could get him to come home. Then everything would be all right,* I kept telling myself.

At 10:00 p.m., I started to dial again, then stopped. *He's totally out of control,* I thought. *But I have eighty people coming tomorrow. Instead of getting ready, I sat here all day calling a number that's not being answered. He might be crazy, but what I'm doing is crazy, too.*

I got a miracle, but not the one I wanted—my husband getting sober. My miracle was when I finally stopped looking at the other person and saw myself. Even if I talked him into coming home, our marriage wouldn't be fine. It would be like it had been—a codependent trying to control an alcoholic. I worked as a chemical dependency counselor. I'd been recovering from addiction myself for nine years. Alcoholics couldn't control their drinking. How could anyone else control them? The only person I can control is me, and I wasn't doing that. I was letting his drinking control everything I did.

That was the moment I let go of him and began taking care of myself—my self-care anniversary. I went to bed, woke up early, got the house ready. My neighbor deserved a beautiful celebration. In the middle of the party, the telephone rang.

"I'm at the airport and out of money. Come and get me," my husband said.

"No, I won't," I said. "I'm in the middle of a party and I'm not leaving. You got yourself to Vegas, then you got back to Minneapolis. I'm sure you can find your way home too, if that's what you want to do."

Click. I hung up the phone.

That was the first boundary I set.

It was the beginning of years of boundary training. Sometimes I'd let feelings build until they exploded. Waiting until we reach our limits is one way to know them—but not necessarily the best.

At first I'd make a big production by formally announcing that I was *setting a boundary*. It must have been annoying, because it annoys me when people do that now. But that's how many of us start. Soon, we can use ordinary conversation to say what our boundaries are. We'll do it so diplomatically that people may not be aware that we set a boundary, but they'll respect what we said.

We don't need to have so many boundaries that people can't get near us, however. We don't want to be doormats, but we don't want to be porcupines either. Doormats get walked on, but porcupines can't be hugged.

BOUNDARIES AREN'T:
- limits we set because someone told us to;
- empty, angry threats;
- power plays to control someone;
- limits we don't or can't enforce.

THE ONLY NONNEGOTIABLE BOUNDARIES ARE:
- don't hurt yourself,
- don't hurt anyone else,
- don't let anyone hurt you.

I have few boundary rules in my writing or when I worked as a counselor. However, because of past experiences, I always state the above three. I probably always will. Once I didn't, and I will never forget the woman's bashed-in face as she lay in the bed in the hospital's emergency room. Another time I used them with a man going through a crisis. He still remembers to call and thank me for the rules at least twice a year.

Here's one more rule of thumb and good advice for protecting yourself: Call 911 to report abuse, then don't get close enough to an abuser to be hurt. It's easy to think that most people know not to allow themselves to be abused. But statistics on abuse from a wide range of sources are staggering. Although the numbers vary, about six people every minute in the United States are seriously hurt by someone they know and love.

Is it a Boundary or Controlling?

Boundaries concern our behaviors. We don't set them to control or interfere with people's free will—unless someone is harming us. Boundaries may involve consequences. We say, "If you do this, I'll do that." Boundaries give people choices. They can do as they please, but we can, too.

"I really liked this guy," Shelly said. "Then his drinking increased. By the end of each date, he was drunk. Or he'd call intoxicated, late at night.

"Let's back off from seeing each other," Shelly said when he called. "And don't call anymore at night when you're drunk."

"You don't mean that," he said. "Bet you can't say it again."

Shelly put the phone in front of her mouth. "I don't want to date you. Don't call when you're drinking," she said slowly, loudly. "Don't call after ten. Do you want me to repeat it?"

"Heard you clearly," he said.

"It's not my place to tell him to stop drinking," Shelly said. "But being with him or talking to him when he's drunk is my business."

That's the difference between boundaries and controlling. We can't make a person stop drinking. But we can refuse to talk to or date that person. Boundaries concern our behavior—what we will or won't do.

It's not a boundary if we can't enforce it.

Be clear. If people have room to misinterpret, they will. People hear what they want to and what causes the least pain. We won't be clear with others if we're not clear with ourselves. Sometimes we don't like their behavior, but we don't want to lose the relationship, so our boundaries are murky. We can't have it both ways; it's either a boundary or it's not.

QUESTION

✐ Can you enforce the boundary you're setting? If not, can you reword it so your limit concerns your behavior instead of controlling someone else?

Enforcing Boundaries

After he went to alcoholism treatment, a woman's son started drinking again. His mother had said: "No driving and drinking." She asked for the car keys back. He refused to give them to her. So she waited until he was asleep, then took the license plates off the car, and mailed them to a friend.

Enforcing limits can take creativity. It can take energy, too. How much energy depends on how persistent the person is and how consistently we enforced boundaries before.

A man supported his daughter financially after she left home. He wanted to help her get started. But years passed and she still hadn't looked for a job. He was enabling her to be irresponsible financially and he resented it. "What really hurt was she only called when she wanted money," he said. He'd been reading about codependency. It was time to set a boundary, but he wanted to be fair. He said: In six months, I'm cutting you off completely financially. Monthly, he called his daughter and counted down: five months, four, three, two, one. Then he stopped sending money like he said.

She called, asking for her check. He said the day he'd been

warning her about had arrived. He wasn't sending any more money. He canceled her credit card, too.

His daughter called him the worst father in the world. She cried, screamed, sweet-talked. He didn't budge. She hung up. An hour later, she called again.

"The next months were tough," he said. "She tried every trick in the book. Sometimes she called five to eight times a day. Enforcing that boundary was exhausting. So many times it would have been easier to mail a check. But I knew if I gave in, I'd have to go through the whole ordeal again. Enforcing the limit was so hard that even thinking about going through it again made me determined not to give in. When she finally understood I meant business, she moved in with her boyfriend. A month later she was pregnant. Three months later she got married. Those are her choices," he said. "Not supporting her is mine."

Expect people to test our boundaries. The more they stand to lose, the harder they'll push. They often won't stop pushing until they know we mean what we say.

QUESTIONS

⟋ Have you set boundaries that required creativity or endurance to enforce? Which ones? How did you do it? In the future, draw on the creativity and endurance you've already used.

⟋ When setting a boundary, think about how you'll enforce it. Talk to friends to get ideas. When we're on track, we'll get the strength and creativity we need.

AFTER SETTING BOUNDARIES, PLAN ON:

- being tested to see if we're serious, especially if previous boundaries were empty threats.
- feeling "after burn" (guilty) for saying what people don't want to hear.

- needing to be creative to enforce some limits.
- some boundaries taking enormous amounts of energy to enforce.
- people being persistent if they're obsessive, dependent, or spoiled.
- losing some relationships when people can't use us anymore.
- people trying to guilt us into changing our mind.
- people becoming angry when they realize the boundary is real.
- people lying or behaving desperately to get us to back down.
- some boundaries hurting us (to set) as much as they hurt the other person.

QUESTION

✐ Are we willing to do what it takes to enforce a boundary? If not, we'll have to start over. Then the person will push harder. By giving in, we teach people that if they push enough, our boundaries collapse.

Weak Spots

We may be expert boundary setters. Boundaries roll off our tongues like butter. People barely know a boundary was set. We know we have a right to express ourselves—except with one particular group of people or one person. For some reason, that's our weakness with boundaries.

Many people say that romance comes and goes, but friendship is forever. However, friends can be the hardest to set boundaries with. Although many people expect to argue in romantic relationships, there's an unspoken agreement not to argue with friends.

Don't resist your weak spots. Awareness and acceptance bring change. The harder it is to set a boundary, the more important the boundary probably is.

QUESTION
🖎 Who is the person or group that's your boundary weakness? Do you know why?

Boundaries That Hurt

Sometimes we deeply love people whom we need to separate from unless their behavior changes. Even if it's our child who's doing something that harms or disrespects us, we may need to distance ourselves for a while.

The day arrives when a child isn't our baby. When they become adults, our children need to take responsibility for their behaviors. Setting limits will be good for us and good for our children, too.

No doubt, some boundaries can hurt us as much or more than they hurt the other person. Maybe that's why it's called "tough love."

QUESTIONS
🖎 What's the most painful boundary you've set?
🖎 Is there a boundary you're delaying setting because you know how much it'll hurt?

Boundary-Setting Tips

Say "Can I get back to you on that?" if someone catches us off guard asking for something. Don't blurt out, "Yes." Retreat until we know what we want to do.

Prepare for setting difficult boundaries by writing or rehearsing what we'll say.

Don't explain or justify our actions unless people ask and we want to tell them. Excuses weaken our power.

Don't forget: Boundaries include saying what we want, enjoy, and like, too—not only what doesn't feel good.

If we spent years not knowing we could say no, we might spend years saying no after we learn we can. If we didn't get to experiment with power as children, we may go through the terrible twos when we're adults.

If we feel our boundary collapsing, write a reminder letter to ourselves about how it feels when we let someone do what the boundary concerns. Write the letter when the feelings are fresh. When we're tempted to give in, read the letter. It may stop euphoric recall and help us remember how much that behavior hurts.

If a boundary involves people doing something differently, be specific about what needs changing. Then, everyone involved can clearly tell if and when the boundary is met.

Set tough limits in blocks of time to reduce the sting. Set a boundary for six weeks or six months. Then, review the situation. Boundaries don't have to be forever. They can be "until."

Someone sending hostile thoughts at us for saying "no" can be extremely disruptive. The more bonded we are with people, the more likely we'll feel what they're feeling whether we're talking to them or not. If we react by sending back angry feelings, we'll be even more disrupted. Unhook from unspoken or silent hostility. When we send only loving thoughts to people, it makes those tough boundaries easier to set.

If a boundary involves complaining about a service delivered, stay focused on the issue. Don't attack the person. Be specific about how we'd like the problem solved. We won't always get satisfactory resolution, but our chances improve when we don't put people on the defensive by attacking them. Besides, who wants an angry dentist drilling our tooth or a resentful stylist cutting our hair? They may be working at a job role, but they're people and they have feelings, too.

Sometimes we may think we've reached our limit. We may want to be done with a relationship, but when the person calls, we give in and see him or her again. Sometimes the more we resist the person, the more we get pulled back in. If that happens, accept we're not ready to enforce the boundary yet—or we would. It's like the Chinese finger cuff trick. The harder we try to pull apart our fingers, the more stuck we get. By relaxing instead of resisting, we set ourselves free.

We don't have to yell to show power. The more certain we are about our limits and our right to have them, the softer we'll speak. When we're serious, people know we mean business no matter how loudly—or softly—we talk. Sometimes if a person is being aggressive, or a salesperson is trying to bilk us, we may have to stomp our foot and loudly insist that the behavior stop. We may have to call the authorities. When we need to raise our voices, we'll be more effective if we do it like an actor playing the role of an angry person than if we're screaming because we're out of control and our anger is controlling us.

We may find ourselves in difficult situations—legally and emotionally. We either get a divorce or let a spouse ruin our credit. It's a decision only we can make. If we can't decide, maybe it's not time. But remember—not deciding is choosing. Do we want the consequences we'll get? Laws are constantly changing. Check—maybe you can legally protect yourself in ways you didn't know existed.

Other circumstances have legal complications. We have responsibilities for children until they're adults. "Living with my teenager was hell," many parents said. Call the school or police. They may be able to tell you what your responsibilities are; they will probably have the most current resources. Or consult a competent attorney. Knowing your legal responsibilities and options is part of taking care of yourself.

Get support from a group whose members have similar problems as yours. Don't attend a group with women talking about being married to alcoholics when you're dealing with a teenager engaged in abusive behavior. Whatever you're going through, you aren't alone. Others are going through a similar experience. Support will help more than you know. A group equals more than the total of its members. Something happens that strengthens us in ways we won't know exist until we have the experience.

If we ask for help and look for answers, we'll find the information, clarity, guidance, and power to set and enforce the limits that are right for us.

✐ ACTIVITY

1. Keep track of the boundaries you set and the limits people set with you. Write about your feelings and how people respond to them. Write about your experiences with enforcing boundaries. Be detailed. You may be surprised at how easy, fun, and smooth boundary setting becomes.

2. Recognize when it's boundary-setting time. When you complain or feel upset, ask yourself if there's a boundary you need to set. Wait for the right time, although we sometimes need to *make* our opportunity. Don't rush but don't avoid setting a boundary either. Your ability to set boundaries will grow along with your ability to take care of yourself and knowing that you deserve respect.

"Saying no was almost impossible for me for thirty years. Now saying no is easy. Boundaries roll out of my mouth with such ease that people barely know a boundary was set—yet they

respect my limits. I'm doing things that I thought I could never do. Hang in there. It's like anything else. It takes practice, trial, error, and time. Most of all it takes courage. Set boundaries even when you're scared, and when it doesn't feel comfortable to do. Eventually setting boundaries will happen naturally for you, too."

—Anonymous

---

3 • Caretaking

THE HEART OF CODEPENDENCY

"I was the firstborn child," a woman said. "Then my mother had three more children. It was my job to take care of them and take care of my mother. Then I got married and had children. They grew up, got married. Then my grandchildren moved in with me and I took care of them. Taking care of other people is all I've known. Nobody ever taught me how to take care of myself."

Taking care of others and neglecting ourselves is what codependents do. There are many reasons people neglect themselves. Why we didn't take care of ourselves isn't as important as taking care of ourselves now.

CARETAKING IS:
- doing what isn't our responsibility and what we don't want to do.
- doing what people are capable of doing—and need to do—for themselves.
- meeting people's needs without them asking us for help.
- getting involved in what isn't our business.
- doing more than our share when someone asks us to help.
- forcing our help on people, when they don't want it.
- giving more than we receive instead of mutual giving.

- taking care of people's feelings or problems; neglecting our own.
- facing people's consequences so they can avoid them.
- speaking for people and not letting them speak for themselves.
- pouring more interest into joint efforts than the other person does.
- not saying what we need.
- taking care of others' feelings as a substitute for taking care of our own emotions or unresolved issues.
- giving that attaches ourselves to others—needy giving.
- making excuses for others, but not understanding ourselves.
- not standing up for our rights, but advocating for other people.
- not getting paid what we're worth.
- compulsively caretaking and not knowing how or when to stop.

Caretaking Is What We Do Best

It's what we do over and over; what we've been trained by religion and family to do. Caretaking is what we think we have to do to be a good person. It fills the emptiness inside and compensates for feeling like we don't have a life. It allows us to hide low self-worth and attaches us to people. It makes people look like they're dependent on us when we're the ones who need them.

We take care of people's feelings, problems, needs, and desires. We do a good job of it, too. We usually know what people want before they do. Some of us take care of people at home, and we work as caregivers, too. "Your wish is our command," is our theme. "Your problem is my problem," is our motto.

If we're unsure how to take care of ourselves, treat ourselves the way we treat others and most of us can't go wrong.

Helping That Doesn't Help

Rescuing is related to caretaking, and that doesn't mean saving someone from a burning building. Rescuing often helps people be irresponsible, negligent, or addicted. Instead of letting them face the consequences of their behaviors, we take their consequences for them. What we're helping people to do is hurt themselves and us.

"Aren't we supposed to take care of sick people?" a woman asked. "Alcoholism is a disease. Why shouldn't we take care of alcoholics?" For the same reason we don't bring sugar cookies to diabetics. Caretaking doesn't help; it hurts other people and us.

Rescuing stops people from learning the lessons Life is trying to teach them. We jam ourselves between people and God. We make it easy for people to avoid taking responsibility for themselves. They don't have to grow up, even when they're fifty. People think, *Why should I be responsible if you'll do it for me?*

We rescue people, then get mad at them when we do something we don't want to do or something they need to do for themselves. Then they get mad at us even after all we've done for them. Caretaking sends the message that we think people are incompetent. We feel used and unappreciated. Rescuing creates victims—us!

We tell people "no problem," "happy to help," and then we complain about what we do. Caretaking is based on the belief that we're responsible for others and others are responsible for us. We take care of them, and then stand there feeling needy, wishing someone would take care of us. Caretaking often results in us neglecting ourselves so much that people have to rescue us. We give away our rent money and then need to borrow from someone else. We overextend ourselves and then don't have the time or energy to take care of ourselves.

If it's not our business, don't do it. Ask if our help is needed before we assist. If people create consequences, be kind: Let them face the results.

Needy Giving

Caretaking is often giving based on our need to be wanted and loved.

We're giving to get. We give to get people to need us because we don't feel loveable. Caretaking attaches people to us, creating dependent relationships.

Sometimes we're taking care of our needs by taking care of someone else. Most of us have seen examples of this. Maybe a parent abandoned us. We grow up, get married, and find ourselves in a dreadful relationship. From day one, the person we're in a relationship with talks about how he or she was abandoned as a child and how much that abandonment hurt. We vow we're not going to abandon that person the way other people did. We know how horrible it feels to be abandoned, and we haven't dealt with our feelings yet. So we stay in the relationship. We're determined not to give that person any feelings of abandonment—no matter what it costs us emotionally, physically, financially. It looks like we're taking care of the other person's feelings, but we're taking care of our own. We're treating the other person the way we wish someone would take care of us. Indirectly, we're taking care of our feelings by caretaking the other person's abandonment issues. We're going to make sure they don't feel the way we felt.

It's our job to take care of our feelings and let other people take care of theirs. It's okay to give to people—but don't give to get people to like us. Give because we want to, when giving comes from our heart. Speak up for other people, but speak up for ourselves, too. Stick to our responsibilities and let other people take care of theirs.

Getting Our Needs Met

Often caretakers get their needs met by getting sick. If we have a migraine or cold, we can stop taking care of other people, and take care of ourselves. We finally have an excuse. Some people are so locked into caretaking they even become happy about having a fatal illness because it sets them free. "I'm dying of cancer," a woman said. "But to tell the truth, I'm relieved. At least I won't have to keep taking care of everyone. People are finally taking care of me."

She was twenty-eight years old.

We don't need an excuse to take care of ourselves. We don't have to get sick. Start giving ourselves what we need. Life will work with us and start to feel good.

QUESTIONS

✍ Are you able to take care of yourself without getting sick or making excuses? Do you have a favorite pattern that you use to justify self-care? What is it? Migraines? Cramps? Back pain? You don't have to be sick to pamper yourself. You don't have to feel guilty about letting yourself feel good. But every time you get sick doesn't mean you're being codependent. Lighten up on yourself!

Minding Our Business

If we're taking care of others and not taking care of ourselves, reverse the pattern. Stop doing what isn't our business and start taking care of ourselves. When I first started taking care of myself, it was hard at first and for years afterward. I'd spent so much time obsessing about people, I didn't know what my true responsibilities were. Okay, get up. Brush my teeth. Comb my hair. Wash my face. Get dressed. What's next? I faced a huge empty spot that should have been my life. The empty spot outside me reflected the emptiness within. My only identity came from the wedding ring on my finger and from being a mom. Some people get their identities from their careers. I didn't know how to be me or how to have a life other than taking care of other people.

Sometimes it's normal to center our decisions around other people—when we have children or we're caring for an elderly parent or an ill spouse. Healthy caretaking means we meet our responsibilities to others and still keep our center where it belongs—in ourselves. That's not being self-centered in a negative way. We stop focusing on and obsessing about other people and live our lives. We find ways to build time into our busy schedules so that we can recharge our batteries. We find something we're passionate about, and then we do it. We make our best decisions, get our clearest guidance, and move through life most naturally when our center is in ourselves and we're not exhausted and depleted from giving everything away.

ACTIVITIES

1. **Work the first step.** *I am powerless over others and my life is unmanageable* is a mantra based on the first of the Twelve Steps. Saying or thinking it can keep us grounded in the truth whether we attend Twelve-Step groups or not. Say it over and over. We can make a conscious decision to detach.

2. **Get in your body.** Breathe, three or four long, slow, deep breaths. Do it several times a day. Do Yoga. Meditate. Pray. These activities connect us to ourselves. Go for a walk; stay present for each step. Feel what it's like to live in our bodies. Many of us escaped from ourselves because there was so much pain inside us we couldn't stand being in there. The only way back into ourselves is by feeling all the feelings we left our

body to escape. We clean house, then we come home and live in ourselves again.

Victimizing Ourselves

At first people thought they had to be "codependent on" some-one—an alcoholic parent, child, or spouse. That meant they were caretaking that person. But we don't need to "be codependent on" anyone. We can be codependent all by ourselves, without involving anyone else. Being codependent can mean that we're neglecting ourselves.

"I had an alcoholic parent," a woman said. "That qualified me for Al-Anon. All you need for membership is to be affected by someone's drinking. But the real reason I went to Al-Anon wasn't my father; it's my relationship with my husband. He doesn't drink or use drugs, but he's always angry. I tiptoed around his rage. I spent my life taking care of his feelings and not taking care of mine." Codependency manifests many different ways.

Can we be codependent on a codependent? Absolutely. We want them to stop controlling everything (or at least us), and look at themselves. They are always right and we're wrong (according to them). They don't want facts to interfere with what they believe. While they're spinning wildly out of control, they're trying to con-vince us they know what's best for us. Some of them are sticky. They cling to us. They tell us they have abandonment issues so we can *never* go away. The sighs, the whining tone in their voice, their determination to be victims drives us insane. They stick to us like flypaper. They need so much that we want to run when we see them coming. We can be codependent on anyone, but codepen-dents are the neediest. They're the worst.

Living in the Mystery

A man who was so codependent years ago that he didn't think he'd ever get a life or keep one told me this story. He lives in Massachusetts, his only sibling, a brother, lives in Toronto, and their elderly father lives in Florida. Two years after the father's wife passed, the man's brother moved his son from Toronto to Florida to keep an eye on his aging grandfather. Some time after that, the man's brother called him. "I'm worried about Dad," he said. Their father had given power of attorney to the grandson. Then he left everything he owned (a sizable estate) to the grandson in exchange for helping him. In the meantime, the man's brother and his son had become estranged.

"What's the problem?" the man asked his brother.

"The only person my son is helping is himself," his brother said. "Can you go see Dad and straighten this out?"

The man wondered why his brother couldn't intervene—it was, after all, *his* son who lived in Florida. But the man agreed to do what his brother asked—not because he felt he had to, but because doing it felt right. That night he got on a plane. The next day he knocked on his father's door. His dad was so undernourished that he couldn't get out of bed. The man called an ambulance. The doctor did a five-minute exam, decided his father was of sound mind. But the man didn't buy it. He suspected his father was also suffering from malnutrition. Later it came out that the grandson had been spending shockingly little on food for his grandfather. Apparently he had little regard for his grandfather's health.

While his dad was being examined, the man looked at his checkbook. Many checks were made out to the grandson for large amounts of cash. This was something the man knew his father wouldn't do; he didn't believe in using cash or keeping money around the house. But he'd had several strokes and had lost his short-term memory. That's why he originally made the arrangement with his grandson. His father was terrified of going to a nursing home; the grandson promised to take care of him and never let that happen.

Later it came out that the grandson had convinced his grandfather that everyone but him (the grandson) wanted to take the grandfather's money and put him in a home. That was his grandfather's greatest fear. The grandson used typical abuser tactics: isolate the person, poison his mind, make him dependent, and gain control of the person's mind. His dad couldn't drive—he'd forget where he was going and whether to put the car in forward or reverse. He was dependent on his grandson for everything. The man's father was a vulnerable adult. Later the grandfather admitted that his grandson said if he complained, he'd lock him in his bedroom, deprive him of food, and threaten to put him in a nursing home. He said he remembered going to bed hungry many nights because all he'd had to eat that day was bread and water.

His son went to every agency in town: family services, the police, and the social service workers at the hospital. They all said the same thing: Because of the durable power of attorney, there was nothing they could do. Plus his father insisted he wanted everything to stay the same. The man could see his dad wasn't in his right mind—no matter what the doctor said.

"I was a raving caretaker in my codependent years," the man said. "Nothing could stop me once I decided to help someone. I didn't like what I saw and heard. My dad was in trouble. But something clicked inside me. I assessed the situation instead of obsessing, like I used to. I knew I'd done everything I could. Anything else and I'd be 'crossing the line' from helping to caretaking. I hugged my dad good-bye, flew home, and then told my brother what I saw.

"I felt horrible about leaving my dad like that, but I felt grateful I wasn't the person I was before. I was given the wisdom to understand what I could and couldn't do. I'd also learned that detaching and letting go were loving, conscious decisions I could make. If I've done everything I can, it's time to Let Go and give the situation to God. That's what I did, although I wished I could have done more."

He felt like he wasted money on the trip, but he'd listened to his inner guidance. Going on the trip felt right even though he didn't accomplish anything. He didn't understand what the experience was about. Maybe he never would. Over the years, he'd learned that he didn't always get to see how things worked out. Sometimes he had to live with mysteries and this was one of those times.

The man had his own family problems that required him to stay close to home for a while. Then one day he got a feeling *out of the blue*. Go to Florida to visit his dad. When he knocked on his father's door, he couldn't believe what he saw. His dad had lost thirty pounds. There was no food in the house. His father stunk—obviously he hadn't bathed in months. His house was as filthy as he was.

It broke his heart. The only good thing was that in the son's absence, the grandson became careless. He had enough rope to hang himself, and that's what he did. Now, he was writing checks to himself for thousands of dollars instead of hundreds. There was something the man could do now and he did it. He got the grandson's power of attorney revoked by the court.

"It was good that I had made that trip before," the man said. "I proved that I had tried to do everything possible. I wish Dad hadn't suffered at all. But at last we could undo the damage. We cleaned Dad up, fixed his house, got him help. He gained weight—and to this day, he eats like a twenty-year-old man. His cheeks went from ashen gray to a healthy glow, and he smiles instead of looking depressed. With proper nutrition, even his memory improved. The experience turned into a blessing for us all—especially Dad."

It took this man many years to get to where he could detach from what he couldn't do and take care of himself, and to trust his guidance whether it made sense or not. He had learned to live in the mystery by letting God do what he couldn't do himself.

We can each only start where we're at.

What feels impossible in the beginning—letting go of people we love and taking care of ourselves—grows easier with practice. It's not the caretaking behaviors that cause the problem. Feeling and believing we're overly responsible for other people—and for what we can't do—causes the pain. It's not codependent to care about people we love. It's normal. When we see someone in trouble, we want to help.

It's also not as much what we do as how and why we do it. Two people can engage in the same behaviors in similar situations. One will be acting codependent; the other will be exhibiting healthy behavior. If we do what we want to do and take responsibility for our choices, we won't end up victims. Taking responsibility for our actions is how we determine if what we're doing is codependent or not.

CARETAKING ISN'T:

- genuine acts of kindness and love that come from the heart.
- fulfilling our true responsibilities to others.
- clear contracts to help, in which all people hold up their end of the bargain.
- relationships where both people give and receive.
- giving to receive good feelings from giving, not because we're needy and want to make people dependent on us.
- acts of service we do because "to keep it we have to give it away."
- helping people after we ask if they want help, they say yes, and we want to give them the help they want.
- any behavior we take responsibility for that doesn't result in us feeling victimized.

Legitimate Caretaking Duties

Sometimes caretaking *is* our responsibility. We're responsible to take care of our children. It may be our responsibility to take care of an aging parent. Having young children can be exhausting. Taking care of an aging parent takes tremendous amounts of energy. But we don't ever have to do more than we can. If we're doing what we're meant to do, we'll get the Grace, guidance, and power to do it.

When we feel overwhelmed, exhausted, and burdened, it's our responsibility to make time for ourselves. It's also important to stop and evaluate: are we doing too much for others and not enough for ourselves? It's easy to start neglecting ourselves when we're busy with young children. We need to make a conscious decision—a choice and a commitment—to give ourselves what we need and want, too. A little bit of self-love can go a long way.

If we don't take care of ourselves, we won't be able to help other people. We'll get sick—our bodies will force us into it. Taking care of ourselves isn't optional; it's essential.

Sometimes we come first.

When Addictions Are Involved

When other people are addicted (drugs, alcohol, gambling, sexual addictions, eating disorders), it may help us and the other person to:

- get information about the particular addiction or illness the person has.
- attend a support group for caregivers of people with that problem or for people affected by that addiction.
- learn and practice principles such as detaching and letting go in love.

- stop reacting and begin taking action.
- stop centering ourselves around the addict and get centered in ourselves.
- when it's appropriate, work a Twelve-Step program. Yes, the other person has the problem, but if you're hurting, your pain is your problem. You deserve to heal from it.
- admit what we're powerless over—what we can't do—then start doing what we can.
- keep taking care of ourselves, no matter what.

When Our Child Is in Trouble

"I could divorce my alcoholic husband, but I can't divorce my daughter," a woman said. "It's different when the addict or alcoholic is your child."

Parents have legal and moral responsibilities for minor children. We can't walk away. Children can get into trouble with eating disorders, gambling, sexually acting out, or gang or criminal behaviors. All these problems cause pain for the child and the family. Taking care of ourselves means learning to walk the fine line between meeting our responsibilities to our child, and letting go and taking care of ourselves. Not only is it difficult, it may be one of the most difficult situations we'll go through.

"Whenever I was in the same room as my daughter, when she was drinking or using drugs, she started screaming at me," more than one mother said. "It felt like being in prison. I couldn't stand living under the same roof."

"I put my daughter through treatment twice," another woman said. "I attended Al-Anon. But sometimes I couldn't control myself. I knew better, but I'd start screaming back. Many nights I'd drive around in my car, not going anywhere—just crying. I didn't know what to do. It felt like this would never end. Eventually my daughter grew up. Then she got clean and sober. I don't ever want to go through that again and I feel sorry for anyone who has to."

No parent wants to lose a child to addictions or any serious problem. "Everyone is nagging me about codependency," another woman said when she discovered her daughter was a heroin addict. "But it wasn't only codependency. I was in deep grief. I knew my child might die and I couldn't do anything about it. I lost my relationship with her when she was addicted. My sweet daughter was a completely different person—a monster—someone I didn't know, when she was using drugs."

It's heartbreaking to see our child in trouble. We feel like we should protect our children. We think about every mistake we've made as a parent, and wonder if that's why our child became addicted or got into trouble. The guilt can be unbearable even when we know intellectually it's not our fault. We didn't cause it. Feeling guilty is part of grief and it goes with the territory of having an addicted or troubled child. When we let go of the guilt, we'll be better equipped and able to help ourselves and our child.

It's difficult and confusing to know what steps to take and when. Maybe an intervention is the answer. But if we intervene too soon, we'll waste time and money and need to do it again. Some experimentation with alcohol and drugs is natural. But when does a child cross the line from experimentation into addiction? When does concern with looking good turn into an obsession with weight watching and self-starvation. When is fighting with a sibling normal sibling rivalry and anger, and when does it cross the line into abuse?

Educate ourselves about the problem. Educate our child. Ask for help from knowledgeable people. Find out exactly what our responsibilities are. Keep taking care of ourselves. Find help for our child when it's time. All resources of help aren't the same. Get references from people you trust.

"I scrambled and got thousands of dollars together to pay for two weeks in treatment for my daughter," a woman said. "They kept her on drugs the first week. The second week they allowed her boyfriend—a drug dealer—to visit her every day. At family group, my daughter blamed me for her addiction. Then the other group members—including the counselor agreed. Nobody held my daughter responsible for her behavior. I got so angry I walked out," she said. "Two weeks passed quickly, then they released my daughter. She never came close to getting sober and it cost me a lot of money. One of the counselors pulled me aside the last day my daughter was there. She told me next time I put my daughter through treatment, I should find a better place."

Don't assume that treatment centers or counselors are good because they're expensive. Take time to check references. You'll be glad you did.

We can't control our children's destinies, but we can teach them when they're young about problems they might face, based on their genetics. We can tell them what the signs of addiction are: loss of control, blackouts, and continued use despite negative consequences. "The problem isn't that drugs don't work," a counselor said. "The problem is they work too well. The truth is for a while, children have fun getting high."

It may feel like we're failed as a parent or that we should be the one to help our child. But when our child needs dental work, we take him or her to a dentist to do the job. If we stop reacting insanely, it'll be better for us and our children. If they're not busy reacting to us, there's a better chance they'll see themselves. If we're not taking their consequences for them, they can learn what Life or their addiction is trying to teach them. If we're taking care of ourselves, we'll know what to do and when. If we're not obsessed, we'll hear the guidance we get.

Getting and Keeping a Life

After my son died, I spent years grieving. My daughter came home from school when I was finishing a crossword puzzle. If I could finish one puzzle, I felt like I'd had a successful day. "You need to get a life," she said. "I have one," I replied. "It's just not a very good one right now."

We can focus on other people and live our lives through them. Or we can keep living our own lives—through the worse, bad, and better days.

I can't count the number of times I've had to start over, whether I wanted to or not. After a loss I'd stare at the big empty space that used to be my life. All I could see was what I didn't have. Then I'd start doing something to fill the time. Before long, what I initially thought was "time filler" became the next chapter in my life.

Attachments or Connections?

Taking care of ourselves doesn't mean not caring about other people. We've begun the journey of learning to love ourselves and others in a different way—we're learning the meaning of true love. We're learning about love that isn't needy. We'll no longer take care of people so they'll like us, or so we can attach ourselves to them. We stop confusing love with controlling. After connecting to ourselves and giving up the illusion of separation, we'll see that we're already one with everyone and everything—but not in a codependent way.

We won't have to pretend that others are dependent on us, when all along we've been dependent on them. We won't obsessively glom on to people by caretaking—something that looks like giving but isn't. A light will go on. We'll see that while we've been complaining about how much we do for others, caretaking is how we take energy from people. Caretaking others is really about meeting our needs, not taking care of them.

When we start taking care of ourselves, we won't have to take care of people or have someone take care of us. What we can't do for ourselves, Life and God will do for us. It really gets good when we see how much we're being guided and cared for—and have been all along.

Often I've heard people regret the years they wasted "being codependent." But our codependent years aren't wasted time. Codependency isn't about how much someone else drinks or does drugs. It's a gateway to enlightenment, a path to our Higher Power, a vital spirituality, and a new way of life. Many things that happen won't make sense. It won't be one big holiday. We'll watch people suffer, and wonder why God lets that happen. The longer we walk a spiritual path, the more that will be required of us. Instead of trusting what we know, we'll be called on to trust what we don't know yet. We'll walk into the unknown, one step at a time. One thing we can count on is that even when we don't know what it is, there is a Plan especially and uniquely created for and by us.

More shall be revealed, but not until it's time.

✐ ACTIVITIES

1. **Know your true responsibilities to and for yourself, and to and for other people.** If you're uncertain, ask. If you don't know what your responsibilities are to your children—especially if addictions or problems are involved—take steps to find out from school, the police, or an attorney. Before spending a lot of money on attorney's fees, check references. Don't let yourself be taken. Start protecting yourself.

2. **Is there someone you're "being codependent on"?** Whom? What are you doing to take care of the other person that isn't

your business? Do you feel responsible for someone? Whom? Why? Go over the list of what "Caretaking Is" (see page 40–1). Mark the problem behaviors. Then work on changing the feelings and belief system underneath. You're responsible for other people only in certain situations. You are always responsible for yourself.

3. Get information. If letting go and detachment are behaviors you haven't yet learned, read or reread *Codependent No More, The Language of Letting Go,* or any good book on the subject. Then begin practicing these behaviors. Think of this as going to college; you're getting a degree in healthy love for others and yourself.

4. Stay aware of caretaking and self-care behaviors. Are you healthy enough to love other people without getting lost in their needs? In your notebook, keep track of what you do for others and what you do for yourself for two weeks. Then evaluate. Are you tending to your true responsibilities? Is there a healthy balance between what you do for yourself and what you do for others? Do this activity as often as needed. Even if you've been taking care of yourself for a while, do it once a year. You may be surprised at what you see. Do this activity more frequently when you're beginning recovery. Do it whenever you're in emotional pain. A light may turn on; you might see why you're hurting. Awareness brings change.

5. Attend a support group. It can be a support group for caregivers who have an ill spouse, or for people who love someone with Alzheimer's Disease. It can be Al-Anon, Codependents Anonymous, or an Adult Children of Alcoholics group. Never before has so much support been available, and most of it is free. Find a good group, then attend it as often as you need. If you don't like the first group, search until you find one that works for you.

6. Set goals. Setting goals is a basic, powerful tool that helps us get and keep a life. Always keep a constantly updated goal list of our wants, desires, hopes, and dreams. Include what we want to do, get, attain, and accomplish. Be specific. Then put the list in a special place and let go. Trust that God and Life will bring us what we need when it's time. Use visualization, too. Clearly imagine yourself living the life you want. Include as many details as you can—how things look or how you feel. These tools sound simple, but the basics work. Often when we have a strong desire or dream, it's God talking to our heart about what we can have. But unless we're aware of and open to receiving it, we won't even notice when what we want comes to us.

7. Detach and let go in love. Feel our feelings. Sometimes we'll instantly and automatically detach after we feel a blocked or denied emotion. Also use the gratitude activity to help us let go. Be thankful for what we don't want to let go of and that we don't want to detach—if that's where we're at. Acknowledge and express gratitude for whatever is honest and real. Be grateful for how difficult life is, if it's hard for you right now. Be thankful that we can't fix what we want to change and for how frustrated we feel about that. Write and say thank you until our gratitude becomes real (which it will if we're diligent). We can choose to let God take over (or at least decide to get out of the way). Detachment is a decision we make. Be patient. Mastering this tool takes time. It's worth the effort to learn.

8. Cut back on your caregiver duties. Are you a caregiver at work and at home? Make time to take care of yourself. If you don't make self-care a priority, nobody will do it for you. If you're resenting your job, it may be time to reevaluate your vocation or find more ways to gentle up and relax at home.

4 • Chemically Dependent and Codependent

DOUBLE WINNERS

"Welcome to Al-Anon," a perky woman said when I walked into my first Twelve-Step group for people affected by someone's drinking.

"I'm not an *Al-Anon*," I said. "I'm an addict, alcoholic." I wanted to make it clear I wasn't one of these hand-wringing, obsessive women. I thought it was nice that the wives had somewhere to go while the addicts and alcoholics—the people with the real problem—got help. I didn't consider Al-Anon real recovery— more like a Ladies' Aid society. My sour mood didn't slow down the perky woman.

"Oh! You're a Double Winner," she said.

My husband was drinking. I'd been sober for years, yet I'm the one getting help? I'm watching my marriage go down the drain. Double Winner? This felt like one big loss.

I started drinking when I was twelve. My mother didn't drink, but she kept big bottles of alcohol—booze—in the cabinet underneath the kitchen sink in case she dated a man who wanted a drink. While other students were on their lunch hours eating a sandwich, I was home alone slamming straight shots. I'd pour a little water back into the bottle so I wouldn't get caught. I was young; it didn't take much straight whiskey to get me drunk.

The glow from the whiskey warmed my whole body. It was the first good feeling I had felt. By thirteen, I met all the criteria for alcoholism: loss of control, continued use despite negative consequences, and blackouts. Despite the negative consequences from drinking, alcohol still gave me the only good feelings I had. Blacking out was scary, but it was better than remembering what I did when I drank.

The signs at church say "God is Love," I thought, walking to church one Sunday morning. *But nothing that happens in my life feels like love.* I looked up at the heavens. *If You're love, then You don't love me.* I stopped walking, lit a cigarette. *Thanks but no thanks for Your help,* I thought, saying a good-bye prayer. *I can do as good a job as You've done, so from here on out, I'll handle my life by myself.*

When I was younger—before all the abuse and the family dysfunction—I thought God was the greatest. Not anymore. I skipped church from then on and lied about where I'd been. I started drinking almost daily—as much as I could. Twelve years would pass before I'd talk to God again.

Staying Normal

I continued to get straight A's in grade school and at the conservative religious prep school academy I attended. It took two hours and three buses to get from St. Paul, where I lived with my mom, to high school in Minneapolis. My entire childhood was lonely, hard, and confusing. I didn't fit with other students. I didn't fit with myself. I wasn't allowed to have friends. The drinking and consequences worsened. I still graduated on the Twin Cities Honor Roll, but something was wrong and nobody—including me—knew what the problem was. Everyone said I should behave but by then, I couldn't stop drinking. What started out as medication for my pain turned into a problem of its own.

Bill Wilson cofounded Alcoholics Anonymous long before, but AA was still underground. People didn't know teenagers could be alcoholics. I didn't know I had depression. We each have a "normal"—a way we're comfortable feeling, a way that feels like "us." I didn't know how badly I felt, but I knew other people felt better than I did. It would be decades before I knew how bad my normal really was. A month before graduation—the day I turned eighteen—I left home. I'd been counting the days for years until I could leave. That's when I decided: No more drinking. Alcohol made me crazy. From then on, I'd only use drugs.

People think Minnesotans talk funny—that they talk like people in the movie *Fargo*. It's true, we have an accent, but we're smarter than we sound. By the time street drugs reached us from the coasts, they'd been cut so much we couldn't get stoned. Pharmaceuticals were the only game in town. Dilaudid, used by doctors to treat severe pain, was better than heroin. Ear, nose, and throat doctors had cupboards full of vials of pure liquid cocaine. When you used pharmaceuticals, you knew what you were getting (quality control). I'd wanted to be a writer since I was five or six years old, but I started robbing drugstores with my boyfriend instead of going to college for a journalism degree. This was the old days, before burglar alarms. The revolution was just beginning. It was the start of peace, love, drugs, sex, rock and roll. Equal rights for everyone. We felt entitled to get high.

It was fun for a while, but there was a trick to this getting high thing: You only got high a couple times. After that, all drugs did was make you feel normal. But the normal from using drugs was still better than any normal I'd ever felt.

When I was twenty-four, a district court judge gave me a choice: chemical dependency treatment at a state hospital for as long as it took to get clean and sober or up to five years in prison. I chose treatment but didn't plan to stop using drugs. I thought I could manipulate my way through. I'd already been arrested for possession. Each time, the charges were dismissed. Judges couldn't understand why a nice girl like me—a straight-A student with big horn-rimmed glasses—was doing this.

"Do you know you're responsible for your behavior?" a wise

judge finally asked me in the courtroom in 1973. I said yes, but didn't mean it. I thought if the people supposed to love us abused, abandoned, and betrayed us, we could do whatever we wanted. What I didn't understand is we could, but we had to face the consequences of our behaviors, too—once the codependents got out of the way and stopped taking our consequences for us.

I became the poster girl for narcotics. By the time my run with burglarizing drugstores ended, the police said my tracks were the worst they'd ever seen. They took pictures of my arms for drug prevention programs in schools. Tracks are needle sticks that become scabs, then scars. On each arm, three thick lines ran from my shoulders to my fingers, covering up where veins used to be. By then, there weren't any visible veins left or attainable ones underneath. During those years, I had a child, but had to give him up. I didn't want to abort the baby, but I knew I was incapable of being a mother, and I didn't know I could change. The losses were mounting. I still didn't want to stop using drugs. Narcotics gave me the only good feelings I had. Getting clean and sober felt like dying—the death of the only happiness I'd ever felt.

A surprise waited for me at treatment: a spiritual awakening. I was on the lawn getting stoned one day when the sky turned a purplish color and the world looked like a Monet painting. Everything was connected; the boundaries were blurred between everything that was. In that moment, I knew God was real and I had no right to keep filling my body with drugs. In that moment, I lost my free ticket; I no longer felt entitled to get high. A thought occurred to me: *If I put half the energy into doing the right thing as I have into doing the wrong thing, and put half as much energy into staying sober as I've put into using drugs, there isn't much I can't do. Being a junkie was a lot of work.*

I took one more hit off the joint, then threw myself into recovery with as much passion as I'd used drugs. God and I reconciled. We starting talking again. I had one slip in treatment a few weeks later, but I was honest about it. I learned if you don't want to slip, don't go where it's slippery. Years passed before I told anyone about the day that the sky turned purple and I saw God. I figured if I did, I'd never get out of the state hospital I was in; they'd diagnose me as crazy and lock me up for life. But the day the world turned purple and I knew God was real was when and how my sobriety began.

The judge meant it when he said "as long as it takes." I spent eight months in a six-week program. By the time I left treatment, I felt like I was leaving home and graduating from college. Instead of getting a journalism degree, I got a Ph.D. in being a junkie, and then one in cleaning up.

My child's father and his parents refused to let me have my son, even though I was sober. People were beginning to understand more about alcoholism and addiction. It wasn't a matter of will-power. Addiction is a disease. Anyone could get it: rich, poor, men, women, children. The next stage of the revolution began. Treatment centers were opening in almost every major city. We learned that if we cleaned up alcoholics, they make decent people. But we didn't understand yet that women were fit mothers after they got sober. I stopped the custody battle over my son. I didn't want my child ripped in half. He'd already been through enough.

God gave me a new beginning. Finally, I had enough sense to be ashamed of my past. From my perspective, this new life was the only part that counted. I felt guilty about the past and giving up my son, but I knew stopping the custody battle was one way— maybe the only way—I could show my child true love.

Two years later, I married a tall, handsome man of Irish descent—a chemical dependency counselor at a major treatment center in the Twin Cities. He was in recovery, too (only he preferred alcohol, not drugs). A month after our wedding, I became pregnant. Within three years, we had two children: Nichole and Shane. I had everything I ever wanted: a real family of my own with two children and a mom and a dad. My new life made up for every painful experience I'd had. I thought this was my reward— my prize—for getting clean and sober.

By then, I worked at the same treatment program where my husband worked. I wanted to help other addicts, but they made me work with the spouses. We didn't have the word *codependents* yet; we called them "significant others." But they weren't significant to anyone, including themselves. I didn't know what to do with this group of overly helpful women. They were so obsessed with their husbands and boyfriends they couldn't see anything else. Simultaneously, something was going wrong with my marriage. It had been since our wedding. But I didn't know what the problem was. I didn't know what a real family looked or felt like, and I didn't know how love felt. When I told my husband something was wrong, he agreed. He said the problem was me. That made sense; I'd felt there was something wrong with me all my life.

I saw all the red flags—in retrospect. But it all became clear the day the toilet kept running. I jiggled the handle. When that didn't work, I removed the lid. In the tank was a bottle of vodka. My husband had been sneak-drinking since before we met. That's what was wrong. I'd married a practicing alcoholic who'd been lying to me since the day we met. I began to see that the reason I didn't understand those hand-wringing, anxiety-filled, overly helpful women—the significant others—was that I didn't understand myself. From then on, I began to catch my husband drinking regularly. I became the sobriety police.

A neighbor encouraged me to attend Al-Anon after years of listening to me complain about his drinking. I refused to go to those meetings at first. Why should I get help? My husband had the problem. I was already in recovery for chemical dependency. I didn't want or need to work two programs. Yes, I'd been feeling somewhat suicidal. (It happens as codependency progresses.) But I wouldn't kill myself. Too many people needed me. Besides, if reincarnation was real, I'd have to come back and do this horrible life over again. So I lived life vacillating between wishing I or my husband was dead.

Lately I'd been trying to teach my husband lessons. I wanted him to know how much I hurt. I wanted him to think I was using drugs again. I wasn't—but I wanted him to feel the pain I'd been feeling. I didn't understand that the person I should be telling how I felt was me. Then I had my second spiritual awakening.

Many people have spiritual awakenings after attending recovery groups for years. Gradually, after seeing the changes in themselves and their lives, they acknowledge the existence of a loving Higher Power—not just "a God," but as Bill Wilson describes it in the *Big Book of Alcoholics Anonymous,* a personal god who knows, loves, and cares about us. I have my spiritual experiences first, then I work the programs. In my first spiritual experience at the state hospital, I realized God was real. In my second awakening, I stopped blaming my husband long enough to see myself. I was real, too! I surrendered. I wasn't happy about it, but I attended my first Al-Anon meeting and let the perky woman guide me to a chair.

I started crying when I heard other people's stories. That doesn't sound like much, but feeling emotions was a miracle to me. Chemically dependent people numb themselves with alcohol and drugs. They don't know or feel what they're feeling. Codependents go numb by obsessing, controlling, denying. I hadn't felt anything for so long that I barely remembered what a feeling was. Looking back, I see I was stuck in the first stage of grief.

It's not "sick" to want to save your marriage. It's natural to grieve when you lose something important, and my marriage was valuable to me. My losses had been piling up since the wedding—actually since I was born. Besides the drinking, I knew that my husband had been unfaithful. It's crazy-making when we feel guilty and apologize when the other person does something wrong. When I heard other people talk about their feelings, my heart opened and I began feeling mine. The moment I started feeling, healing began.

I wasn't crazy. I was codependent. What a relief.

Although people might read my story and think change happened in one moment, that's not true. Getting sober, then beginning recovery from codependency were processes that took years of hurting, wearing myself out using drugs or trying to sober up someone else, and trying unsuccessfully to control people and things I couldn't. Many of us are stubborn. It takes a long time to wear ourselves out and get ready to surrender to Truth.

Codependency is subtle, insidious. To recover from chemical dependency, we admit that we're powerless over alcohol. We realize we aren't controlling alcohol; it's controlling us. Now alcohol was controlling me again, but it was the alcohol *someone else* was drinking. That's what made it so confusing. I began to see I'm powerless over almost everything. It's a painful, defeated feeling when we admit we're that powerless and our lives are that messed up. The good news is, when we surrender to what we're powerlessness over, we discover our true power.

Recovering from addictions was grueling. But surprisingly, healing from codependency became fun after I surrendered to the pain. It feels good to take care of ourselves. I became excited, then obsessed—but now I was obsessed with codependency. (Obsession can be positive.) I wanted to learn everything I could—not about the alcoholic, but about this thing that had brought me to my knees. The perky woman who welcomed me to my first meeting was right: If we're alcoholics or addicts *and* codependents, we are Double Winners. Codependency gave me the pieces I needed to make my recovery from chemical dependency complete.

The wheel of life turns constantly. It's the wheel that creates paradigm shifts, changes in perception, and changes in our lives. Often events in one person's life symbolize these larger shifts in the world. His Holiness the Dalai Lama was ousted from Tibet. But many people say that the Dalai Lama's loss was the world's gain. His departure from Tibet symbolized the enlightenment principles spreading from a tiny country atop a large mountain all the way around the world to the United States. These principles became the basics of recovery and self-care: nonattachment (letting go and detaching); nonresistance (surrender and acceptance); present moment living (one day at a time); and awareness (taking inventory daily). Recovery also encourages prayer and meditation. People in recovery learn to live like little monks—they're offered a spiritual way of life.

We connect with ourselves and learn to connect in healthy ways with other people. We develop a personal relationship with God, a Higher Power of our understanding. We find meaning in every detail of our lives; there isn't anything that we did or that happened to us that can't be used for good. We finally find our purpose instead of feeling like a mistake. Plus we get the tools to handle any experience we encounter. These are some of the gifts of recovery. That's what we win, and it's a lot more than two things.

Codependency: The Primary Problem

Al-Anon and Adult Children of Alcoholics meetings *are* real recoveries. Although I wrote four books about the subject between 1986 and 1991, it wasn't until 2003 that I understood how important codependency is. I don't know how much longer I'll be here; none of us do. There were some issues I wanted to clear up, some additional ideas I'd learned, and some misconceptions people had about my earlier writings that I needed to clarify. I wasn't finished with writing about codependency until I covered these ideas. More had been revealed.

There are no accidents, preached a cofounder of the treatment program where I worked in the seventies. I thought he was crazy when he said that. Of course, accidents happen! Later I realized he was really saying, *Everything happens for a reason.*

In 2002, a man approached me at a book signing and asked, "Remember me?"

I didn't.

"We rode the same bus to the academy in Minneapolis," he explained. He was still involved with the high school and asked if I'd please speak to the students. I had stopped almost all public speaking after my son Shane died in 1991 in a ski accident; I hadn't gone near that school since the sixties. I still pretended that part of my life—everything that happened before I got sober—didn't count and wasn't real. Now this man I didn't remember wanted me to travel back in time to a life I didn't consider mine? At first I thought *No way.* Then something tugged at me.

This wasn't accidental. It was part of a pilgrimage.

Most people take pictures of moments they want to remember. I didn't have any of those moments until after I got sober. I had destroyed or avoided pictures of myself from age four (when the first abduction and molestation happened) until twenty-four. I especially went out of my way to destroy all pictures of myself as a teenager. That was the peak of my self-hatred. If a word stronger than *hate* existed, I'd use it because that's how I felt about myself. Since age three, Mom said I was an accident, a burden. I felt bad that she got stuck with me. I had my life divided in two compartments: everything before I got sober and everything that happened after. I wanted to forget the "before" part. But now I was going back.

I walked up to the podium at the high school I'd attended. Most of my teachers who were still living came that morning to say hi. I was touched by their kindness. How much love did my self-hatred stop me from seeing and feeling all my childhood? Maybe it wasn't that God didn't do His part; maybe I didn't take care of business by not caring for and loving myself. The school's curriculum—an emphasis on creativity combined with spirituality—impressed me. I'd been so resentful those years, I missed a rich experience. Now I regretted that my senior year I went to the public high school in the neighborhood where I lived. I only needed two credits—I was that close to graduation. I got a rich education from that school, but I still wonder how much richer it would have been if I'd been a healthy person and could have made the most of those years instead of making myself numb.

The principal introduced me, then said he had a surprise. "I found two pictures of you," he said. Using the overhead projector, he flashed them on the wall behind me. I turned and stared, struggling to maintain my composure. There she was, bigger than life—that girl I hated so much, the one I'd left behind. I didn't think any traces of her still existed. The students laughed. "You look so different now," a girl said. I looked at that ugly girl on the wall wearing thick, horn-rimmed glasses. I saw so much pain and darkness in my eyes. Seeing myself knocked the wind out of me. I felt something untwist inside. Luckily, I'd done enough speaking, I pretended that everything was okay (I could do a speech in my sleep). I turned back to the students, made a joke, got them laughing, then spoke to them from my heart.

"Some of us have this disease, but it's still okay to be who we are," I said. "That's who God created. There aren't any accidents. In the end, it all works out." I said we were lucky; now students could get help that wasn't available when I attended school. I said not to feel ashamed if anyone had that disease, and couldn't stop drinking or using drugs, or if they'd been abused. Asking for help takes courage. "The things we do that we hate ourselves for can become the gifts we use to help others heal. That's what true love is. That's what God's love is, too. We're all part of it—God's love—by being ourselves."

Afterwards, some students thanked me. Some wanted to tell me their stories. If I helped one student not to hate themselves as much as I had hated myself, it would be the most important speaking engagement in my career.

In Tibet, devotees walk in circles on pilgrimages. They believe that Life moves in circles. Other people believe *If we run fast enough, we run into ourselves.* I'd been running since I was a child. Now I'd come full circle. I'd run so fast and far I'd run into myself. It was also part of a pilgrimage that had just begun.

I'd spent years working on my feelings—past and current. I know how important feelings are. Releasing one emotion can bring instantaneous change by bringing us into balance. After Shane's death I didn't take antidepressants (not that it would have been wrong, but I wanted to feel my grief). I thought I'd cleared my emotional past until the day I walked out of that school.

The thing that untwisted when I saw that picture released something so thick, dark, and heavy it was beyond my comprehension at first. I couldn't even cry. Later when the tears came, they didn't bring relief. I'd sink into depression. It felt like an anchor was pulling me to the bottom of the ocean. I was drowning. I couldn't break loose, swim, or float. I didn't understand the feelings or what they connected to. They were relentless. I'd start to feel normal, then the feelings pulled me under again. I was gasping for air. It didn't compare to grieving over Shane's death. That's comparing apples to bananas. But in thirty years of doing "emotional work," I hadn't experienced anything as heavy and confusing as this.

It lasted for months. A friend who takes antidepressants told me to take them, too. I refused. This was more than depression. Then one day I understood. This was how I felt as a child and teenager. This is what I'd medicated against since age twelve; this is what I had been running from—the part I'd cut off and left behind. *It's a miracle I didn't kill myself,* I thought, although I'd attempted suicide several times. *It would have been impossible for me to deal with these emotions back then. There wasn't help for problems like this—the understanding and healing wasn't in the consciousness yet. With all my skills, I could barely deal with these emotions now.*

That's when I understood how important codependency is. Although drinking and using drugs became a self-destructive addiction and a primary problem, alcohol and drugs also saved my life. I'd been medicating myself, only there wasn't enough medication to make all this pain disappear. Using alcohol and drugs is another survival behavior—but it can become a disease of its own.

That's not an excuse or justification; it's an explanation. There's a reason everything happens, including why some children become alcoholics or addicts. They're medicating emotions. The problem is, the medication becomes a potentially fatal disease. No matter what we call them (Al-Anons, Adult Children of Alcoholics, codependents), the problem of codependency isn't secondary. It's a dangerous, potentially fatal and primary problem that often comes *before* the chemical dependency. Codependency is as deadly as chemical dependency. It's a *real* problem, as confusing and insidious as alcoholism to the people who have it. When we're addicted, we know we're messed up. With codependency, we only see other people and we look good, compared to them.

Another gift happened from returning to my high school. I forgave myself for being an addict and alcoholic. I set myself free. I didn't have to pretend that part of my life never happened because I finally saw how important it was. There was value in my childhood addiction. There's value in all parts of our lives, even those parts we call mistakes.

At one time, addicts weren't allowed in AA meetings. Now, most AA groups welcome addicts. Then we went through a time when many recovering addicts (like me) were biased against Al-Anon and codependency. Some of that bias still floats around, but finally some of it is lifting.

Just as options to codependency behaviors such as letting go, not controlling, and setting boundaries mainstreamed into the nonrecovering culture, they've now become part of many AA groups. Some members of AA groups feel free to discuss codependency issues there; some are officially called Double Winner Meetings. Although many fundamentalists want to follow all the original rules and keep recovery exactly the same as it was in the beginning, others realize that recovery and healing from all kinds of issues is experimental. Part of taking care of ourselves is staying open to new ideas while still practicing the basics.

Most recovering addicts and alcoholics have codependency underneath.

I wrote that in *Codependent No More*. Now I'm writing it again, this time in bold print. By year seven, codependency can create serious problems for recovering alcoholics and addicts. Sometimes people can't get sober until they deal with their codependency first. Sometimes people deal with their codependency by year two of sobriety. But the seven-year mark is a generally accepted recovery rule of thumb.

Addicted or Pseudo Addicted?

Codependency—an already complex issue, may become even more complicated when someone we love is an alcoholic or an addict. We can become so overly engaged in addictive patterns that we become addicted, too. The Classic Codependent, people say, becomes addicted to being surrounded and victimized by addicts and alcoholics. That energy and way of relating becomes miserably comfortable. To us, it feels like love.

Eventually, we may drink or use drugs to be with the alcoholic. Or people may engage in pseudo addiction—drinking or taking drugs to ease emotional pain caused by codependent behaviors that hurt. We look like we're drug seeking or drinking alcoholically, but we're drinking or using drugs to medicate pain that really hurts. When the pain is adequately medicated or stops, our drug-seeking or alcoholic drinking stops, too.

Sometimes the emotional pain escalates, turning into true physical problems with legitimate physical pain. In *Codependent No More*, chapter 4, you'll find a chart of codependent characteristics. At the end of the characteristics, I write that codependency is progressive, leading to serious physical, mental, or emotional illnesses. As the pain from these illnesses increases, the person often increases self-medication.

We each need to decide if addiction or alcoholism is a primary or secondary problem, or if we're suffering from pseudo or true addiction. The easiest way to decide is to see if we can stop drinking or using drugs without help. If we can, we're not addicted. We should consult a doctor if a physical illness has become chronic and the pain we're medicating doesn't stop. Ideally, we need to consult a doctor knowledgeable in addictions and codependency, although doctors like that are rare.

If we've lost control of our drinking or are addicted to drugs, we need to deal with that problem, too. Some of us may need to take medications for legitimate, chronic physical problems. We may be dependent on medication to be able to function and for quality of life.

This is how to tell if we have a healthy dependency or an unhealthy addiction, according to Dr. Forest Tennant, an addiction and pain management specialist who understands codependency and chronic illnesses:

a) Healthy dependency on anything *improves* while addiction *destroys* quality of life and ability to function.
b) Loss of control accompanies addiction.

"I did an informal survey of people in Alcoholics Anonymous," Dr. Tennant said. "Although it doesn't qualify as a controlled study, I learned that about seventy percent of the people in Alcoholics Anonymous began drinking or using drugs to medicate physical or emotional pain."

If addiction or pseudo addiction is a problem, we will probably need to deal with that first—although there are no rules. Some people need to tackle their codependency issues before they're able to stop medicating the pain and become ready to let go of addiction or alcoholism.

Codependency isn't minor. The problems from it can progress, become fatal, or cause relapse unless we address those issues. It's common for codependents to medicate emotions. Codependency hurts. Again, it's about crossing lines. When we cross the line from social or problem drinking, or pseudo addiction into true alcoholism and addiction, alcoholism becomes a primary problem of its own. But at some time to continue our healing, we need to address the issues underneath. Codependency is one.

Dual-Addicted

We can have any combination of issues or addictions: gambling, sex, love, drug, alcoholism, codependency, obsessive-compulsive disorder, depression, bipolar, anorexia, bulimia, other eating disorders, manic depression, or attention deficit disorder. The issues and combinations are nearly endless.

Back in the seventies, when people got sober and stopped self-medicating, the problems they medicated would suddenly appear. They'd just pop out. Sometimes they would come out of nowhere. We didn't have answers for them yet. We hadn't named the pain. When an unnamed problem without a solution appeared, the recovering person with the underlying problem felt disappointed, confused, and crazy. Sobriety—which promised so much—let them down.

I remember some of these people vividly. Many had their initial breakdowns in the middle of an AA meeting. They'd begun self-medicating because the problem hurt so much. Now they'd taken their medication away with nothing to replace it. Some people killed themselves. Others spent years in deep despair. Some went into institutions. They worked a good program so when these underlying issues surfaced, they didn't understand what was happening or why. We stood by helplessly and watched people suffer, and didn't know what to do. The surfacing of other underlying problems nearly destroyed some people and killed others.

It's time to forgive ourselves for having issues. It's not like addicts and codependents are the only people with problems. We don't live in a "we" and "them" world. It's one big "us." We're people learning lessons. Everyone has something and some of us have two things. Some have three or four.

Don't rush it. If you've recently begun recovering from alcoholism, don't force another recovery on yourself. When the time is right, it'll happen. When and if another recovery issue presents itself, or if you're in recovery for one issue and your recovery stops working, see if there's another problem underneath. If trustworthy people say it quacks and waddles, check to see if it's a duck. Ask. We'll get answers because now the answers are here. Welcome Double Winners. Stop resisting. Surrender. Win two or three times!

QUESTIONS AND ACTIVITIES

1. Are you a Double Winner? Have you identified yourself as having more than one issue? Have people suggested that you look at another issue, but you refuse because you don't want another problem? What is the other problem? If you're feeling suicidal, repeatedly relapsing, depressed, stuck, or confused but don't understand the problem, maybe you do have two issues—whether you want two or not. Are you willing to become willing to surrender to the second problem? That's a yes or no question. Write your answer here: _____.

2. Love yourself for your illnesses, disorders, or problems. If you haven't forgiven yourself for issues, problems, or illnesses, start using this affirmation or write one yourself. I forgive, love, and accept myself for having _____ and/or _____. I'm grateful for the lessons these issues have taught me and the gifts they've given, and all I'm going to learn. Then look in the mirror—into your eyes. Say the words out loud three times daily for twenty-one days or until you know you're speaking the truth. It's easy to feel guilty for having issues like addictions or codependency, but it's time to forgive yourself.

3. Find your way. Are you prejudiced against any programs? Are you unsure what your secondary problem is, or if you even have one? Are you ready to let Life show you what it wants you to see? Here's HOW: Honesty, Openness, and Willingness to try. It's an old saying that's been around so long because it works. Write your request, "Please show me in a way I can understand what the problem is. Thank you." Then let go and wait. Your answer will come. Ask sincerely and you'll be shown.

4. Find the right resources. If you need help from another resource, group, therapist, or treatment center, continue looking until you find the right one. Now there are more resources available than ever and some are better than others. Each group has its own personality. Treatment and therapists cost money.

Ensure that you get your money's worth, that the resource has an excellent reputation, and that it's right for you or the person you love. The initial help we get is the foundation for our recovery and the rest of our lives. Make sure your foundation is solid. Investigate. Get referrals. (A rule of thumb: Attend groups three times before deciding and trust *your* intuition.)

5. Don't overdo. We don't have to spend our whole lives in therapy, treatment, or groups. In the beginning or in a crisis, attending ninety meetings in ninety days can help. But the goal is to go to meetings and get help so that we can have a life. Trust our guidance about how often we need to attend which group or use a particular resource. Don't attempt so much that you become overwhelmed and give up. We may need more help from one resource temporarily because that problem hurts most at the time. Adjust our schedules according to what we need. The goal is balance. Sometimes we outgrow a group or sponsor. It's okay to do that without guilt as long as we're not in denial. As we grow, our recovery needs will change. Be flexible and open, and Life will show you what to do.

6. Enjoy a healthy self-image. Alcoholism and other addictions are diseases. Codependency is a problem. We don't need to label ourselves "sick." We have alcoholism for life, but healing doesn't have to take forever. Don't reinforce a victim self-image by saying how sick we'll always be. Words are powerful. Our bodies respond to what we say. Don't program ourselves into being sick people even though we have a disease for life. We can be healthy, whole, and complete in the moment we're in now. If we have codependent behaviors, we don't have to label ourselves at all. Deal with the behaviors that hurt and call yourself whatever you want.

5 · Communication

FAX OR FICTION?

"I don't like your tone," a web message board manager wrote to a member.

"HOW CAN YOU TELL MY TONE FROM READING?" the member asked. "TONE CAN ONLY BE HEARD."

"I feel like you're screaming when you write emails using all capital letters," one friend said to another.

"I'M NOT HOLLERING," the friend wrote. "SOMETIMES THE CAPS LOCK KEY ON MY COMPUTER STICKS."

Some people are being conned into believing that well-chosen words exchanged on the internet represent *true love*. While many great things are made possible by the internet, we can't believe everything we read any more than we can believe whatever we hear.

Emails and text messages are unique forms of communication, requiring special care. When I wrote *Codependent No More*, communication options included: speaking in person or on telephones; the written, spoken, or typed word; media transmissions via satellite, radio, or TV; telegraphs; faxes; Morse code; smoke signals; and ESP. Now emails, websites, text and instant messaging, cordless and cell phones need to be added to the list. Some cars have phones in the ceilings. Push a button, say the number, and the phone dials itself. But beware. Many people now consider lawsuits a profitable vocation. People can openly discuss ideas in some states without fear of legal repercussion. In others, the spoken word or emails constitute binding legal agreements.

The oddest evolution in communication is this: After working hard to prevent verbal (and all) abuse—not that abuse is eliminated—people now stand in line waiting to be verbally abused publicly on some radio and TV shows. (Most of us have seen women stand in line waiting to be degraded on television for their fifteen minutes of fame. Who hasn't listened to a radio show where the host—supposedly a source of healing information—calls her phone-in guests names that a decade ago we were "trying to heal from because our mother or father called us that?") Codependency mutates, adapts to the culture, and finds a way to stay alive in the same way that viruses and bacteria continue to survive despite new cures.

What hasn't changed is that communication is the art of self-expression. We communicate in many ways: body language, sign language, looks, touch. Whatever form we use, communication is how we connect with ourselves, God, people, animals—the world. But one of, if not *the* most powerful form of communication is words. According to the Old and New Testaments, and Kabala (the mystical side of Judaism), words created the universe. Whether spoken, written, or thought—words continue to create our world.

Words also have the power to hurt or heal. For better or worse, words have a physiological effect on people and their bodies, according to *The Worst Is Over: What to Say When Every Moment Counts*, by Judith Acosta and Judith Simon Prager. We don't need to speak words for them to have power. Pass a stranger. Think a positive thought. Then notice the stranger's instantaneous reaction. Words are living things. They can heal, but they also can hurt and deceive. How many of us have been hurt by words spoken in anger, or felt betrayed by believing lies? Who hasn't had to undo the damage done by being tagged with a certain adjective—from stupid to dumb to unforgiveable?

The following ideas will help improve communication, no matter which form we use. The biggest barrier to communication is again repressed emotions. Sections Three and Four will cover that. Like setting boundaries, communication is connected to overall growth. The more we love ourselves, the easier it becomes to express who we are.

Communication Tips

1. Go Fish. "When you fish, find out what level the fish are at and what they're interesting in eating," a teacher said, using fishing to teach me about communicating more effectively. In my naïveté, I expected people to come to me—adapt to my point of view and what I wanted to talk about. We'll be more effective and more interesting—and more able to talk to a wider range of people—when we learn to go to them. Find out where people are in their growth; find out what interests them. Discover what we have in common with others. Learn to value and appreciate the differences, too. Like my friend Ginny says: "If two people are the same, one of them isn't necessary." Often, especially if we feel insecure or need to control, we won't be comfortable unless people agree with us. Go fish when you talk to people. We may learn something new.

✐ ACTIVITY

When I first began working on codependency issues, communication was painful. I loved writing. But talking to people face to face was something else. I didn't know what to say—how to make small talk or chat and be myself. Talking about more sensitive issues was even harder. If communication is difficult, use the fishing exercise the next time you meet someone new or attend a gathering.

2. Harmonize. Confrontation is a form of communication used in groups, treatment centers, therapy, and personal relationships. People *tell it like it is.* Some people pride themselves on being confrontational and not speaking with compassion. We can confront if we want, but there's a predictable result: Most people become defensive when attacked. Harmonizing is an alternative to confrontation. It's a powerful way to communicate when people have opposing points of view (POV) or when we want to discuss something delicate. Aikido, a soft martial art, teaches about harmonizing. (*Soft* means it can be used only defensively, not to attack.) Harmonizing sees and acknowledges the validity of both people's POVs. We feel secure enough to allow ourselves to see the world—at least for a moment—the way others do. Instead of telling people what's wrong with how they see things or what they do, we acknowledge their POV. Then we gently segue into our POV, explaining why it has value, too. Because harmonizing doesn't attack, it eliminates the need to defend. We're not dogmatically positioning ourselves *against;* we're agreeing with as much as we can. We take the time and have the maturity to know that how we see things isn't the only legitimate way. Everyone wins because we're not fighting. We're making peace and possibly new friends.

Someone pounds on our door. "Turn that bleeping stereo down!" a neighbor in our condominium screams. "I can't sleep!"

"I'll do what I want. I own a condo, too," we yell back.

We could say, "I can see how aggravating this is if you're trying to sleep. I'll lower the volume or use headphones after ten at night. I want living in this building to work for both of us. How can we make this work?"

It's not difficult to know which approach might start a war and which one might bring peace.

Switch roles. Become the person disrupted by the noise. We could respond the way the aggravated neighbor did. Or we could harmonize. Harmonizing requires releasing emotions such as anger first. Then we can say calmly, "I live next door. You've got a great stereo system; I wish I could afford one like that. But I've got to get up in six hours and go to work. Your stereo's bass is so good it's rattling my walls. Is there some way you could enjoy your music and I could get my sleep?"

There are some qualifications. If we're asking someone not to make noise during daytime hours, we may be out of line. Maybe *we* need to wear soundproof headphones or earplugs instead of asking the person to not make any noise during daytime hours. Whatever the circumstances, take time to see the situation from the other person's POV. Harmonizing demands setting aside ego *and* our need to win or be right. It doesn't mean we're weak, passive, or being doormats. The more powerful we are, the more we can use diplomacy to harmonize, negotiate, and live in peace. We'll have enough esteem to be able to compromise and meet most people halfway. Walk in someone else's shoes. A tendency people often have is thinking our POV is the only one that exists. *How can they do that?* We ask. *How can they say that or think that way?* We assume because we see things this way, everyone else does, too. Spiritual maturity means acknowledging each person has a unique POV. Being different doesn't equal being wrong or right.

✎ ACTIVITY

When facing an argument, follow these steps to harmonize but also use intuition to adapt these suggestions to your circumstance. They're suggestions—not rules.

1. Immediately (or as soon as possible) let go of resistance to the problem. Accept that it exists.

2. Release emotions first, before talking to the other person. We're more effective if we're calm and clear. When we communicate from an emotional base, our emotions are controlling us.

3. Set aside ego. Do you want to win or do you want peace?

4. Consciously see the other person's POV. How would we feel if we were him or her?

5. As much as possible, acknowledge the validity of the other person's POV. If you were going through what that person is going through, or came from where he or she did, maybe you'd feel and see things that way, too.

6. Propose creative solutions so all people get what they want. Is there a solution available that allows both people to win?

3. Communicate Authentically. Are we talking to manipulate, control, or alter someone's perception instead of to honestly express ourselves? We can't simultaneously communicate who we are *and* control or manipulate. When we're manipulating or controlling, we're not speaking our truth. If we're numb or disconnected from ourselves, we may not know what our truth is! Maybe we're not lying, but we're not being who we are. It's not deliberate. Some of us have been codependent chameleons for so long we don't have a sense of ourselves at all. Our intuitive responses to people—and how they talk to us—can give us real hints to what other people are up to, and where they're at. But that requires trusting ourselves and knowing what we're feeling. If people are trying to control us, we'll feel like we want to back off, run away, escape. If we're being manipulated, we'll feel confused and cruddy after the conversation ends. Another communication problem is draining energy or power from someone under the guise of "talking." People may act like they want to have a conversation with us, but many people with codependency issues use conversation as a way to get us to take care of them. They're draining our energy the way thieves siphon gas from someone's car. People segue from asking how the other person is into begging the person to tell them what to do, listen to them complain, or take care of them emotionally. If someone is "taking power" in communication, it can be detected by how the person who is robbed of power feels when the conversation ends—exhausted, drained, or depleted. When someone feels incomplete and thinks another person holds the missing piece to them, they drain other people's energy or take their power. Is someone controlling, manipulating, or draining you? Does seeing someone's name on your Caller ID evoke a groan, or do you hide in another aisle when you see the person at the grocery store because (whether you have the words to describe it or not), you know he or she wants to control, manipulate, or suck your soul? Or is the situation reversed? Are people avoiding you? Do you want something you're not honest about or aware of from them? Do you want them to fix you, validate you, make you feel better? Do you believe they have some magic, insight, answers, or power you don't? Do you think that someone else has the power to make you feel whole and complete?

✐ ACTIVITY

Pay attention to how we feel when conversations end.

4. Talk After Releasing Emotions. Picture a woman throwing herself on the hood of her husband's car. "Please don't go. I can't live without you," she pleads, slipping off the car while he drives away. That's talking from an emotional base. Usually our conversations aren't that dramatic. But we'll still communicate more effectively if we release emotions first, then communicate. Communicating from an emotional base means emotions are controlling us. We're not in balance—we haven't acknowledged, felt, and released our emotions yet. Many people with codependency issues babble. This is anxiety and fear coming out as a continuous (annoying and irritating) string of words. That doesn't mean we can't talk *about* feelings to help us get in touch with them. It means we're mastering our emotional selves instead of letting feelings control us. We feel and release emotions, come into balance, then peacefully say what we have to say. When we're clear, we'll know what that is. When we talk from our center instead of speaking from an emotional base, our words will be more powerful. Expressing what we're furious about in a calm manner is usually more effective than screeching like a shrew.

ACTIVITY

If emotions are causing communication problems, read and do the activities in Sections Three and Four.

5. Talk from the Heart. When Life thrust me from being a hack reporter for a daily paper to speaking to groups of up to five thousand people and appearing on radio and TV shows, I learned the value of talking from the heart instead of from the ego or the head. When I tried to impress people or get a standing ovation, I'd fail miserably. But when I forgot myself and what I wanted to *get,* and sincerely asked my Higher Power to love people using me as an instrument, my talks were good; they worked. People responded well to what I said. Plus I felt so good giving, I didn't care what I received in return.

ACTIVITY

Instead of worrying about what we're going to say, use a prayer or mantra first. My favorite is a Bible verse: "Let the words of my mouth and the meditations of my heart be acceptable in Thy sight." That can be rephrased to reflect the religion or beliefs of our choice. What we're doing is asking God to keep our intentions pure, and love people through us by using our words.

6. Don't Bounce Words. Responsible people don't write checks without sufficient funds in the bank. If they do, they get a bad credit rating. Reputation is worth more than gold. Are we good for our word? Sometimes we offer assistance too soon. We hear about a problem and instantly offer to help. Before the words leave our mouth, we regret what we said. Instead of being honest, we call at the last minute with a lame excuse and don't do what we committed to doing. Most people see through us. We become known as someone not good for our word. Don't volunteer so quickly. If we do jump in too soon, use the truth to get ourselves out of a commitment we regret making. A check is a promise to pay. Our word is a promise of what we'll do. Don't let our words bounce. Either make good on them, or take them back.

✐ ACTIVITY

Make being good for our word a boundary for ourselves and people in our circle—when we're prepared to enforce it. If what people do doesn't match what they say, it's a sign that they may not be people we want in our lives.

7. Censor Ourselves. I don't endorse censorship, but we'll be more effective communicators when we censor ourselves. We don't have to tell people every thought we think. We can also censor what we think and say about ourselves. Many of us wouldn't allow someone to verbally abuse us. Yet the way we think or talk about ourselves is worse than how we'd let anyone else talk about us. Another area for self-censorship concerns talking about feelings. When dealing with feelings became popular, many people thought they needed to share every feeling with whomever the feeling involved or whomever would listen to them. It's not essential to always tell people how we feel. Learn when to censor ourselves—otherwise our communication will be a lot of noise. Note: The opposite of this may be true for some people. Maybe we don't talk enough. If it's true, reverse the above ideas. Stop censoring yourself so much. Let yourself go; open up your mouth and talk. Don't worry so much. Most of us stick our foot in our mouths now and again. If that happens, take the foot out and apologize. That's why we've been given the concept of making amends as a relationship and living tool.

QUESTIONS

✐ Do we need to censor ourselves? Or are we censoring ourselves too much? If you're unsure, write out your question: Do I talk too little or too much? You can ask Life and your Higher Power to please help you see yourself clearly. This request asked sincerely gets answered. Also, observe yourself. Be aware, conscious, when you have a conversation. Are you tense? Do you out-talk the other person? I spent years assuming people knew what was going on inside me because I knew. I didn't want to speak too much. When it was time for communication to be my lesson, people began prodding me to speak up about how I felt—to say what my answers were, and what I had to say.

8. Practice Verbal Nonresistance. If people accuse us of something we didn't do, if they attack or confront us, or say anything unfair, it's instinctive to become defensive. That's an excellent opportunity to practice nonresistance. Almost everything I needed to learn about communication, I learned writing for the daily paper. When people wrote letters to the editor bashing a reporter, we weren't allowed to respond. It was hard to stand there and not defend myself. Ultimately, the training was so valuable I should have paid my employer for it. When we defend ourselves, we look guilty—especially if the person has made up his or her mind about us. The only way I've been able to win when verbally attacked is by practicing nonresistance. That doesn't mean we can't speak our truth. When it's time to do that, we will and we'll be guided.

We don't ever allow people to verbally abuse us. But if someone is being antagonistic or trying to start an argument, practicing verbal nonresistance will help. Instead of making mountains out of molehills, nonresistance makes the mountain or molehill disappear. "You're overweight and ugly," someone says, trying to provoke an argument. What if we said, "Hmm. Maybe I am a few pounds over my desired weight. Maybe not. Heck, beauty is skin deep. Who doesn't want to be prettier than they are?" When we respond that way, there's not much anyone can say. If someone does keep going, we can continue practicing nonresistance. (This is usually true unless it's aggressive abuse.) Nonresistance goes against every instinct we have. But when we learn to do it, we'll be aligned with power; people won't be able to take away our Peace. We can't control what people say or write, except by suing for slander, libel, or getting a verbal restraining order. (I had to get one once; my ex-husband would come to the house to see the children and say nasty things about me. The restraining order specifically said he couldn't say certain things to me. It's not something we hear about often, but this verbal restraining order worked.) But restraining orders are last resorts, not initial responses. What if we don't respond at all to lies or slander? Eventually, Truth comes into the Light. In comic strips, writers put character's words in "balloons." Verbal nonresistance will take the air out of people's word balloons. It's impossible to argue when one person refuses to fight and instead responds only with peace.

✍ ACTIVITY

If you're interested in learning more about harmonizing and nonresistance, read about translating Aikido practices into spiritual living principles. Helpful books on the subject include *The Way of Aikido*, by George Leonard, and *The Practice of Freedom*, by Wendy Palmer and Jack Kornfield.

9. Speak from the Middle. *Talking out of both sides of our mouth* means saying one thing to someone—usually what we think that person wants to hear—then the opposite to someone else. Talking out of both sides of our mouth is cruel. We can't trust people who talk out of both sides of their mouths any more than we can trust people pleasers, which means we can't trust them at all. If people gossip about others, it's not a big leap to believe they're talking that way about us, too. The more sensitive and aware we become, the more we can feel the presence of the words around a person—negative or positive. Even people not spiritually evolved react to the field created by a person's words and thoughts. If someone is angry and bitter, we can sense and feel it. If someone is at peace, we feel that, too. This doesn't mean we can't talk to a trusted friend to release feelings or sort something out, but that's different from engaging in malicious gossip. A good boundary is to talk about a person the same way we talk to the person. Speak only from the middle, not out of both sides of our mouths. If we stick to our Truth, we'll say the same thing, no matter who we're talking to.

QUESTIONS

✍ Are we talking out of both sides of our mouths? Do we know someone who is doing this? If we're doing it, what are we gaining from it? If someone else is doing it, how does it affect how we feel about the person?

Note: As you go through these questions and activities, you may get ideas about boundaries you need to set. Take a minute and write these ideas in your boundary book so you don't forget. You also may get ideas about behaviors you want to change. Or you may decide that you have people in your life who you've been calling friends who aren't behaving friendly toward you. Make notes and you'll find yourself addressing these issues when it's time.

10. Make Saying the Hard Stuff Easy. The more we say the hard stuff, the easier it becomes. What's difficult to say may be different for each person. It can include saying no, saying what we want, or saying what we know people don't want to hear. Sometimes we'll have to make an opening to speak, like carving a path through a forest, or we'll need to muster the courage necessary to speak. It helps to know beforehand what we're going to say, but we shouldn't rehearse the words too much or it will sound like we're reading a script. Learn to say the hard stuff and the easy stuff. Before long, all of it will be the same: We'll be expressing our Truth, who we are, and what we honestly have to say.

QUESTION

✍ What's the hardest thing for you to say or to talk about? Do you have something you'd like to say to someone now that you've been avoiding, denying, resisting, or repressing? What and to whom? Turn saying that into a goal. You might want to give yourself a month to tell someone something important, something you need to say to him or her.

11. Practice Presence for Others and Ourselves. With so many forms of communication available, it's common to see people talking on the cell phone with one person on hold. They get rid of the first person, talk to the person on hold, then another call breaks in. They finish talking to both people, then call someone else. Before getting two sentences out, another call beeps in. If they do get a break, they send a text message or check their email. This isn't communication. It's compulsive babbling. People aren't present when their communication and conversations are scattered all over that way. They haven't listened to anyone—not even themselves. Communication is a two-way street: talking and listening. Be present for ourselves. Be present for our conversations—what we say and what we hear. Listen to the spaces in between the words, too. A lot is said there. Take time to put silence between our conversations. We may even start remembering what was said.

✎ ACTIVITIES

For a week, spend an hour each day practicing silent presence for ourselves: how we feel, what we're doing, our breathing, our feelings, and thoughts. Shut off the phone or don't answer it. No email either. No TV or music on headphones. We can go for a walk. Pray. Meditate. But no reading books or magazines, or doing crossword puzzles or Sudoku (a popular numbers game). If we live with people or have children, we may need to talk to them. If so, be present for those conversations. It doesn't count if we do this activity at night while we are waiting to fall asleep. During the time frame (a week or month) that we're doing this activity, practice presence for all our conversations, even after the hour is up. Instead of waiting for people to stop talking, listen to what they say. When we're done with conversations, recap what was said. If we can't, we didn't listen. Stop answering call waiting for a week. Let people leave messages unless you're waiting for a true emergency or important call. After a week, if silence is still uncomfortable, do the activity until we enjoy silent presence as much as communication. Be present for ourselves, our conversations, and the spaces in between.

12. Wrap a Golden Ribbon Around Each Day. Communicate with God in the morning and at night (and as needed throughout the day). Praying is talking. Meditating is listening. Bless each day by taking time to wrap it in a ribbon of meditation and prayer.

✐ ACTIVITY

If you do only one activity in this book, this is the one I would recommend. When I asked a teacher what activity would most increase spiritual power, she immediately answered, "Meditation and prayer." Is it any coincidence that these behaviors are suggested in one of the Twelve Steps? A few minutes a day is enough to start with, although it may feel so good, we want to spend more time. But don't make your goals so difficult you don't do them at all.

13. Talk on the Light Side. Do we wait until our romantic partner is almost asleep, then nudge him or her, and say, "Can we talk?" Are we constantly saying, "We need to have a *talk*." These statements can be death to a relationship. Lighten up. If we have something to say, say it. But don't beat that horse to death. If we want him (or her) to adore us, stop asking, "Where is the relationship going?" Instead ask ourselves, "Where am I now? Am I present for the other person and myself and the time we spend together? Do I enjoy being with him or her now?" This concept applies to friendships and other relationships, too.

ACTIVITY

Become aware of our communication with romantic partners and friends. Are we constantly talking about heavy topics, or do we stay on the light side at least sometimes? Or, in the reverse, do we avoid talking about anything important or in depth?

14. Let Our Words Be Like Wind Chimes. Tone is something we hear, like wind chimes blowing in the air. What sounds do our words make? Do we sigh, moan, whine, complain? Is our voice dripping with sarcasm, anger, fear? Have we ever known someone whose voice was like fingernails on a chalkboard? Communication is more than what we say; it's how we say it and how we sound. As much as possible, and without forfeiting what we have to say, let our words be music to people's ears. We can even use a pleasant tone to say the hard stuff. We can become so skilled at communication that people may barely realize we've said something difficult, set a boundary, or said something they'd prefer not to hear.

ACTIVITY

Be aware of how we and other people sound. We can't change our voice but we can change our tone.

15. Let Life Speak through Us. Before we can communicate who we are, we need to know who that is. When we're present for ourselves and the moment, free from agendas, we open our mouths and Life speaks through us. That's when we become a channel of love.

✍ ACTIVITY

If communication is a problem, have a "communication awareness month." Pay attention to how we communicate with others and how they communicate with us. Don't focus on change.
Practice awareness. Let change take care of itself. Besides the
points covered above, here are a few more. Do you tell people
how much you appreciate them or do you complain? Do your
words reflect self-responsibility, respect, victimhood, or blame?
Do you have a sense of humor? Do you allow other people to
speak disrespectfully to you? Are you easily swayed or sucked in
by sweet talk or by people stroking your ego (telling you how
pretty you look, how talented or smart your are) so they can
manipulate you?

When we undertake the journey of becoming free from
codependency, we start walking the road to freedom. It's a paradigm shift and a revolution. But eventually every revolution
becomes an institution. Ideas become rules. I've heard people
talk about their pain, and get cut off before they could finish.
"Stop being a victim," someone interrupts. In the beginning of
the codependency recovery movement, people listened to people while they told them their stories, and listened as often as
people needed to share. Sometimes telling our stories over and
over is more than obsession; it's an important part of grief. It
helps us make sense of losses that aren't yet acceptable to us.
On the other hand, we have the right to set boundaries and not
listen when we don't want to—for instance, if someone constantly complains about the same thing but doesn't do anything to change. We start feeling used.

Trust ourselves to be present each moment and respond
spontaneously. The times we help others most is when we're
not consciously trying to help. Instead, we're being who we are.
After the communication month ends, ask: What did we learn?

What would we like to change? Turn what we'd like to change into written goals such as *I'd like to be more honest; I want to stop apologizing so much.*

We can also make it a goal to talk better to our body. How many of us have looked in the mirror and thought, *I hate what I see.* Or *Ick.* Instead of degrading our bodies and how we look, tell our body we want it to be healthy. Thank it for being there for us. When looking into the mirror, consciously say something kind to ourselves. As we become more comfortable with ourselves, our communication skills will increase. The more we know ourselves, the better we'll communicate. Our voice will be one in the chorus of Life.

6 · Control

THE CONTROL TRAP

A codependent person is one who has let another person's behavior affect him or her, and is obsessed with controlling the other person's behavior.

Of all the behaviors that hurt us and destroy love, peace, pleasure, creativity, relationships, and our skills—control takes first place. But if not controlling someone's behavior was all that recovering from codependency required, healing from it would be a snap. The catch is, there's an almost endless list of things we encounter that we can't control. These "things" dare, defy, and entice us into trying to control them—in the name of being loving and solving the problem. After wearing ourselves out by trying to do the impossible, we finally realize we weren't solving the problem by trying to control it. We got suckered—tricked—into the control trap. While we thought we were controlling something or someone, it (or that person) was controlling us.

When we step into the control trap, we step out of Grace. We're tense and frightened. We lose our connection to ourselves, people, God, and Life. There's an indescribable gift that helps us get through our worst and best days: Grace. We can't have it both ways. We either try to control or we get the gift of Grace. Which one is it going to be?

Out of Focus

When I wrote *Codependent No More,* I had no idea how much I tried to control. Each time I'd surrender to something, along came another problem. Like cheese on the mousetrap, it tempted me. "Come on. Try to control me," that problem would say. When I was diagnosed with hepatitis C after a pre-op physical for some cosmetic surgery, I went into shock. My liver scores were normal; I was in excellent health. I didn't feel sick. By listening to my intuition and guidance, I'd been taking vitamins and supplements for years that are helpful to people with hep C. Had I known the doctor was going to test for it, I probably would have asked him not to. I don't know what I was angrier about: having it or knowing I had it. I didn't want to have this disease. I wanted it out of me. The truth is, part of me knew I'd had it all along. Upon hearing I had HCV, I instantly got sucked into the control trap again. I spent the next two years holistically trying to make the virus go away. Some days I took over one hundred fifty supplements, plus I spent a fortune.

Looking back, I can see I was going through the stages of grief. Most people don't like to hear they have an incurable and potentially fatal disease. It's a loss.

I spent two years staring at my liver, like it was going to explode, going in for blood work every six weeks. Each time the lab tech would draw my blood. I'd ask him how long it would be before my lab results came back, and would he please call me the instant they did. Finally, the umpteenth time I did this, the lab tech said, "Quit worrying about your liver. Go live your life."

It was some of the best medical advice I've ever received. I wasn't "taking care of my body." I was obsessively trying to control the hepatitis C.

Even how we dress can be a form of control. "I can feel when I'm into my control mode," a woman said. "I put on twenty different outfits. None of them look or feel right. That's because I'm trying to control how others perceive me instead of dressing how I want to, in a way that feels comfortable to me."

When we're in the control trap, nothing feels right. Seeing anything through the eyes of control takes it out of focus. We can't be who we are and be controlling at the same time. Control eliminates any possibility of being real.

Is It Love or Control?

Some of us have lived with extremely controlling people. We became so sensitive to control then that the second we feel someone trying to control us now, we react. When someone tries to control us, explained James Redfield in the *Celestine Prophecy,* they're stealing our power.

If control was what we received from people who were supposed to love us, that's what we think love is. We can confuse love with dependency, manipulation, and neediness. None of those are love. Love is when we want other people to be who they are.

Control is an attitude as much as an action. We even bring control into our work. It takes all the joy out of our vocation— the same way it takes the fun out of relationships, recreation, and sex. Everything we do is for the moment ahead, not for the one we're in now.

Control is an illusion, a trick.

Spending time with a controlling person is one of, if not *the* most unpleasant experience there is. I've been through the death of three ex-husbands and the death of my son. I'm recovering from chemical dependency. I had two artificial discs put in my back. I spent fifteen years living in poverty and have traveled all over the world. I've jumped out of airplanes even when it's all I can do to parallel park a car. Now you're going to stand in my living room and tell me what I should do, how I should live my life, and what to think? Give me a break.

Some people find it seductive to be controlled in a romantic relationship at first—especially when they're young or if they don't have a sense of who they are. Sooner or later, as B. B. King sings, the thrill is gone.

I despise being controlled. Of all my pet peeves, that's number one.

It's normal to want to control someone we love who's hurting themselves, whether they're destroying themselves by shooting drugs or by doing something else. But the knowledge that we can't control anyone but ourselves is almost as common now as how to fasten a seat belt. There was a time in our culture when we believed that controlling was appropriate. Parents should control their children. Men should control their wives. Bosses should control their employees. People had preset roles. Then we went through the sixties. It was a revolution. Control had to go.

We began to understand it didn't work.

People control for many reasons: habit, because we don't want someone we love to hurt themselves, or because we think we can. But the biggest reason we control is fear. We're afraid of what will happen if we let people be who they are, ourselves be who we are, or let Life keep evolving without our influence or help.

Control is also part of grief. Elisabeth Kübler-Ross defined the stages of loss: denial, anger, negotiation, sadness, and acceptance—or peace. Control is the negotiation part. We're trying to make a deal, make the loss go away. Occasionally we can but usually we can't.

Maybe there isn't an impending loss now, but some of us have experienced so much loss that control became a habitual way of life. It became a way to keep ourselves safe (we thought).

Losing control is frightening. But the idea that we have control is an illusion. We can't lose something we don't have.

The parent who loves children when they're babies, when they can put the child in the corner but starts to have problems when children learn they have power and say "no"; the woman who looks into the man's eyes and says, "I love you with all my heart," then spends twenty years trying to make him do what she wants him to do instead of letting him decide that for himself; the friend who sends the card ending with "friendship is forever," then gets so frustrated that she ends the friendship when that friend doesn't do what she thinks the friend should. Is it love or control?

"Love suffers long and is kind; love . . . does not seek its own." That's how the Bible describes love. It also sounds like the opposite of control.

"Love is presence and awareness," explains Eckhart Tolle in *A New Earth: Awakening to Your Life's Purpose.*

"Love happens after our hair has been rubbed off and our joints are wobbly. Love makes us real," reads *The Velveteen Rabbit* by Margery Williams and William Nicholson.

Maybe all those years of being so angry at God, hating myself and life, and feeling like everyone hated me is what I had to go through to get real and know what love is. I don't know what you had to go through to learn love, but I know what I went through. I wouldn't trade one second of it, even if I had known how much it would hurt.

We don't learn surrendering and letting go by following rules or intellectualizing. We learn these behaviors by going through all those experiences we didn't know were coming. In the end, we learn that Love is the only thing that's real. Love isn't control. It's not even close. It doesn't matter if you understand what I'm saying. If you don't, someday you will. Ultimately, it's the only lesson we're here to learn.

Crossing the Line

There's a difference between taking responsible actions to solve a problem and controlling. When do we cross that line? We each need to decide that for ourselves. We need to know we've done everything we can before we surrender. When the doctors said they had to turn the machines off because my son Shane wasn't alive—he'd been dead since he hit his head on the ski slopes two days after his twelfth birthday and knocked his brain stem loose—I knew I'd done everything I could, from calling in the best neurosurgeons to consulting the best ministers, healers, and holy men I knew. Nobody and nothing could make my son breathe on his own. But still, some nights I lay in bed and wonder, *Is there something more I could have done?* We each need to decide when we've crossed the line from responsible problem solving to control, and then get back on the other side of that line.

Feel the feelings underneath the controlling. Then surrender to it—whatever it is. Let go and detach in love. The more impossible it feels to surrender, the more important surrendering is. We can learn to live each moment from that surrendered place. With our hair rubbed off and our aching joints, we'll be more full of joy and peace than we were before all those things happened that made us sad and made us think we had to control to keep ourselves and our loved ones safe.

Just as controlling is an action and an attitude, so are surrendering and letting go. Control makes us feel tense, rigid, and uncomfortable inside. Resignation makes us feel hopeless. Cold detachment makes us bitter, mean, uncaring, insensitive, and callous. It closes our hearts. True surrender and detaching in love bring Perfect Peace. Life will take us there by sending us whatever experiences we need.

The funny and miraculous thing is, even if we don't tell people we're letting go, they can feel it. They can feel our control gestures, too. Control pushes people away. People can feel how good it feels, how free they feel, how much nicer it is to be around us, when we've stopped trying to control them and we've set them free.

The problem with trying to control addicts and drunks is that when we try to control them, they use it as an excuse to drink more. While we are aware that they're drinking and using drugs because they have a disease, they don't know it yet (or if they do, for whatever reasons they aren't ready to get sober and clean). If we stop trying to control them, we take away the excuse that we're nagging and who wouldn't want to drink or use drugs if they were around someone like that. Letting go in love doesn't guarantee that someone will get sober, but it gives them a better chance. It's like releasing a fish from the hook and letting it swim free.

When we stop controlling others and set people free, we get our freedom back, too. Sometimes detaching in love is all we need to do, then people admit they have a problem and ask for help. But we shouldn't detach for that reason, otherwise detaching is controlling. We're not really letting go. Some alcoholics and addicts don't ever get clean and sober no matter what we do. One man drank horribly—even antifreeze—when he couldn't get alcohol. He lived to be seventy-nine and barely drew a sober breath most of his life. After his funeral, all his ex-wife said, "I told him that drinking would kill him someday."

There's no way (yet) to predict who'll recover from addictions and who won't. There's no way to predict who's going to recover from most other illnesses either. Doctors and counselors are regularly surprised by who makes it and who doesn't. We aren't here to control life. Our purpose is to live it.

Life and the people sent to us—the people we love—are gifts. Love people for who they are. Let yourself be you. Feel whatever you feel. Do the work for the sake of work instead of for the results you hope to get. When you let go of control, you bring the joy back into relationships, life, and work.

Surrendering isn't something we do. It happens to us. Get out of the control trap. It's an illusion. Get some Grace instead. That's about as good as it can get.

✐ ACTIVITIES

1. Log your efforts to control and the results. Is there someone or something you're trying to control? Who or what? What's your desired outcome? Keep a journal or log of everything you do to try to control. Carry a notebook around. Write down anything that's a control gesture, whether it's something you say, do, or think. Maybe you've got yourself convinced that worrying will help. Most of us have heard the line, "Worrying doesn't change anything." Not all the things you worry about happen. Then someone says, "The reason they didn't happen is because I worried about them." We know that's not true. Worrying doesn't keep trouble away. We actually attract problems with fear.

2. Make surrendering, detaching, and letting go in love written goals. Are you ready to let go, surrender, detach? Do you still have things left you need to do to solve or control the person or problem that's bothering you? If you're ready to let go, detach, or surrender, make that a written goal. Be specific. Write what or whom you want to detach from, or what you want to surrender to. Don't make your goal (or list) too big. For instance, I may never be ready to surrender to Shane's death. But each moment, I can surrender to how I feel about his dying. It's good enough for me. It must be good enough for God, because it got me the Grace to get through.

7 • Denial

TELL ME IT'S NOT SO (OR I'LL TELL MYSELF)

Denial is like the blind spot on our car. We can't see what's there. *Why do people stay stuck in denial so long?* was a question I had before writing *Codependent No More*. While we're wondering why people can't see that elephant standing in the middle of the room, denial is busy doing its job: protecting people from seeing something too painful to accept.

Denial can be a gift. It gives people time to gather their resources so they can face the truth. The strongest people can have something that's too much to accept at once. People don't deliberately use denial. They need its help. For some, it's a hotel—a temporary place to stay. Other people dig in and make denial their home.

Most of us know what's going on, whether we admit it or not. Pounding on people to see things clearly usually doesn't help. Instead of seeing what we're trying to show them, all they can see is their anger at us. Unless we're therapists, breaking through people's denial isn't our job. It's our job to deal with our own blind spots. Forcing people to acknowledge the truth can be dangerous. Denial is the first stage of grief, according to Dr. Elisabeth Kübler-Ross. The stages are: denial, anger, negotiation, sadness, and acceptance (forgiveness or peace). Because the stage following denial is anger, how people react after giving up denial is unpredictable. It's better to not play God. The way to crack through denial isn't with a hammer, anyway. Do it with love. People see the truth when they're ready, when they feel safe. Willingness is important. Do we want to see the truth? Sometimes the truth can hurt a lot.

Living in denial makes us feel murky, confused, and out of touch with ourselves. Staying in denial can cause illness. Blocking the truth takes enormous energy (or a lot of pills and alcohol). Denial can be exhausting. When we're doing it, we may feel like all we want to do is sleep. Feeling drained, edgy, and tired can signal two things with denial: either we're in it, or the truth is about to be revealed.

Denial is a protective device that blocks out many losses—big and small. Don't underestimate its power. We may think people in denial are lying to us. Sometimes that's the case but usually people are lying to themselves.

If we suspect we're in denial, one way to safely move through it is ask God (or Life) to reveal the truth. Moving out of denial brings us closer to acceptance. Letting go of denial makes life easier because we won't have to control everything so our fantasy doesn't become exposed. We can let the truth come into the Light. While denial takes a lot of work, so does acknowledging losing our dreams or something or someone we love.

Unless we make denial a way of life, we'll see the truth when it's time. When we see clearly, we align with God and Life's formidable power. The truth will always set us free.

⌁ ACTIVITIES

1. Ask to see truth. Here's a prayer I use when I'm confused about reality. "God, I'm real slow. Please show me what the truth is about _____. Please show me clearly, in a way I can understand, what I'm supposed to see, learn, do, and know. Thank you." Ask however we want, then let go. If we're sincere, the answer will come—often more quickly and with more Grace, than we think.

2. Strive for habitual awareness. Spend a few minutes a day making a list of what's going on with you. What are you feeling? What's taking place? What's upsetting you? What's bothering you? Who is bothering you? What are you doing or not doing to take care of yourself? What are you feeling? If you don't know, write a goal: I want to become aware of what I'm feeling. Spending quiet time, or engaging in prayer and meditation help increase awareness. We can tell ourselves we're too busy, we're already overworked, we don't want to do one more thing. But staying busy may be how we're avoiding what's going on with us. Invest ten minutes a day in taking inventory of our most valuable asset: ourselves.

8 · Dependency

NEEDY OR NORMAL?

People with dependency issues think they need people as much as they need air. People are the source of their energy, strength, money—whatever they think they need but don't have and can't get themselves.

Some experts say that dependent people didn't bond with their parents when they were children, and when they grew up, they compensated by bonding with anyone they could.

But not all dependency is codependent. Children depend on parents and then gradually learn to depend on themselves. Most of us enjoy being needed a little. We need people, too. The difference is that when it's healthy dependency, we love and want people more than we need them. We'd miss the people we love deeply if they left, but we'd know we could take care of ourselves. Many dependent people don't know that yet. Some dependencies are legitimate; we may be disabled and unable to drive a car. We legitimately depend on people for quality of life and ability to function.

Dependency is another line. Are we on the normal side, or have we crossed over to the Codependent Zone? Are we depending on people to do things for us that we can and need to be doing for ourselves?

Being Dependent and Needy Isn't Attractive

Dependency gets people in trouble. People who are dependent walk around with a sign reading, "You don't have to meet my needs. Throw me a few crumbs and I'm yours!" If dependent people get someone to take care of them, they don't feel grateful; they resent asking for everything they get.

Being dependent and needy is a downward spiral. It drives people away. Neediness is easy to see, easier to feel. People avoid needy people. The dependent person's needs go unmet. As they become needier, people run away from them farther and faster.

Dependent people often jump into relationships too soon. They aren't selective enough. Usually their needs don't get met, but they stay anyway, thinking it's better than being alone. When they leave, their pile of unmet needs has grown. Then they jump into the next relationship too soon because they're even more unfulfilled because they've gone longer without any needs being met.

Dependent people are vulnerable to people with devious intentions. They're driven by the fear that they can't take care of themselves. They throw themselves into anyone's arms, so focused on what they want they don't know whether they even like the person they're with. All they want is anyone to make up for everything they didn't get since the day they were born.

What an awful job!

"I have this dream about my soul mate," a woman said. She described everything this person would do for her, how great this relationship would make her feel compared to how miserable she felt.

"Would you want to be the person who makes up for all the needs someone has that haven't been met?" I asked.

"No," she said. "Ick."

Usually the only person willing to be with someone that needy is someone who is also that needy. Frequently, when two dependent people get together, their neediness explodes and drives them apart.

It used to be mostly women who behaved dependently. Women thought men had the power. Now it's common to see men being the needy ones.

Dependent people are too easy to get. Besides being draining and demanding, needy people are manipulative and controlling. They're not real; they're being who they think they have to be to get their needs met.

Loving and being loved is part of happiness. But love isn't "getting." True happiness doesn't depend on something transitory or external. Happiness is surrendering to each moment as it is and as we are.

Want your choice of anyone? Be happy as you are.

Are you running from relationship to relationship so you don't have to be alone? Do you feel deprived from years of going without? Do you trust God and Life to meet your needs? Do you trust yourself to take care of you? If we feel needy and unfulfilled, don't deny it. Surrender to what we feel. There's a difference between feelings and actions. We can feel dependent without behaving that way. Stop looking for wholeness and happiness in something or someone else.

⌒ ACTIVITY

1. Fill up your tank. Where do you get energy? Do you look to people to fill your tank? When feeling depleted, do you cling to someone or gaze at the stars, watch the sunset, hike up a mountain and feel its power? Do you sit at the beach, letting the waves energize you? Have you ever leaned against a tree, letting it support you, instead of leaning on a human being? Do you get massages, visit hot springs, and attend groups? Climbing a mountain in China (which meant walking up thousands of steps), I'd become so tired I was ready to collapse. Once when this happened, four women approached me. They didn't speak English; I didn't speak Chinese. We were strangers bonded only by our common goal: getting to the temple on the mountaintop. Two women stood behind me and one stood on each side. Together we climbed to the top. Their power surrounded and strengthened me. There's power in groups. If you don't know what energizes you, make learning it a written goal. Ask people you respect how they get strength. Answers will come. Begin to make a list of what fulfills and strengthens you. When you feel needy, do something on the list. Discover true sources of energy, and you'll begin to find true power from your Oneness with the world where you live.

2. Tell yourself the truth. What or who are you telling yourself you need to be complete? Do yourself a favor. Start telling yourself: *I'm complete as I am.* Tell yourself that. Say it until you know it's real.

3. Be aware of dependencies. Are you dependent on someone? Whom? For what? Why? Be specific about what you depend on people for, what you think you can't do for yourself. Then turn each issue into a specific written goal. We all have some legitimate dependencies, and it's natural to need help, but without being too independent, do as much as you can for yourself. Don't go too far the other way, never allowing yourself to need or receive from anyone. That's not being healthy; it's the flip side of the dependency coin. Being overly independent can be just as codependent as being too needy. Both behaviors are based on fear.

9 · A New Legacy from Our Family of Origin

When the codependency movement began, a new therapy trend called "family of origin" work emerged. Many people and groups thought of the idea about the same time. Family of origin work is the description that stuck that covers them all. Different therapists designed different approaches: family role (oldest, middle, youngest child); family rules (it's not okay to think, feel, rock the boat); beliefs; repressed emotions; uncovering abuse. The goals are all similar: to become aware of how our family negatively conditioned us and then to recondition ourselves.

While people now tell family secrets on TV, in the past what happened in families was kept hidden from others and often from ourselves. How could we know we were abused if we hadn't experienced anything else? To us, abuse equaled normal treatment. It was love.

In the beginning, some people went to extremes dealing with abuse, in the name of family of origin work. Innocent parents were (and some still are) incarcerated. Children were badgered by officials (because there weren't any rules guiding interrogation) into saying abuse happened that didn't occur.

Other times family of origin work hurt instead of healed. Traveling therapists gathered groups of people together for weekend workshops. The workshop leaders used techniques to expose uncovered or denied secrets quickly, then sent people home forty-eight hours later without resources for follow-up—often with disastrous results. Many people had breakdowns or needed to be institutionalized after having a lifetime of secrets or severe abuse suddenly exposed. The workshops were playing with fire.

One good understanding that emerged from family of origin work is we recognized how sensitive and vulnerable children are. But some people went overboard with this belief. They decided their children would never feel an uncomfortable emotion again. Other people—opponents to this work—argued that the past is over, so why relive it.

Most moderately and carefully done family of origin work achieves positive results. We know that until we examine the past, we will re-create it and continue living in it. It's not gone and done; it's still happening today. Although the number of children, women, and men who are still being abused is astonishing, we became aware of abuse and that it isn't okay. People (children or adults) have a right to be protected from strangers and from people we trust. Abuse doesn't end when it stops; the effects go on for years—sometimes for a person's life or for generations.

Some people incorrectly think the goal of family of origin work is to blame parents and stay victims. Society doesn't want to hear about how awful families are, unless the abuse is over the top. Many people didn't take their family of origin work far enough, which is another reason I needed to write this book. I wanted to make my feelings about that clear. For these people, blame is as far as they got when they did their therapy. Letting go of the victim self-image is challenging for most victimized people. But until we do it, our healing isn't complete. We're only partway there.

We don't want to live in the past, but it's important to look at what happened. The firstborn child doesn't always have to be a caretaker, even if they've been one for forty or fifty years. Abuse victims can give the shame back to the perpetrators instead of blaming themselves. Like it or not, freeing our inner child by releasing repressed feelings and acknowledging what really happened as children is the only way to ever feel joy. But we won't feel joy if we stay stuck in blame and anger.

There's another important aspect of family of origin work. I don't enjoy feeling repressed, painful emotions, but the process of feeling these emotions began—almost on its own—as my recovery progressed. I made an effort to change unhealthy beliefs and patterns I formed as a child such as "I'm separate from God" or "I'm not good enough." I didn't obsess about doing this work; Life brought me the events I needed. New beliefs formed organically. Life reconditioned me.

Then a friend insisted I hadn't felt enough anger about the injustices I'd suffered. She said I needed to become righteously indignant. Listening to a CD of chanting Tibetan monks, I sat cross-legged on the floor trying to muster anger at people who'd treated me badly. The harder I tried to become indignant, the more I felt an overwhelming sense of gratitude for and peace about everything that happened. I could see that each detail of my life was a choreographed part of a magnificent universal dance. Every step, each detail formed who I am. I saw that what I didn't get from one person, I got from someone else. I'd never been alone. God and Life had cared for me all along. Even the hardships served a purpose. It all worked out perfectly in the end.

My friend said I obviously did the activity wrong, but that feeling of perfect peace about my life has been with me ever since.

Shortly after that meditation, a therapist encouraged me to look at the legacy I received from my family. This part was easy. Mom had been through the Great Depression. Women were supposed to suffer. My therapist suggested that instead of accepting the legacy I received from my family, I write my own.

I didn't have to hire an attorney to write this will. I knew what I wanted to leave to myself: I didn't want to suffer anymore. There's a difference between feeling sadness and pain, and suffering. While I cannot control events that trigger feelings of sadness, I can decide how much I want to suffer about it. Suffering is how we feel about how we feel.

Then another therapist had me make a family tree to honor my ancestors. She told me to go up five generations maternally and paternally and fill in the blanks with names. I knew few relatives outside my nuclear family; I'd met only two grandparents and didn't want to know any more. I tried to talk her out of it, suggesting I fill in the blanks with "Great-Great-Grandma Jane Doe" instead. She said taking the time to learn their names was part of how I honored them.

"Before you're finished," she said, "something important will happen. It always does."

After I began, I became genuinely interested. I found a website, www.ancestry.com. On it, I pulled up old census sheets. By then, I had learned my father's mother drowned when he and his sister were young. My great-grandmother raised them. Then I saw her name, Annie Vaillancourt, written in her handwriting on the census sheet. She was head of the household. For dependents, she put my dad and his sister.

What a hard life, I thought. A single woman whose daughter dies, then she raises her grandchildren herself. A blank space suddenly became a person. I wondered if Grandma Annie knew that raising my dad would affect me and influence my life someday. I could almost feel her presence and her love. In that instant, my heart opened. I started crying. I opened to the beauty of my ancestry and my heritage.

The therapist was right.

Each ancestor plays an important part in shaping who we are. If it were not for them, there wouldn't be us. A piece of them is in each of us. If we don't honor our ancestors, we can't love ourselves.

The only way to stop being a victim is to forgive everyone in the family. It's important not to forgive before feeling emotions. But many people stay victims forever. It's in their voice, what they do and say, and what they don't do. It's in those codependent sighs followed by "I guess I'm hanging in there," when we ask how they are.

I finished by memorializing a few family members. For one, I planted a tree. I had another's name engraved in a park bench that was put it in a national forest. I wanted my ancestors to know— wherever they are—that their lives mattered. The time they spent here was important. I wanted them to know that they were forgiven and loved. My therapist also encouraged me to pray for forgiveness for each of them—from others, for others, and from God.

We each need to know our lives count and matter, she said. We need to know we're forgiven. Many people die thinking their life was insignificant or a mistake, but we each have a purpose. If we're looking for that big brass ring, we miss the purposeful moments we live each day. The world wouldn't be the same without each of us—exactly as we were and are.

Honoring our ancestors honors us.

Scientists discovered that everybody has a small particle of DNA from each race and culture in them. That means our true family of origin is bigger than we thought. All people really are our brothers and sisters. As long as we're honoring and forgiving our family, why not include everyone? We belong to the family of men—and women—who have been here since the beginning of time. Oneness is more than a cliché: We are truly connected to everyone.

Have you done your family of origin work? Have you let go of the victim role? Don't worry about it, if you haven't completed it. I wasn't looking for it; unraveling my family conditioning found me.

Life will bring us the right family of origin work at the right time.

Write your own legacy. Give yourself what you want and desire. Remember to leave the victim role behind.

Leave yourself a legacy of health, love, forgiveness, peace, and self-esteem. Some things money can't buy.

✐ ACTIVITIES

1. Make a family tree. For five generations up on each side—maternal and paternal—make a family tree. Fill in as many names as you can. Put energy into doing the work. Like my therapist said, that's part of honoring the people. Then select a few ancestors to honor. Maybe plant a tree in one person's name. Or dig around through family pictures, find a picture, and have it framed. Get creative. We could even write the person a letter, then put it in a private place. We can't mail deceased people letters but the act of writing the letter—telling the person about us, then thanking him or her for the part played in our formation and creation—will get the job done. Do something that symbolizes respect, gratitude, forgiveness, and appreciation for everyone's life—including our own.

2. Write your own legacy. What are the main family traits passed down in your family? Many of us have parents who went through the Great Depression and who passed suffering to us. Maybe in your family women weren't important. If you aren't certain how your family conditioned you, turn learning that information into a goal. Write: "What has my family conditioned me to do, be, or believe?" You'll get answers. After you do, decide if you want to accept that. We don't have to accept any legacy we don't want. We can write our own. If you want to impact your life, write a will from members of your entire family tree to you giving yourself everything you want: the right not to suffer, the ability to feel joy, compassion, and love. If you were left some legacies you don't want, you can write what those are, then cross them off and refuse to accept them. I changed my legacy from "Women are supposed to suffer" to "It's okay to nurture, comfort, and take care of myself." I changed "I'm in this all alone" to "God meets all my needs."

It's also helpful to look at how Life brought us what we needed when we didn't get what we wanted. When we can see that, we'll know that we've always been cared for and guided.

3. Forgive our entire family. We belong to a universal family that includes all of creation. A healer and friend taught me this prayer: "Help me forgive them, help them forgive me, and help us all forgive ourselves. Please God. Thank you God." © Howard Wills. Howard, who authored the prayer, suggests saying it as often as needed. We can forgive and still have boundaries. Forgiveness means we set ourselves free by releasing blame and resentment. While we're doing our family of origin work, why not take it all the way and forgive everyone and anyone we still resent?

10 • Giving and Receiving

THE CIRCLE OF LOVE

Here are some ideas about giving and receiving.

1. Balance giving and receiving. A goal of healthy living is balanced giving and receiving. We want reciprocal giving and receiving in some relationships. I'm not suggesting that we keep score, but we do need to pay attention so that one person isn't doing all the giving while the other only takes in relationships that are supposed to be reciprocal. That's codependent. Sometimes we give to be of service. We don't want anything back except good feelings. Balance doesn't mean giving and receiving the same amount daily; it means the scales don't tip too far in either direction overall. We may go through periods in relationships in which one person does most of the giving, then later, the other person does. Or we contribute one thing, and the other person gives something else. If we've spent twenty years giving to others, we need to stop for a while and give to ourselves. The way to test if a relationship is balanced is ask and observe: Do we feel drained, manipulated, or used by giving to this person?

2. **Abstain until we're giving cleanly.** It's said people can't outgive God, but codependents come close. That's not healthy giving. If we're compulsively giving, stop until our giving comes from the heart. Abstinence from giving is the best way to do this. No giving until our giving and receiving is clean and balanced.

3. **Know when to start giving again.** Some people associate all giving with codependency and permanently stop giving. *Not giving at all is as unhealthy as compulsively giving too much.* Both behaviors are codependent. Giving is a personal choice. But never giving breaks universal law. Giving too much or too little means we're not trusting ourselves. Know when to give again. Life will nudge us. We might notice a blockage or decrease in our receiving. Or we'll become aware that it's been too long since we've been of service. Healthy giving is choosing freely when we want to give, how much, and to whom. Not giving blocks the flow of Life energy. If you've learned to say no, then maybe it's time to learn when to say yes.

4. **Learn to receive.** While it's more blessed to give than get, it's important to receive. For some people, giving puts us in the driver's

seat. Receiving leaves us vulnerable and we feel like someone is controlling us. Some of us were abused by people who gave to us, and to protect ourselves, we don't receive from anyone anymore, which guarantees people can't control us by giving. Also by not receiving, we don't feel guilty, like we owe people because they gave something to us. Learning when to receive means listening to and trusting ourselves. It's even okay to ask for what we need. Asking is different than demanding. Asking for what we need means people have the right to say no.

5. Know your boundaries. The same way some people give compulsively, without boundaries, other people receive without boundaries. Neither is healthy. Boundaries aren't static. They're based on how we feel and what feels right or wrong to us in each situation. Be aware of what feels right to us concerning giving and receiving. If we're unsure, wait until we're clear.

6. Give cleanly and clearly. Give without ulterior motives or conditions. If we have conditions with our giving, then be clear about what those are, otherwise it's manipulation. If we expect something back from God or the person, then we'll likely be victimized by ourselves again unless the person we give to is aware of and agrees to the condition.

7. Saying no is loving. God needs people to be vessels to give to and care for people. If we don't want to give, it means we probably aren't meant to (unless we're stuck in our fear about compulsively giving). Knowing when to give, how much, and to whom, are as important as knowing when not to give. Our giving can be God's hand touching people—or it can block them from learning a lesson. Don't give unless it's something you feel led to do, and you are willing to take responsibility for your decision.

8. Don't be afraid of giving. Sometimes when we don't have much to give, we're able to give freely. When we have more, we may become stingy. We may be afraid of manipulation. Sometimes people are trying to manipulate us. Or we may be financially insecure. No matter what our budget, our Higher Power is taking care of us. Clean giving takes practice. We'll probably make mistakes. If we take responsibility for what we give, then we won't be victimized.

9. Give and receive more than money. There are things we can give and receive that are as important or more valuable than money: time, skills, compassion, encouragement, and listening. Sometimes it's easier to give money than to give of ourselves, but giving of ourselves is important and brings with it a special blessing.

10. Beware of crossing the line. Our goal is giving that's pure. If we cross the line from giving clearly and cleanly—no matter what we're giving—into the Codependent Zone, all we need to do is step back over. But don't forget that giving is essential to being a healthy, loving person. Until we can say yes as freely as we say no, we're still on the codependent side of the line.

Freely giving and receiving completes the circle of love.

✍ ACTIVITY

Become aware of your giving and receiving. Log your giving and receiving for one month. Note how much you give, who you give to, what the feelings are that motivate it, and how you feel afterward. Log when and what you receive and how you feel about it. Do you feel like you have to give back each time someone gives to you? Are you afraid to give? Are you caught up in compulsive giving? Are you giving to manipulate? Are you able to ask for what you need? Awareness is the first step toward acceptance, peace, and change.

11 • Self-Love Is Contagious

LOW SELF-WORTH

"Do you really love yourself, or is it words you're mouthing?" a woman asked.

Self-loathing is like a virus. If we were exposed to low self-esteem in our families, we caught it from them. Our parents caught it from the people who raised them. It's hereditary, genetic, and contagious. It's in our DNA and our cells. It's also present in our feelings and behaviors. With stem-cell research on the horizon, maybe we could grow self-love in a Petri dish and have it transplanted?

Self-esteem and self-worth feel like quantities we need to measure up to. They're dualistic, dependent on being good or bad. Who's "good" all the time?

People say we can't love other people until we love ourselves, but how can we love ourselves if we don't know how to love? Songs, movies, and poems make love confusing. "Love hurts," country-and-western singers wail. People confuse getting, controlling, sexual chemistry, and yearning with love. We don't long for ourselves. How does self-love fit into the picture?

Some people give self-love a bad reputation. The lazy employee who calls in sick but isn't, then justifies it with, "I'm taking a 'me' day," (as if every day isn't) confuses self-love with selfishness. Other people stand on a pedestal, judging others harshly. Whatever they say is "right" and everyone better know it. That's not self-love; it's narcissism.

People have a hard time with self-love for many reasons. It's difficult for people from fundamentalist backgrounds to get a handle on self-love after being steeped like teabags in the boiling water of original sin. My biggest fear was loving myself would make me lazy. But the real reason I have a hard time loving myself is I'm not sure I'm deserving.

The answer to the woman's question is, *It takes a long time for some people—including me—to love ourselves.* But there's a trick that makes it easy: practice self-appreciation. Self-appreciation is gratitude and love rolled into one. Self-appreciation is motivating. It makes everything better because it helps us see how good everything already is.

Self-appreciation doesn't depend on deserving. It happens when we let ourselves be who we are. How we feel about ourselves affects how others feel about us. We create a field around us with our thoughts. When people look at us, they see this field like a cloak we wear. Let our beauty shine from the inside out so the world knows how beautiful we are. Give ourselves a confidence boost. Let ourselves feel our emotions instead of telling ourselves what we feel is wrong. Tell ourselves we're forgivable, no matter what we've done.

If anyone is going to "catch" something from us, let it be self-appreciation and self-love.

Deprived and Undeserving

Low self-esteem is a stage of grief that hasn't been talked about enough. We didn't get something or we lost it. Then we told ourselves the reason we don't have it is we don't deserve it, so we stop ourselves from ever having whatever it is we lost. Being deprived and undeserving is a downward spiral.

Some of us have been deprived so much, our first reaction to our desires is that they're wrong. That's not thriving; it's barely surviving. It's thinking that helped us keep going after the losses we endured.

Instead of watching TV or listening to music, someone deprived and undeserving will sit uncomfortably in silence. I know. I've done it. If Life hadn't taught me enjoyment—made it one of the lessons in my course in codependency—I'd deprive myself of every pleasure.

Things don't make us happy. But some things are also gifts. When we're in the Codependent Zone, we don't enjoy the gifts we're given. We'll sit and obsess about what we don't have and not appreciate what we have.

Most of us know someone who went through the Great Depression and bought furniture and kept it wrapped in plastic. We make jokes about people who do it. Deprived and undeserving are easy to see in others but more difficult to see in ourselves. If we don't enjoy and appreciate the gifts around us, why would God send us anything else? Deprived and undeserving becomes a way of life. The less we let ourselves receive, the less we'll be given.

The opposite side of the coin is over-consumers. They buy everything just to tell other people they have it, keep up with the Joneses, and create false esteem.

We'll lose everything and everyone someday. Things begin deteriorating the second they're made. Everyone heads toward death the second they're born. Accomplishments are fleeting. If we base our esteem on what we do, how we look, or what we have, our worth is fragile. When we grow older or lose that thing, we think we lost our value.

We live in an abundant world. We can have almost anything we want. Many things are free. Do we enjoy a sky full of stars? Do we see the beauty in the trees? We're not meant to get our esteem from things and people; we're meant to enjoy the person we're with and the gifts surrounding us each moment.

It's easy to see what we don't have; harder to see what we have. If we're deprived and undeserving, it's even harder to enjoy it.

We can bring ourselves out of hiding by self-appreciation. It's like sunshine. The more we appreciate ourselves, the more we'll appreciate others. It's an upward spiral.

One thing leads to another, which leads to abundance, true gratitude, and love.

✐ ACTIVITY

1. Rate our self-appreciation. On a scale of 0 to 10, how much do we love ourselves? 0 means not at all; 1 means a little; 5 means half the time; 6 means more than half the time; 10 means all the time. Anything under five means self-appreciation is a problem.

2. Practice self-appreciation. When we look into the mirror, say that we appreciate ourselves. Thank our body. When we go someplace and don't feel like we have a right to be there, tell ourselves we do. Appreciate how we do things. Perfectionism is self-torture. Be aware of what we like, what triggers a strong reaction—positive or negative. Reactions reveal who we are. If we feel we'd like to do something, respect that feeling. If something feels wrong, don't do it. If we can't stand doing something, then we're probably not meant to do it. We can't set boundaries if we don't appreciate ourselves. We won't know what we do and don't like, and that's the key to knowing what our boundaries are.

3. Grieve our losses. If we lose, or never had, something, do we tell ourselves the reason we don't have it is because we don't deserve it? Start telling ourselves we deserve it. Read *The Grief Club* if loss is a problem. It covers seventeen different losses, from losing love from a parent to not having enough money to losing a child.

4. Ask for self-appreciation training. Ask God to send the teachers and lessons we need to learn self-appreciation. We'll get our answers. Usually the form they take will catch us by surprise. We learn best when we're caught off-guard and when we're not certain of what we're learning.

5. Separate things from self-esteem. List things or people we attach to self-worth. A car, a spouse, a certain weight, living in a particular neighborhood? Money in the bank is net worth, not self-worth. Attaching self-worth to things or people causes many problems. We start worrying about what we'll do if we lose what our esteem is attached to because when we do, we lose our value, too.

6. Enjoy what we have. Enjoy something we already have. Listen to music. Watch the sunset. Every few hours, stop what we're doing. Look around. Take in the beauty of where we are.

7. Create beauty. Fix our home. Make our bedroom comfortable. Plant a garden. Pay attention to texture, color—what feels and smells right. The universe will give us what we need when we know we deserve it, and then we can let go and know we're complete and can be completely happy without it.

8. Be aware of deprivation. What do we feel deprived of? Sunshine? Clothes? Friends? God speaks through our heart's desires. Instead of denying what we feel deprived of, become aware. This awareness of what we feel deprived of will help point us toward where we're going. By loving and valuing ourselves, we align with God's will for us and our lives.

12 • Manipulation

I WANT WHAT I WANT WHEN I WANT IT

We've just finished talking to someone. Our head is tangled. We aren't sure how we feel; the best way we can describe it is "cruddy." Something's wrong, but we don't know what it is.

It's not that confusing. It's a clear sign that we were just manipulated.

Skilled manipulators turn the tables when we confront them, and then we feel more confused, plus guilty. Manipulation and control are cousins. People try to get people to do something they don't want to, or try to get what they want indirectly. What they want may be as simple as getting people to like them. It may be closing a million-dollar deal or getting married. A manipulation can be one transaction. An entire relationship can be built on manipulation. Manipulators tell lies; victims believe them.

We're either the manipulator or the victim. Sometimes we're both. When we're manipulating, we're not being real; we're not honest about who we are and what we really want from someone—what our intentions are. Manipulate long enough, and we'll lose touch with ourselves. Manipulating makes us vulnerable to being manipulated. We're so busy covering our tracks, we're not aware of what others are doing to us. We're so busy trying not to get caught, we don't see anything clearly.

Some people manipulate occasionally. For others, it's a way of life. Some people blame themselves for being manipulated, but if someone lies to us, we didn't do anything wrong. We'd have to live in a bubble not to encounter manipulators. Odds of encountering manipulation increase faster than the cost of living. If we're being manipulated over and over by the same person or for the same thing, we may have crossed into the Codependent Zone where we're living in denial, dependency, or not trusting ourselves again.

Healthy behavior means taking care of ourselves immediately when we recognize manipulation.

Worry and obsession can be forms of manipulation. We think worrying hard enough will make something happen. A friend was worrying about whether he was going to get something. "If it's God's will, it'll happen. If it isn't, you don't want it anyway, do you?" I asked.

"Yes," he said, "I do."

Most people on a spiritual path don't want anything unless they acquire it honestly and it's what they're meant to have. It can take years to know that a job, relationship, or possession needs to be obtained by right action to bring pleasure or peace.

First-generation codependents and children whose parents went through the Great Depression often feel like they deserve suffering. But second- and third-generation codependents sometimes feel entitled to whatever they want, whether they work for it or not.

The best way to prevent manipulation is to be and stay aware of what's happening. It helps to deal only with reputable people and corporations. But we still need to pay attention.

A businessman got three written bids for computer equipment. The minute he decided to go with a particular company— a reputable one—they transferred him to a different department. The price doubled for less equipment. He stopped negotiations and went to the head of the corporation. By standing up for himself instead of resigning himself to being manipulated, he ended up getting more merchandise for less money than on the original bid.

Sometimes manipulation is intentional. Some people aren't fully conscious that manipulation is what they're doing. "If I don't hide my purchases from my husband," said one woman, "he'll scream and make me miserable." Manipulation was a survival tool; the only way she knew how to get what she wanted and needed.

It's manipulative to date someone who says he or she doesn't want to get married and pretend we don't want to either, when that's really what we want. We think if we cook, nurture, are good in bed—prove we're *the one*—we'll get a wedding ring. The other person may be aware that we're trying to coerce them by what we're doing. Instead of giving us what we want, they go ahead and use us for all they can get. When we realize we're not going to get what we want, we feel used and victimized. But we weren't victimized by the other person—we did it to ourselves. We're upset because we didn't get something we said we didn't want! It's not logical thinking.

People may accept a lesser position than they want, then work hard and longer hours for far less pay than they're worth, hoping they'll get more money or a promotion. Sometimes that happens. Sometimes not. Some employers make a practice of using employees up. When one employee gets angry and quits, realizing that no matter how hard he or she works or how much that person gives, the employer has a line of people waiting and willing to be used and willing to work for less than they're worth.

Living in the moment—free of agendas—is the best way to avoid setting ourselves up to feel used. If we aren't happy with the situation now, we probably won't be tomorrow. Today is as good as it gets.

People dangle many things to get what they want: money, power, love, or sex. "Give me what I want, then I'll give you what you want" is an unspoken promise. The problem is, they don't mean it.

"You don't have to give people what they want," one man said. "Just let them think they're going to get it." When people *know* they won't get what they want—game over.

When people dangle something in front of someone—something they know the person wants—even if they say clearly that they're not going to give it to the person, it can still be manipulation. They're not directly telling us we'll get what we want: they're manipulating us, and we're telling that to ourselves. The other person knows what we're doing. If we're busy manipulating, we don't see we're being manipulated. Sometimes we don't even want the person or thing. We're so out of touch with ourselves, we don't know how we feel or what we want. It's an idea in our head—not a desire of our heart.

One evening I went car shopping with a friend. He'd seen an advertisement in the paper—good deals on new cars with low interest. When we arrived, the dealership had sold out the advertised deals. We looked at other models. My friend had the salesman run the numbers on a car, and then he decided to wait to buy one. We walked to his car. Both back tires were flat! Coincidence or manipulation? I'll never know for sure, but I believe it's the latter. The manager had the papers prepared. My friend just needed to sign and drive away in a new car. He decided it was easier than fixing the flat tires.

Prices are high and getting higher. People need money, and everyone's selling something. But there's another movement taking place. People are also deciding right action is more important than getting rich. Some people and businesses are caring about people, quality, and service. They're living by values and trusting money to follow instead of following the money. The wheel of life constantly turns. It's bringing people back to their hearts. Help give that wheel a push. Be honest and clear ourselves.

If you're feeling cruddy and confused and your head isn't clear, end the conversation. Don't let yourself be manipulated, even if that means changing two flat tires at midnight or taking a taxi home from the car lot.

⟋ ACTIVITIES

1. Be clear about intentions and desires. If the employer hasn't promised a raise or promotion upon certain conditions, or if the person we're dating insists he or she doesn't want marriage—listen to what we hear, not what we tell ourselves we want. Are we happy with the job—what we're doing and getting paid—whether it changes or not? If the relationship doesn't result in a wedding, will we feel betrayed, like we wasted our time? Are we comfortable with the job or relationship the way it is now? Do we have an agenda? Have we told the other person? Have we told ourselves what our true desires and intentions are?

2. Trust our gut feelings. The best way to prevent manipulation is awareness. What is the person saying? How do we feel? Does the situation feel "right"? Trust our intuitive emotional responses. When something feels wrong, that "wrong" feeling makes a loud emotional sound. Guilt and not trusting ourselves make us more susceptible to manipulation. If we feel guilty, we think what's wrong is us.

3. Take responsibility for our choices. Don't sign contracts until reading and understanding the fine print. Insist on clear answers. If we have qualms, make people address the issues in writing. If there's no cooling-off period, don't sign unless we're certain. Don't let people pressure us, for example, by saying that we'll lose the opportunity. That's the oldest trick in the manipulation book. Know our boundaries and bottom lines.

13 · Let's Play

ONE SIZE DOESN'T FIT ALL

One trend that became popular in the eighties was *healing the inner child. "Inner" as compared to what*, I wondered. Inner child work might be great for some, but I didn't have time for teddy bears; I had two children to support. It took a long time to see that although I felt alone, Life had supported me all along.

When I turned fifty, my inner child was ready to have fun. Recovery isn't one size fits all. Some people are passive; they need to learn to assert themselves. Some people are aggressive and need to gentle up. We don't find our lessons. They find us.

Freeing my inner child was the best time I ever had. Some people like quilting. Some collect antique cars. Some ride horses. What's fun for you might not be my idea of a good time. I like to jump out of airplanes.

I lived in a tent at the drop zone while I got my skydiving license. During the day, we went through the maneuvers: exits, going forward and backward during free fall, and landings. At night, we sat around the campfire. It didn't matter what we did for a living or how much money we made. What mattered was: Were you alive? Did you have fun?

After I got my skydiving license, I bought a house by the drop zone. We called it the Blue Sky Lodge. For the first time ever, I had roommates—something else I always wanted to do. Whatever pieces we don't get, we need to go back and retrieve if we want to experience joy. Recovery is like putting together a jigsaw puzzle. The picture is our life. We need to find the missing pieces to make the picture complete. There was a big chunk missing in mine. I'd started drinking at age twelve; using drugs by age eighteen, robbing drugstores and shooting narcotics at twenty, until I ran out of veins and ended up in treatment facing five years in jail by age twenty-four. I spent two years working hard to save my life by working a program of recovery and "clearing the wreckage of the past." I worked, went to recovery meetings, made amends, and ate bologna sandwiches after going to the grocery store by bus. I had a lot of debts to pay off. Then I immediately got married and began having children. Now, at age fifty, I got to be a child, a teenager, and a young adult for the first time.

Impermanence is a hard concept to grasp, and even harder to become comfortable with—but it's a truth and a universal law. Everything comes to pass. Even our lessons end once we learn them. We don't stay in the classroom after we pass our final exams. We can try to hold on after our lessons are finished, but things won't be the same. Next to letting go of being Shane's mother, letting go of that time in my life was the saddest thing I'd done.

Painful lessons feel like they last forever. This one was fun. It passed way too quickly. We don't know it's the good old days until the days are gone. That's one reason it's so important to make every moment count.

I still talk to my roommates from the Blue Sky Lodge. Even with artificial discs in my back, I can still make tandem jumps—doing barrel rolls out the door and relative work during freefall. That time in my life is finished, but I can still go back and visit. When the class is over, we're meant to remember what we learned.

When I was growing up, children played—except children of alcoholics. By age four, we were adults. Now children have "play dates." Parents make appointments for their children to have fun. When you feel bored, or if people say you're a wet blanket, when life loses its sparkle, or you go numb, maybe it's because you lost something important. Look around. Did you lose your inner child? Don't make a play date. Bring him or her with everywhere you go.

Ready, set, jump!

QUESTIONS

⊘ **Keep track of our lessons.** Can you see how your lessons were perfect for you? Have you learned to carry your lessons forward wherever you go? So far, what's been your hardest lesson? Your favorite? Write a list of the lessons you've learned.

⊘ **What's your approach to life?** Do you have a passive, help-less approach to codependency? Do you need to become more assertive? Do you have an aggressive approach to codependency? Is that how you have protected yourself—by being surly and mean? Could you benefit from learning to be more gentle, softer with others and yourself? Be aware of how you've protected yourself. You don't have to survive anymore. It's okay to thrive.

⊘ **Let your child come out to play.** We can be alive and still be dead if we haven't learned to have fun and enjoy being alive. After my son died, I spent eight years doing everything I did "to heal from my pain." I spent most of my life doing what I had to do. When I turned fifty, my motivation changed. I learned to start doing what I wanted. That's when I learned to have fun. I'll never have to say, "I wish I would have done that when I could." Now that I have two artificial discs in my back, I can no longer bungee jump. My spine could decompress and the discs could come loose. But whenever I pass a bungee jumping site, I remember what it felt like to get to the edge of the platform with my heart in my throat from fear, then close my eyes and let myself topple over the edge. I did it (bungee jumped) when I could. If I forget what it felt like, I paid the extra few dollars and had videotapes made.

Look around—in the attic, the closets. Where did you put your inner child? Keep looking until you find him or her. Once you do, hold tight. You've found a treasure. Don't let your inner child go.

14 • Nurturing

A WAY TO LOVE THAT WORKS

Nurturing wasn't included in *Codependent No More*. I didn't know what nurturing was when I wrote that book. Compartmentalizing fragmented me, and I lived a series of roles.

My roles as a child and teenager were: alcoholic, student, and family member. Until I was twelve and turned my back on Him, I was a child of God. Part of my identity was being sickly. Four times in my life I became deathly ill; twice illness kept me home from school for a year each time. I didn't have "friend" as a role. Friends weren't allowed. I didn't know how to socialize. I was also a musician, studying classical music for thirteen years.

From the age of eighteen to twenty-four, I had one role—junkie. Then I became a recovering person on a spiritual path, legal secretary, and student getting my chemical dependency counselor degree. The roles shifted when I became a counselor. Then I added wife and mother to my roles. I had a child when I was a practicing drug addict, but I gave up custody of him. I didn't know how to compartmentalize that, so I filed it—and my first divorce—under "guilt."

The roles continued to shift. I became a reporter. Then I wrote my first book (with Carolyn Owens). It took two years. I made $900, amounting to twenty-one cents an hour. I returned to journalism, vowing never to write another book. When I understood how much codependency affected me and other people, I crossed off "never" and wrote *Codependent No More*. Gradually I became: author, speaker, single parent, woman, and recovering person. I was no longer a wife. Now, I had two divorces filed under "guilt."

Compartmentalizing cut off my feelings.

As a child, I didn't understand emotions, and even if I had, they weren't allowed. I didn't have time for them as an adult. Occasionally a feeling came along I couldn't avoid. "You're the only woman I know who doesn't cry when she needs to," a male friend said. When my marriage ended, I felt sad but didn't cry. I grieved the loss and end of my marriage while I was still in it, like many women do. When I filed for divorce, my husband's grief began. I was done feeling sad.

If we don't feel, have never felt loved, lived according to roles, and weren't nurtured, how could we know what nurturing is?

During my marriage, I was in so much pain from codependency (but not consciously *feeling*), I wasn't present for my children the way I wish I'd been. Losing someone often makes us who we wish we were when the person was alive. I held Shane the first year of his life. I sensed how important each moment was. At ten months, he hit the ground running and didn't stop until he died. Holding him was as close to nurturing as I came.

I wrote from the heart but didn't consider myself an expert. When requests for media and speaking engagements arrived, I was in a dilemma. I didn't know how to be on radio or TV. I knew roles. I didn't know how to be the expert some people thought I was— and I didn't want to be. All I did was write what I wanted to say. I punted, and asked God to help me speak in love. That was close to nurturing, but it still wasn't it. Love motivated me to write. I wanted to serve people by writing stories, by being their eyes and ears. But I was so shy; people easily mistook my shyness for coldness. When my writing career took off, I was *in over my head*. I loved my children and readers (in different ways). I was learning to love myself. But nurturing? I was clueless. I didn't even know what it had to do with sex. Nurturing didn't fit into any compartments or roles.

When Shane died, feeling emotions stopped being optional. Grief is more than the five stages outlined by Elisabeth Kübler-Ross; grief is thousands of feelings: horror, disbelief, overwhelming sadness, white hot rage, missing who you lost—and that's the first few minutes each day. I stood on the riverbank. On this side, Nichole. On the other, Shane. I wanted to swim across to spend one more minute with Shane, but I couldn't abandon Nichole. I committed to life and feeling each feeling I had.

Soon, a teacher came—the first person who showed me what nurturing is. Life became more than roles. The compartments dissolved. I was who I was and who I am. I do different things—mother, write, recover. Once I learned about nurturing, I couldn't return to who I was and how I used to be. I began to bring myself and my feelings wherever I went instead of living out roles and intellectualizing life—living it from my head.

Nurturing is action and attitude. Many recovering people think nurturing means being codependent. It's not (unless we use it to get our needs met). Codependency "gets." Nurturing gives. Nurturing is love—plus. It's a way of being. Nurturing changes how we speak, touch, are. We go to where the person is and offer comfort. My teacher was the only person unafraid to come to me when I was in the dark cave of grief after losing my son. He understood permanent loss; an illness similar to polio had disabled both his legs. If we've been in the dark cave, we aren't frightened to go back into it to be with someone else. Wherever people are, there's Light. When we nurture, we adjust to the person's velocity—whether nurturing someone else or ourselves. Velocity is the speed at which we move. After Shane died, the whole world kept spinning and people continued to go on with their lives at full speed. My life slowed. It almost stopped. The rest of the world was on a merry-go-round. I sat on a bench and watched it go around—until nurturing began to heal my heart.

Nurturing is a mixture of compassion, awareness, love, acceptance, honest caring, and surrender. We can only use real, pure ingredients to make it, though. Nurturing is a gift. It comes through presence. Nurturing changes us and the people we touch. It brings heaven to earth.

We may never be happy we lost someone, but we'll become happy again. It's a different happiness from what we have experienced—more profound. Nurturing doesn't judge. I cried wherever I was if I needed to cry. If I didn't have a tissue, I'd use my sleeve. The only way I got through was by nurturing myself, and letting Life and God help. Nurturing doesn't push, although it encourages people to take the next step. Nurturing doesn't deny feelings. It doesn't come with rules.

It can come through touch, eyes, voice. It respects pace. I was a superachiever. Grief slowed me down. Nurturing helps us sink into wherever we are. The rest of the world moves at its speed. We have our own. Grieving people move like turtles. How do we reconcile moving forward with understanding we'll never have what we want, no matter how long we wait?

A pet peeve of mine is people saying they're "hanging in there," followed by a sigh. Stop hanging. Let go. Another pet peeve is hearing, "It'll be okay." No, it won't. It's okay now.

After spending most of my life barely crying at all, I cried for eight years. I cried whenever I needed to, and wherever I was. Now I'm happier than people who haven't lost as much as I have (if happiness can be compared). That doesn't mean I don't cry. It means I don't care if I cry. That's the secret to happiness and life: we don't resist what is. We know there aren't any real differences between sadness, joy, anger, and fear. Each is a feeling—emotional energy. Happiness is the peace we get when we surrender to it all— being aware of and present for each moment as it comes.

Let each person be who they are. Ask God and Life for what we need. We'll see that Life knows before we do what's best for us. Asking makes us aware that the answer is here. I'm not a hugger. I don't run around with teddy bears. But nurturing is the best, most healing, and comforting lesson I've learned.

⌒ ACTIVITIES

1. Make learning to nurture a goal. Do you know what nurturing is? Has anyone nurtured you? Put "learning nurturing" on your goal list. Then see what lessons and teachers Life brings.

2. Become aware. Do you come off as icy cold, mushy touchy-feely, or somewhere in between? Be aware of how we respond to people and ourselves when we hurt. Are we tough (stop being a baby) or have we learned to respond with gentle, compassionate love? If you are uncertain, ask a few people you're close to but also observe yourself.

15 • Obsession

CURSE, BLESSING, OR BOTH?

Here are a few things I've learned about obsession since writing *Codependent No More.*

a) **A Red Flag.** Obsession can be a sign that something is wrong. Maybe we want something we can't have—at least not now. Obsession can signal that we're trying to control the situation and force it to be what we want instead of surrendering to and accepting life the way it is. Obsessing isn't a conscious decision or a choice. Try to make yourself obsess. Put down the book and spend five to fifteen minutes obsessing about something or someone. Doesn't work. Obsession is also something that we can't stop until we learn the antidote: understanding that we've run into something we can't control.

   Obsession can be an involuntary reaction to not getting

what we want. When we're obsessing, we may think that if we think long and hard enough about something or someone, we'll get what we want. But obsession doesn't contain power or magic. All it does is wear us out—sometimes to the point of exhaustion. Not only does obsession not get us what we desire, sometimes it has the opposite effect. People can feel us obsessing no matter how far we are from them and it drives—pushes—them away. Ask obsession what it's telling us. Are we pretending there's a relationship when there isn't one? Are we denying something? Is obsession masking the truth, keeping us busy so we don't have to accept the loss of something or someone we want?

b) **Part of Grieving.** Obsession is an important part of grieving and healing our hearts from loss. We need to tell the story of our loss repeatedly to make it real and to believe the story ourselves. When we're telling the same story over and over, what we're really doing is working hard to integrate and accept something that's not yet unacceptable to us. We look at what happened from every direction. Is there something we could have done differently? Would that have prevented the loss? We make peace with the senseless by telling the story ten, twenty, one hundred, or one thousand times to anyone who'll listen. Obsession is part of the path to surrendering to loss.

c) **How We Express Feelings.** Sometimes obsession is emotional expression. Saying the same thing over and over can be how we act out anxiety or fear. It's a roundabout way of dealing with feelings. We can take a shorter route to dealing with our emotions by acknowledging, feeling, and releasing the emotions underneath.

d) **Part of Passion.** Obsession isn't necessarily unhealthy behavior. It's closely connected to passion; it lives in passion's neighborhood. Some creations are the result of someone having passion for and obsession about an idea. It's creative energy. Things aren't good or bad—it's the use of them that makes them so. Turn obsession into passion, then use it to get the job done—beautifully, brilliantly, and with excellence. The things that have worked out best for me are small ideas I had a lot of passion for.

ACTIVITIES

1. Determine what your obsession is. If obsession is a problem in your life, read more about it in *Codependent No More*. Understand it, and learn to identify when you're doing it. Also, determine if it fits into another category above. Find out where your obsession fits.

2. Stop obsessing. Ha! That's like telling someone to start obsessing—we can't. Most of us would stop, if we could.

Sometimes obsession is an expression of passion and we want to keep it alive. But unhealthy obsession can drive us and others crazy. Even when it's part of passion, it's an intense emotion and too much of it can wear us out.

Working the first three of the Twelve Steps can help us stop obsessing if we're out of control. We admit we're powerless and obsession has made our life unmanageable. Then we acknowledge there's a Higher Power that can do for us what we can't do for ourselves—restore us to sanity and help us let our obsession go. Then we surrender our will and our lives to God. We consciously "work" these three Steps by meditating and thinking about them instead of dwelling on the object of our obsession.

Other activities can help us calm our mind and become centered: yoga, exercise, meditation, a long hot shower, conscious breathing, taking a walk, prayer. Here's another trick that can help. When we start obsessing and can't stop, cease whatever we're doing. Go someplace private. Then force ourselves—make ourselves—spend thirty minutes obsessing about whatever we're obsessing about at least three times a day.

If it's an unhealthy obsession, we won't be able to do it. We'll also see how ridiculous obsessing is. If it's a healthy obsession, connected to something we want to do, we'll become excited. Telling ourselves to obsess will generate more passion. Even if it's a positive obsession, it's sometimes so intense we still need to calm ourselves and let obsession go. If we don't, we won't be able to get anything done.

I was absolutely obsessed with understanding codependency after it brought me to my knees. I went to recovery groups, but I wanted to know more. I wanted to know exactly what behaviors were involved, and what behaviors hurt the most. I wanted to understand why we did what we did, even though what we did didn't work. I wanted to know how it affected this person, and that person—men and women, both. I wanted to hear people talk about why they did the codependent things they did.

I became so obsessed with codependency that I changed my vow to never write another book to I wasn't going to write another book unless I had so much passion for the subject that I'd write it even if I was only going to make ten cents an hour.

For five years, writing a book about codependency continued to be a goal. Every New Year's Eve, I'd transfer it to my goal list for the coming year. People told me to forget it, just go to meetings like everyone else and stop trying to learn something I obviously didn't need to know. After being rejected by twenty publishers, one contracted with me to write the book. I was thrilled; I'd waited five years for this. A book is an ambitious project. Words don't flow out of your fingertips. It took every ounce of my obsession and passion to get the job done. Obsession and passion are powerful fuels.

Figure out what your obsession is telling you. If it's unhealthy, do something that restores you to sanity and peace. If it's a healthy obsession—ride that wave of passion until you reach your goal.

3. Write about your obsession. If obsession is part of grief, we may need to keep telling the story about our loss until it becomes acceptable. Instead of only talking it out, write about it, too. We'll probably run out of people willing to listen to us tell our story over and over, but we need to keep telling it anyway. We don't control grief; grief controls us. Writing about our loss gives us a time and place to grieve, and gives us some sense of control while Life heals our heart.

16 • The Secrets to Power

Wouldn't it be great to have money, beauty, fame—any of these powers? Celebrities can have almost anything they want. Some people think if they meet a celebrity, the power will rub off on them. But the only people impressed with name-droppers are the people dropping names. While it's true that celebrities, beautiful people, and billionaires have power, these powers can be fleeting. How many times have we heard about multimillionaires dying penniless owing the IRS? Now almost everyone grabs fifteen minutes of fame. Fame means less every day. If everyone has something, it's no longer a symbol of status or power. It's commonplace. Even beauty comes to an end and has its downside. The more beautiful someone is, the more it hurts to age. Some people's lips stretch from ear to ear from cosmetic surgeries performed in vain attempts to hang on to the fading beauty of youth. Some people have more authority than others in certain situations, but age is the great equalizer.

Fame, beauty, and fortune aren't bad. But if we aren't happy without money, we won't be happy with it. And it's easy to trick ourselves into believing power is something it isn't.

"The most powerful person in the world can fall down a flight of steps and break a leg," a martial arts sensei said. "No matter how powerful someone is, someone or something is more powerful."

When people begin recovering from addictions by admitting powerlessness, we're grateful there's a *Power Greater than Ourselves*. When I admitted *powerlessness* over alcohol and drugs, I got my first taste of true power. Some people say admitting powerlessness demeans people who need power. But admitting powerlessness doesn't weaken us. There's real power in *Truth*.

Then I discovered my powerlessness extended to more than drugs and alcohol. I was powerless over people, events, life, and often myself. Trying to do the impossible depletes energy. Whatever we're trying to control, controls us. When we attempt the impossible—trying to control what we can't—we lose our connection to true power and peace.

In the eighties, "owning our power" became a popular recovery theme. Saying no and setting boundaries made many people feel like body builders lifting weights. I ran around beating my chest yelling, *"No!"* It was better than being used. Although I hadn't found true power yet, I was on my way. As *Codependent No More* hit the lists, people recognized me and it was flattering. But for every person who recognized me, over a million people didn't know who I was. "You're Melody Beattie," one acquaintance chirped. "You can have whatever you want." "No, I can't," I finally said, after hearing her say this for the fiftieth time. "I can only have what God wants me to get." That was hard for her to understand. She idolized money, fame, and success.

Shane's death knocked the wind out of me. Any power I thought I had disappeared. I couldn't even keep my child alive! Each year 250,000 children die before their parents. We don't have power over life and death.

Martial arts taught me much about power. Aikido can be used only to defend, not attack. Barely using one fingertip, I took down a man over six feet tall and held him down until he said "uncle." I didn't do it by using my power; I sent his energy back to him.

In *Codependent No More*, I frequently mention Scott Egleston, a coworker and friend. When I was obsessed with codependency, and working in the chemical dependency field, we cofacilitated family groups together. He taught me a lot about codependency recovery. What he really taught me was the concept of *owning our power.* "You can think. You can feel. You can take care of yourself," he said until I believed him. Dissect *Codependent No More* and you'll see that these empowerment techniques are the bones—the structure—of that book. Scott and I lost track of each other after my son died and I moved to California. When I began writing this book, we found each other again. We hadn't talked in fifteen years. Although we took different routes to get there, our paths had led us to the same *place*. People didn't "own their power," we now agreed. We align with power, and it happens naturally, when we know how connected we are to God and Life. Power emerges organically from being who we are.

When we align with power, we don't have to worry about how we'll set that boundary or what we're going to say. When we remove the blocks and barriers—and when *we* get out of the way—*power comes through us.* We speak our truth, take care of ourselves, and do what we're meant to do naturally. But it's not "our" power. It belongs to the universe. *Power is a gift we get to use.*

Something mystical happens when we stop forcing our way through Life and surrender to each moment. Surrender isn't defeat—although we begin recovery by admitting we lost the battle with alcohol and drugs. People can take power from us by controlling, lying, or manipulating. We can block our connection to power by believing lies, buying into the illusion we're separate, not feeling emotions, or being filled with anger, resentments, or hatred. But I don't have your power and you don't have mine.

The only way to accomplish anything of value is to act naturally on the guidance from our Higher Power. This guidance moves us along our path. That doesn't mean we sit back and wait for power to find us. We may have to gather energy for that initial "oomph" to begin. Often we need to demonstrate our commitment and dedication by showing up for Life. Sometimes we have to work hard; other times harder. If we're meant to do something, we'll get the power we need to do it, but usually only if we surrender first. If we don't get the power to do something, it's because it's not ours to do, the time isn't right, we're working on the wrong thing, or going about it the wrong way. Sometimes we co-create by visualizing or setting goals. But we'll get the inspiration and power to do that, too. Everything we do comes through our connection to God and Life, and by *aligning with power.*

How do we align with power?

Accepting our humanity helps, and attending Twelve-Step groups helps many people accept their humanity. *Asking for help from God* or people can empower us to do something we've been trying to do on our own for years. The power we're looking for surrounds us. Breathe it in. Then relax. The way to accomplish the most difficult, overwhelming task isn't to speed up. Slow down. Slowing down is how we speed up.

Empower yourself and others. Tell people and ourselves *we can.* Some people and therapists create dependent relationships, pretending they have power over people. This is an illusion that creates unhealthy relationships. People often buy into the illusion—and spend a lot of money paying for it.

If we're looking for power, stop looking for fame and fortune.

Do the things that help us align with true power. *Become saturated with the universe's power.* Climb a mountain. Touch a tree. Absorb the colors of the sunset. Smell a rose. We'll get the power we need to carry through God's will one moment at a time. Ease into power by surrendering to the moment we're in now. We don't have to search for power, or go on a treasure hunt. There's power wherever we are.

Break whatever we need to do into simple steps. Then take first things first. We each have an inner child, but there's a Warrior inside us, too. We might start recovery by losing, but we'll win through harmony, humanity, and aligning with universal power and peace.

✐ ACTIVITIES

1. **What are we powerless over?** Make a list of whatever we're attempting to control that we can't. Put an X through these things. Then write what we're doing to have power where we don't, how that makes us feel, and the unmanageability it creates.

2. **What are our powers?** What can we do? What skills do we have? If we don't know, write the question: "Please show me the powers I have, what I can do, or change." Then wait and see. Our limitations change, but we become more—not less—with age.

3. **Practice aligning with power.** Spend a few minutes a day practicing prayer and meditation. Or study Tai chi, Aikido, yoga, or breathing. People of all ages can do the activities that align us with power.

17 • Codependency Progression

A POSITIVE ESCAPE

For some people, codependency is a progressive problem. It's general knowledge and culturally accepted that it's not okay to be abused. But every nine seconds, someone is hitting a woman— often in front of children. Many men and children are being sexually or physically abused. Some are killed.

More help is available now than ever before: treatment centers, groups, therapy, school education and prevention programs, books, online help, and support for caregivers in almost every situation. The ways to disguise codependency have increased, too. People know how to sound therapeutically correct. Some are masking emotions with antidepressants. Codependency isn't disappearing. But it's easier to take a pill than change a behavior or grind through emotional pain. Codependency is mutating. It's adapted to the changing culture.

People in the United States have more money, things, and time than people anywhere in the world. Yet the number of people with depression has never been higher. Some people speculate it's because people expect so much. When they don't get it, they're disappointed.

We have another category of codependents whose lives look seamless. They aren't codependent on an addict. They're codependent on society. They're striving so hard to follow rules and be politically correct that they don't know who they are. They're not listening to themselves. They're doing what they think they have to do because they're afraid not to, and because they're trying to please society.

Some people bottom out from codependency. Signs include feeling trapped and looking for an escape; losing faith in God, people, Life, ourselves; suicidal ideation; addiction to illegal or prescribed medications; becoming abusive; developing eating disorders or legitimate physical problems; becoming ill; and dying. We're all going to die. But death caused by codependency is different from dying from natural causes. It's dying without ever understanding how important Life is.

We may have severe limitations—we may be financially limited, or have children we need to support and limited resources with which to do so. When I bottomed out on codependency, I didn't have a car. My husband had run up a $1,000 phone bill; the telephone had been disconnected. All I could find was an old Royal typewriter with an "N" key that didn't work. I started writing. Not having a phone turned into a blessing. I needed to communicate. I remembered my dream of writing. I started writing my way out of dependency to freedom and into my dreams.

Whenever we feel trapped, we look for an escape. Escapes can be negative: thinking about suicide or homicide; using addictions to numb emotions; using religion to deny reality; engaging in magical thinking (next year, things will be better); cutting ourselves; acting out sexually; overeating; compulsive gambling; overspending.

Are you looking for an escape from your current situation? Is your escape negative (using drugs, getting sick, having affairs) or positive (going to school, saving money, getting healthier so we know we can take care of ourselves, creating a positive support system)? Create a positive escape. Life will always have its lessons, but until we know how to take care of ourselves and truly love other people, we'll never know how rich and worthwhile Life can really be.

If we're going to fantasize about something, see ourselves living healthy lives instead of fantasizing about dying.

When I was tangled in codependency, I didn't believe I could get another divorce; I didn't think God would forgive me. How much forgiveness could I expect? I realized it was more loving to divorce my husband than to stay and count the days until his death.

Another codependent behavior that keeps us stuck is telling ourselves our problems aren't that important, and we don't deserve the help we need. If we need help, we deserve it.

No matter how much money we have (or don't), if we're willing to get help, help will come. I've never had money when I've bottomed out. The most effective help is usually free, available to anyone. No car? Go online. No computer? Call the phone number in the back of this book. Ask for the help you need. We'll usually go to any length to help others. How about going to some lengths to help ourselves? I can't guarantee that you'll get money from whomever or whatever you think you should or that calling the number in the back of this book will put money in your pocket; I know that through everything I've experienced, Life and God have taken care of me. At times I didn't have as much as I wanted; but my needs have always been met.

A woman wrote me because her husband was addicted to cocaine. She was playing sobriety police. She decided her best course of action was to buy the movie *The Boost* (a movie about cocaine addiction) and play it over and over until her husband saw the Light. She asked what I thought of her plan. I said attending Al-Anon and getting help for herself was a better one. "By helping yourself," I said, "you're doing the best thing to help him."

Getting help for ourselves is often the best way to help other people.

Ask for help and it will will appear. If the first thing you try doesn't work, try something else. If we put one-tenth of the energy we've put into helping others into helping ourselves, we'll be on the road to recovery in minutes. We don't have to suffer from the pain codependency causes—unless we want to.

Asking for help is often Life's way of getting our attention so we'll be aware of the help that's coming our way. Nobody has a magic wand. We can attend therapy for twenty years, but if we expect our therapist to change us, we'll be disappointed. The point of change is within each of us.

Age isn't a reason not to change. I've seen children learn to take care of themselves; I've seen people in their seventies decide it's time to take care of themselves, even if that meant starting over.

Make our escape hatch positive. That ladder with Twelve Steps is the ladder to freedom. Are you afraid you'll lose someone you love by acknowledging the problem? Recovering isn't staying or leaving; it's taking care of ourselves wherever we are. We can leave one relationship after another and stay codependent. We can live with an alcoholic our entire lives and be healthy. It's not what we do—it's why and how we do it.

Appreciating and taking care of ourselves is the best escape from codependency there is.

✍ ACTIVITY

Gauge our position. Is our codependency progressing? Look at our life over the past five years. Are we getting better or worse? If we've been waiting for someone to rescue us, it's time to rescue ourselves. Make getting help our goal.

18 • Healing What Hurts

Earlier in this book in the section about the New Codependency, I wrote about the woman who was worried that recovery from codependency was disappearing.

When recovery began, our choices were limited. We started out with Al-Anon, then added Adult Children of Alcoholics meetings. Then we identified more addictive problems—Gamblers Anonymous, Debtors Anonymous, Sex and Love Addicts. More groups for people affected by someone with these problems formed. Codependents Anonymous was founded. It caught on in some areas; it didn't in others. Codependents Anonymous isn't dedicated to being codependent on someone; it's for people affected by codependency who want the freedom to develop healthy, loving relationships.

As codependency hit the mainstream, people not in recovery talked about ideas such as self-care and limits. We recognized that if a problem or illness—from Alzheimer's Disease to a spinal cord injury—affects one family member, it affects the entire family, too. What affects one part affects the whole. Support groups for caregivers spread like wildfire. Caregivers need care, too. Internet groups and chat rooms have been added to the list of resources. One shelf of self-help books turned into aisles at the bookstore. (There wasn't a self-help section when *Codependent No More* first came out.) Groups, therapists, treatment centers, support, and information saturated society—from *Oprah* to the newsstands. Less self-help? There's never been more.

I wrote back to the woman and said while some people needed to go to meetings all their lives, others need to attend only during the horrid times. When the hard times end, they didn't need to go. "It's hard to go back to being a doormat again once we've gotten up off the floor," I said, adding that some people stayed stuck in the victim role all their lives. That's as far as they got and it turned off new members.

She agreed, acknowledging all the help available now. But she said that many members can't find sponsors. She also said she realized some people at the meetings are so crazy they need to be institutionalized and often these people scare other people away.

It's similar to what we say in Alcoholics Anonymous: Meetings aren't a hotbed of mental health. The traditions call for principles before personalities, meaning we look at the recovery concepts, not the people practicing them.

"You said we don't necessarily need to go to meetings the rest of our lives unless we're in a horrid situation," she wrote. "For me, the reason I'm not in a horrid situation is I go to meetings weekly or biweekly. If I don't go to meetings on a regular basis, even after fourteen years, I know the disease of codependency will kill me. Being a codependent is who I am."

Other people attend meetings for a while, get the help they need, then go as needed after that. "I only go to meetings if something triggers my codependency," another woman said. "In the beginning I went weekly. Now I might attend groups once a year— sometimes less, sometimes more."

What works for you might not be right for me. Some people may need treatment and have the money and time to afford it. Others may get what they need from reading a book. The important idea is to each get the help we need.

"My mom went to meetings long enough to learn it wasn't her fault," one man said. It made people laugh, but sadly it was the truth.

Don't cut ourselves off from the help we need. But attending groups all our lives may not be right for us, either. Like the old timers say: *Live and Let Live. Take what you need and let the rest go.* Codependent behaviors are normal behaviors, plus. If we're in the Codependent Zone, do whatever it takes to get back across the line. The goal of recovering from codependency is listening to and trusting ourselves, not doing what someone else tells us to do.

⬩ ACTIVITY

Develop a self-care plan. Have you been going to meetings? Which ones? How often and for how long? Do you feel the freedom to develop a recovery plan that's right for you? Over the years, I've talked to many people who feel like they need to "fire their sponsor" (recovery jargon meaning choosing another

program person to be their mentor), but they feel guilty for
even thinking that thought. Other people may want to change
groups or change the number of meetings they attend, but they
feel guilty about that, too. "You feel guilty about everything," a
friend once told me. Excessive and unreasonable guilt is a common codependent trait. We each have the freedom to come up
with a plan that's right for us. Is what you're doing working for
you or is it time for a change? Do you need less or more support? Your recovery plan can change and grow with you. It's
your choice. You can make it guilt free.

19 · The Freedom to Be Who We Are

REPRESSION

In *Codependent No More* I wrote that people with codependency
issues are obsessed, depressed, and repressed. If we don't think
who we are is okay, if we don't think it's okay to feel, if we believe
our emotional responses are wrong, if we're living in a system that
teaches us the codependent rules—don't think, don't feel, don't
rock the boat—or if we get yelled at or punished whenever we express who we are, repression becomes a survival tool. Then it becomes a way of life.

A seven- or ten-year-old child looks at Mom and Dad and has
normal, intuitive healthy responses to what he or she sees. But if
that child acknowledges what he or she feels—that Mom or Dad is
acting crazy, drunk, mean, abusive, or can't be trusted—that means
the child is essentially alone in the world. That's not a comfortable
place for any child to be. It's horrifying. To survive in those situations, children often tell themselves what they think, see, and feel
is wrong. By the time they become adults, repression becomes habitual. Or they've created another situation like the one they came
from—another family that doesn't allow free self-expression.

There's only one alternative to repression: self-expression. We express who we are, how we feel, what we have to say, what our impression of a situation is. We see how normal and intuitive our responses are. The most damaging thing we can do to ourselves is to habitually repress our emotions. Doing so blocks health, creativity, peace, and true power. Repression keeps us out of balance. That's why so often feeling one feeling that's been repressed for years can be miraculous. That one feeling is all we needed to feel in order to come alive and into balance. Get angry. Feel the pain. Get in touch with your fear. Whatever the feeling is that you've repressed—feel it. When you let it go, your beautiful self will naturally shine through. You'll know what to do next, and you'll finally be free to be who you are. By releasing one blocked or repressed emotion, you'll come into harmony with yourself and Life. The second we come into balance by expressing blocked emotions, or by getting our center in ourselves instead of centering ourselves around someone else, we connect to essential power. We'll know what to do and we'll naturally do it. It's not something we do intellectually; it's a natural, easy process. We connect with our Source and with inner guidance.

Repression can also be part of control. We tell ourselves if we repress who we are, how we feel, and what we want, we'll make an impression on other people, maybe get them to like or love us. Or we're afraid if we express ourselves, people won't like us. That may be true. We may be involved with people we don't like that much, either. Maybe we're around people who are manipulating, abusing, or treating us with disrespect. What we'd really like to tell these people is something they don't want to hear, but it may be something we need to say.

Self-repression can become a way of life. Our first reaction to anything we think, feel, want to say or do, is to automatically and instantly repress it. Writers and others in the creative arts can get caught up in this. They write what they think people will want to hear, or what they think people need to hear, instead of writing what they want to say.

We're controlling ourselves, we're repressing ourselves and not being authentic. We're being someone or something else other than who we are. When we are who we are—whether it's how we dress, what we say, what we do—not to control anyone but to be ourselves, we act with integrity and authenticity. When we're being who we are, that's true power.

Give yourself permission to be you.

✐ ACTIVITIES

1. Rate our repression. On a scale of 0 to 10, with 0 being totally repressed and 10 being total freedom of expression, how repressed are you? Can you be yourself at home? At work? In your romantic relationship, if you have one? How about in your friendships? What about with your family of origin? Is there someone in your life you feel particularly repressed with? Someone you feel free with? Who? Do you feel free to be who you are in your support groups (if you attend them)? Rate yourself in all areas of your life.

2. Make expression a goal. Make it a written goal to freely express yourself appropriately, at work, home, school, and in relationships—wherever you are. Practice gently expressing yourself in the relationships where it's the most challenging. Start by expressing a feeling, or saying something you ordinarily wouldn't do. What are you afraid of? Is it something in particular, or a vague fear? Sometimes we can "feel" the rules of repression after being around certain people. Repression is contagious. If people around us are repressed, we often feel repressed, too.

3. Find something that loosens us up. Is there an activity that sets you free to express yourself—listening to music, yoga, running, working out? Experiment. Find something that helps you get out of your head and into your heart—gardening, taking care of a pet, holding a baby, caring for elderly people. Watching movies helps me—especially movies that touch my heart. Find something that helps you connect with who you are.

4. Do something creative for work or recreation. Often dancing, painting, sculpting, writing, or doing another creative activity is a vehicle for self-expression. It carries over into the rest of our lives. "I took up surfing," one woman said. "Being in the ocean, riding the waves, being in the sun, helped bring out who I am. It affected every area of my life," she said. I looked at her. She was tan, her hair was naturally bleached from the sun. She'd never looked more beautiful. Make it a written goal to find something creative that brings you out into the sun. Then do it as much as you can.

20 · Nonresistance

RESISTANCE

Resistance is our first-line defense to anything we don't like—whether it's something happening inside, to, or around us, or to someone we love. It makes sense to try to make what we don't like go away. But resistance does the opposite of what we want to accomplish. It doesn't make anything better; it makes whatever's happening worse.

Resistance is similar to denial. Often we can't tell we're doing it until we're done. Then we wonder why we didn't stop sooner. We resist whatever happens to us, emotions, people's actions, and what they don't do. We resist what people say. Sometimes what we resist most is what we most need to do. We can even resist resistance. Resistance blocks joy. It's the opposite of surrender. It eliminates peace and clogs our connection to power.

I began learning about resistance in martial arts. On the mats, I saw how weak I became instantly when I resisted compared to the power that came surging through me the moment I relaxed and surrendered. If there's a secret that allows life to work smoothly, easily, peacefully—practicing nonresistance is it.

Resistance doesn't solve problems; it makes them bigger. It drains energy. It's also a normal reaction. Stop for a second. Breathe. Become aware of what and how we feel. Tense? Pushed or pulled—pushing or pulling? Trying to make something happen? Or trying to forcefully stop something from occurring?

Nonresistance is simple, easy.

1. Practice awareness. Learn to tell when we move into resistance.
2. Breathe.
3. Identify what we're resisting.
4. If necessary, let go of our resistance to resisting.
5. Peel back the next layer of resistance. Breathe again.
6. Let go of any resistance to whatever's happening, whether it's inside of us or around us.

If it's happening, let it occur.

Surrender only hurts until we do it. Not surrendering is what hurts. Don't try to force our way through resistance because it won't work. Let the layers of resistance dissolve. We may never eliminate resistance completely. It may continually be an initial reaction, but we can learn to move through it more quickly and with more ease.

The patterns for transforming survival behaviors into healthy ones are similar: awareness, acceptance, feeling and releasing emotions, and surrender. Stepping out of the Codependent Zone is simple and paradoxical. We win through losing. Whenever we fight—whenever we declare war—we lose. The moment we surrender, we win. We connect with ourselves, Life, power, and peace. There's a mysterious process taking place. Life is unfolding exactly as it's meant to. If we're in the midst of a loss, this isn't reassuring. It's not comforting to know that someone we love is supposed to die or go away, or that having a chronic illness is part of some "Divine Plan."

We don't have to accept the big picture at once. Often, it's impossible and unnecessary. Practice nonresistance to the small things—the feeling we don't want to feel, what we need to do next, our confusion, numbness, aloneness. Keep it that simple. The second we move out of resistance, we neutralize the pain. It may not dissolve completely, but it hurts less.

Instead of thinking about what to do next, we find ourselves naturally doing it.

Have you ever started to feel the symptoms of a cold? Often, our first inclination is to resist. "I'm not getting sick," we say. "I won't give in." But the more we resist, the sicker we feel. We try to keep going, life as usual. All the while we feel sicker and weaker, until finally we can't deny it. We either call the doctor, go to bed, or both. That's the moment the table turns. We start feeling better. That's what practicing nonresistance is.

Often the action we most need to take is the one that we most resist. Are people suggesting there's something we need to do? Are we feeling led to do something, but we're fighting it? Let nonresistance take over. Then see how naturally we move forward. Somehow we know what to do next. The thing—whatever it was—that we resisted turns into something unimportant or it becomes a gift. We don't have to change anything or anyone, including ourselves. Practicing nonresistance changes us.

✐ ACTIVITIES

1. Stay aware of resistance. Resistance is a natural response to most experiences—the things we don't want to happen. Check in with ourselves several times a day. Does our body feel tight? Controlled? Are we in a battle with something, someone, or ourselves? Don't worry about accepting the big picture; that's usually too much. Keep it simple. Break it down. Practice non-resistance or surrender to each moment—what happens, what we feel, what others are doing to themselves or us. Is there something we feel we need to do next? Is someone suggesting we do something, saying it would be a good next step—but the thought of doing it makes us groan? It's probably exactly what the doctor ordered. Become aware of how resistance feels. When we're unconscious of our resistance, we get tangled up in events. We block emotions. We battle Life. Who are we kidding? Life is going to beat us.

Give up. Give in. Surrender and win!

21 • Sexual Intimacy and Codependency

A POWERFUL TRANSFORMATION

Many (maybe most) people with codependency issues have been sexually abused. For years, we've focused on women, but slowly it's surfaced that many men are victims of sexual abuse, too. Abuse doesn't end when the abuse stops. It can take its toll for years, or our entire lives. It affects trust, intimacy, sexuality, self-esteem. One side effect of abuse is that we take on the shame or guilt that belongs to the perpetrator, which can keep us feeling like victims long after the abuse has stopped.

"I walked into my daughter's bedroom. I'd left her with the

oldest son of a trusted friend for half an hour," a woman said. "The entire family was good friends of ours. There he was, on top of my daughter. She was six years old. He was almost eighteen." The woman started shaking, reliving the experience as she told her story. "I wanted to kill him," she said. "I remember running into the kitchen, chasing him out of the house, then ramming my foot through a cupboard door. I'd been sexually abused as a child. Of all the promises I'd made to myself—the things we vow to never allow our children to experience because we did and we know how much they hurt—the number-one promise I made was my daughter wasn't going to be sexually abused. It can ruin people's lives.

"I called the police, child protection, and this young man's parents. Then I really became angry. My daughter was six. He was seventeen. He was already on probation for doing the same thing to other children! His mother hadn't bothered to tell me that when I said I needed a babysitter. Child protection told me that I'd done something wrong by letting him around my daughter because he was a known perpetrator. How was I supposed to know? My 'friend' hadn't told me this. If I'd known, I wouldn't have let him near my daughter. This was a long time ago, before the laws changed and perpetrators had to make their presence known in a neighborhood. Because he was a minor, his crime wouldn't be public knowledge anyway. I asked child protection how I was supposed to keep him away from my daughter when he lived across the street. Do you know what they told me? They said I had to keep my daughter in the house—I couldn't let her play in her yard or I'd be guilty of neglect."

The woman was still trembling. "I'd be guilty of neglect for letting my daughter play in her own yard? It happened years ago," she said, apologizing for crying. "But right now it feels like it happened yesterday. I asked child protection what they could do to help. They said they couldn't do anything to him because he was already under their supervision. He was on probation. They refused to do anything more."

We've come a long way with sexual abuse but not far enough. When I worked in the chemical dependency field, many things bothered me about the justice system. My decision to quit working as a counselor was influenced by many factors. I was burnt out from working on the front lines. I expected crazy behavior from the clients; but not from the staff. By then I worked for several different programs as a consultant facilitating family groups. Not all the programs had crazy staff, although one program was particularly corrupt. I worked with state licensing agencies to help close it down. But my biggest motivation to walk out the door and not return to work at chemical dependency programs was when I began recognizing sexual abuse in families. I'd report it, but my hands were tied. I couldn't get people to listen. Even if I did, they wouldn't do anything about it. I had to watch it—like an accident occurring before my eyes. I couldn't do anything to stop it and I couldn't get anyone else to intervene. I'd predict the behaviors—tell probation officers that men were remarrying wives to get access to their daughters after being released from prison for sex crime violations. I'd tell the probation officers that if they didn't stop the abuse, the children—the victims—were going to attempt suicide. What I predicted happened almost every time! No matter what I told the agencies, it didn't make any difference. It made me crazy knowing these children were being abused and nobody would stop it. I couldn't handle it. I had to quit. That's not codependency; it's righteous indignation. I haven't worked with "the system" as a counselor for a long time. I hope it's improved. What I saw then was that the system didn't want to prosecute the hard cases, the ones in which children were really being harmed. The tough cases—for example the mother who videotaped her children having sex so she could make money—were too expensive and complicated to prosecute so the system ignored them. (I don't work in that field any longer; it took too much out of me. I don't know if it's changed, and if so, if it's changed for the better or worse.)

Many people in child protection agencies have their hearts in the right place, but their hands are tied. My complaint isn't with the workers—it's with the system. I'd see the signs of sexual abuse; once you know them, they're obvious. Sometimes perpetrators are the last people you'd suspect. Anyone can be one, from the sleazy guy with the beady eyes and potbelly to the gentle person you'd trust with your life—the last guy you'd think would ever hurt anyone, especially a child. It can even be Mister Macho. You cannot tell from faces or demeanor. But once you know the signs of sexual abuse, they scream out from the children, demanding recognition. I'm not going to get into the signs here. You can get a book on the subject if you're interested or read about it on the internet. Recognizing abuse is a combination of training, intellect, and intuition. When you see a young child obsessed with sex, you can be almost certain that something sexual is happening to her or him. When sex offenders are released—especially if they haven't had therapy—you can bet money they'll repeat. There's case after case that would make your stomach turn and the hair on your neck stand up. You'd be kicking the cupboard doors with rage, too. Then we have the other side of that coin—the innocent parents who remain imprisoned for sex crimes they didn't commit. When sexual abuse came into the open, many of the early cases were witch hunts. Information and training hadn't been developed or refined. Some families imprisoned in California are still fighting to be released for sex crimes they didn't commit. One couple was sent to jail after becoming involved in a struggle between friends and a relative who wanted custody of their children. Shortly after the friend asked the husband to be a character witness, the couple was implicated too. This was in the days before there were guidelines about how children should be interrogated. In this instance, when the couple's boys grew up, they said they'd been manipulated into giving false testimony. Both couples were freed because a judge found that improper questioning of the children had resulted in unreliable testimony. But they'll never get back the fourteen years of family life they lost.

If you suspect sexual abuse, report it. But don't do it on a whim; don't do it to "get even" with someone. It's a horrible accusation when it's not true, too. Maybe you can change the course of a child's life. But sexual abuse isn't the subject of this segment; it's the introduction.

The percentage of people with chemical dependency and codependency issues who have been sexually abused is high—guesstimates range from 30 percent to 83 percent. (Other professionals say it's higher.) Chemical dependency treatment now ranges from seven to twenty-eight days. With that little time to treat the primary problem of alcoholism or addiction and even fewer hours devoted to the significant others, time does not exist to treat secondary problems such as sexual abuse. Anyone can be a perpetrator or a victim. Some people are both. It either stops with each abuse victim, or the victim becomes a perpetrator, passing it to the next generation.

Abuse negatively affects males as much as it affects females. Sexual abuse is the most damaging misuse of touch.

Now let's segue into sexual intimacy. Difficult, isn't it? Think how much more difficult it is for sexually abused people to go from abuse to intimacy. Most people with codependency issues have been the victims of abuse and need to make the leap from terrible experiences of sexual abuse to learning how to experience healthy sexual intimacy, sex connected to love, trust, and nurturing. It's a big leap and a long journey.

"I immediately got my daughter into counseling," the mother in the first story above said. "But I never received any counseling.

It affected my sexuality for most of my life—and not in positive ways. But my mother was old-school and also a sexual abuse victim. She didn't believe in talking about things. Bad things happened. People didn't complain; they suffered. Many incidents of sexual abuse happened to me. Some she knew about; others I couldn't tell her. If you're abused enough, you begin to think it's normal. Back then, schools didn't teach children about inappropriate touch or telling someone when it happened. The abuse my mother knew happened to me wasn't discussed because it stopped, as far as she was concerned, when the perpetrator was arrested. For her, it was over. Our family didn't discuss feelings, especially unpleasant ones."

Sexual intimacy is called many things including "having sex" and "making love." It's when two people nurture each other in a special, intimate way. It's a challenge to involve nurturing with sex if people don't know what nurturing is (and many people with codependency issues don't). It's even more challenging to learn about sexual intimacy if our history of sexual experiences consisted mostly of sexual abuse.

Two steps we can take to improve sexual intimacy are:

1. Get help if we've been sexually abused. Write about it. Talk about it. Get the secret out. Give the shame and guilt back to the perpetrator. Don't take it on ourselves. If we were sexually victimized, we didn't do anything wrong. If it's hard to let go of the shame or guilt, write a letter to the perpetrator and return the emotions. If you know where the perpetrator is and want to send it—and if you feel safe doing that—then mail it if you have someone's support and help. Otherwise, write the letter and burn it. Destroy the energy. Get it away from you and your house.

2. Allow sexual intimacy to be a gift by learning to include nurturing—making love—with having sex. Many people with codependency issues have sex with people they don't want to, or

when they don't want to have it. They don't understand what a gift it is. Some people feel it's something they have to do to be loved; other people have learned to "leave their bodies." That means, they've learned how to not be present for and feel touch. Many abuse victims are experts at leaving their bodies. Leaving is a survival tool that's saved many people's sanity and lives.

"For six years in my marriage, my husband barely touched me," one woman said. "When he did, it was repulsive. I left my body. It's a trick I'd learned as a child. I wouldn't feel anything that happened. I'd been abused so often, it was easy for me to do. After I divorced him, and began recovering from codependency, it was hard to learn to be present for intimate, healthy touch."

Stay connected to our bodies. Know how touch feels. Know whether it's touch we want to give and receive. If it's not, stop.

Sometimes we use sex as a tool to manipulate others. We might give sex hoping to receive love or marriage in return. We can do that if we want to; it's our choice. But it's an inappropriate use of the gift that sexual intimacy is. If we respect our bodies and ourselves, we know sex isn't something to be bartered, traded, or exchanged.

Our body has knowledge and wisdom. Listen to what it's saying. Do we want to touch someone? Do we want them to touch us? Do we move away from someone, back off? Do we cringe when someone touches our arm? Pay attention to the body's wisdom in our daily life, not only during sex. Our bodies communicate clearly if we listen. We don't ever have to have sex when or with someone we don't want to. Stay present, aware, in our body, then we'll know what we want, don't want, like, and detest. If we become aware that we don't like how we're being touched—even if we're in the midst of intimacy—listen to and respect how we feel. It's not too late to stop. Never force our body to endure invasive, inappropriate, unwanted touch from anyone, whether it's a friend, lover, or an invasive medical treatment. We don't even have to be hugged if we don't want that. Respect whatever our body tells us. It can inform us when someone is lying, is untrustworthy, or doesn't like us. It can tell us if we don't like someone else. But our body can't tell us anything if we don't listen. Let our body share its wisdom.

We can listen to what our body wants in areas other than intimacy. It'll tell us if we're comfortable being in someone's home, car, or a restaurant. Some of us are so used to forcing ourselves through unpleasant situations that we habitually ignore body wisdom. We make a practice of forcing ourselves through many life situations. We treat our bodies with the same disrespect as the people who originally victimized us did. Learn to treat ourselves better. Protect, respect, and honor our body. Let it become a trusted friend.

Many people with codependency issues have sex with people too early in the relationship. It's the only way some people know how to connect. A phenomenon that's occurred is that men used to use women for sex; now many women are using men for sex. It's the men asking the woman, "Where is this relationship going? Are you only using me for sex?" Whether we have sex only within the confines of a marital relationship is a personal decision. Most people I've talked to tell me they have two conditions for healthy sex: 1) they're monogamous; 2) whether they're married to their partner or not, they only have sex—or make love—with someone they respect, like, and trust. They want more than a "chemical, sexual attraction." Our decisions about sexual intimacy are our own person choices. But as a rule of thumb, having sex on the first date is too soon. Chances are that having sex that soon will ruin any potential relationship. We're allowing ourselves to engage in a degree of intimacy that's higher than any possible level of trust we could have achieved. We're forcing our body to be close to someone it doesn't know yet. It's not possible to be that vulnerable or open that soon. One or both people become embarrassed because they're not okay with what they've done.

Many people are in sexless marriages. They haven't been sexual with their partner for years. Maybe one partner refuses, or both people lost interest and are content being friends, or the couple is staying together for the children and planning a divorce when the children graduate. Staying together for the children isn't necessarily a "codependent decision." Remember—it's not what we do, it's how and why we do it. It's also each couple's choice.

Sometimes one person in the relationship hasn't kept his or her appearance up. How that person looks is a block to making love; whether it's from weight gain, aging, or illness, some people don't want anyone to see their body. Some people who are mad at their spouse punish him or her by gaining weight. Their spouse isn't attracted to them. The people who have let their appearance deteriorate to punish their spouse shrug their shoulders and say, "It's not my fault. My partner isn't interested in me any longer. I can't help it."

Some people become addicted to sex; it's a way to cover up feelings. Others have affairs to hurt or get even with their partner because their partner has hurt them. Some people don't feel complete unless they're sexually active. They're bed-hopping and aren't particular about their partner. Other people could not care less whether they have sex or not. Some studies reveal that disinterest in sex is becoming an increasing pattern. People are absolutely and completely comfortable being sexually inactive. It's not for moral or religious reasons. It's something "that happened."

Loss of interest in, or desire for, sex is a common side effect of many (if not most) antidepressants. Many people say they're comfortable losing interest in sex. Sexually transmitted diseases can be fatal. Some people have sex using pictures or typed words on the internet. Having sex on the Internet counts. If people are married, sex on the computer constitutes betrayal, cheating, and having an affair. It's engaging in sexual activity with another person—whether two people touch each other or not.

Touch is one of the most exquisite senses we possess. Touch can heal. It can nurture and console. It can express as much as words. Promise ourselves to give and receive only touch that feels good to us.

Have you learned what gifts touch and sexual intimacy are?

Nurturing, honesty, presence, awareness, trust, respect, and love are the ingredients that make sexual intimacy a physical *and* spiritual experience instead of only a physical interaction.

If we've been sexually inactive for a long time, we never know when we'll become sexually active again. We also never know when it's the last time we'll make love to someone. People don't stay in our lives forever. It's important to be present; make all our moments count. Be intimate only with someone we want to, and be totally present for ourselves and our partner. It may be the last time we hold that person in our arms. Give the gift of love through touch.

✐ ACTIVITIES

1. **Heal the past.** Are you an abuse victim? Have you dealt with the victimization? If you haven't, the abuse hasn't ended yet. Get counseling, or if you feel strong and safe, begin journaling about it on your own. If it brings up too many issues, get professional help. Be aware of people who insist that you were abused if you absolutely cannot remember it. Some people do repress memories of sexual abuse. People are also impressionable; the wrong counseling can imbed the idea in our minds that something happened that didn't. Make certain it's true before you accuse someone; accusations carry serious implications. Whether to confront the perpetrator or not is a personal

decision. Get professional guidance and give serious consideration to this before you do it.

2. Become aware of touch and sexual intimacy. Practice awareness and staying in our bodies during sexual intimacy. If our partner is willing, have times where we engage in nonsexual touch—give each other massages, touch our partner's hand, rub his or her neck. Sensuality isn't limited to sexual organs. The entire body is involved with intimacy, sensuality, and sexuality. Practice awareness of how touch feels during sex. Journal or write about the experience in a safe, private place.

3. Talk about sex with our partner. Can we openly discuss sex with our partner? It's important to discuss feelings, even if we feel uncomfortable discussing sexuality. It's especially important if you're unhappy with sexual intimacy in your relationship. Is one person wanting an active sex life while the other doesn't, making the person desiring sex feel like he or she is being held hostage? That's unfair and can lead to serious resentment. Sex is a sensitive subject. Ask for the courage to express ourselves. If we're happy with our sex life, why not tell our partner? A wise person can teach his or her partner without words how to become the lover he or she wants; it's not done with constant nagging and negative feedback. Find new ways to bring more romance, fun, and passion into sexual and sensual intimacy. Get creative. There are many good books on the subject. Maybe you and your partner agree—for your own reasons—that you're comfortable not having sex in the marriage or relationship. You're both willing to be loving, nonsexual friends. One person could have a chronic illness that prevents him or her from enjoying sex. Maybe one or both people want to wait for marriage before they have sex. There are other ways to be intimate. Ask God or Life for help. Doors will open to intimacy. Learn to express yourself in romantic, sensual ways. Take responsibility for sexual intimacy being fulfilling. It's your life.

4. Let go of desperation. I've seen many people who are desperate for a sexual partner. They feel incomplete unless they're sexually active. It's unattractive and can also be dangerous. I'm not going to lecture about safe sex; it's been talked about more than using seat belts. Check your attitude. If you're desperate for sex, make it a goal to let go of desperation and feel complete whether you're sexually active or not. The most attractive person in the world—regardless of physical beauty—is someone who knows that he or she is complete as is. The attractiveness comes from within. It can be irresistible. Neediness, desperation, and clinginess are turn-offs. They're guaranteed to make people run—not walk—away. Give up the belief that you have to have a sexual partner. Like attracts like. The best we'll get is someone else who's desperate and needy.

22 • Surrendering Our Way into Grace

TRUSTING GOD, LIFE, OTHERS, AND OURSELVES

"How can I ever trust myself again," a woman said. "Look at all the bad decisions I've made."

When our dreams die and people betray us, it's easy to lose trust in God, Life, ourselves, and others. But by what standards are we judging? *This relationship was a failure,* we say. *And this one didn't work.* Are we sure? Take another look. Often we don't take time to see what we learned, or we come to an inaccurate conclusion, such as *women can't be trusted, stable men don't exist,* or *there's no such thing as love.* Don't judge so quickly. Sometimes the problem isn't that we didn't learn a lesson; it's that we learned the wrong one.

The biggest codependent issue many of us have is our need to control. Underneath that behavior is fear. Under that is lack of trust. We're afraid of what will happen if we don't micromanage (a savvy, new word for control).

In the old days when recovery from chemical dependency first became popular with young people and we hadn't yet discovered codependency, many of us ran around over-helping people. We stayed busy doing all the wrong things for the right reasons. We wanted to help everyone, but we hadn't learned how to help ourselves. When young people first got into recovery (many years ago), we were taught—we had it drilled into us—that we should trust everyone because lack of trust in people was one of our biggest issues. That caused a lot of codependent behaviors. But recovery was in its infancy. Daily we were coming closer to understanding codependent behaviors.

"Our recovery from chemical dependency wasn't working," recalls a woman involved in recovery in its beginning stages. "We thought we were doing everything right. We were trusting everyone, never saying no. The reality was, our recovery from chemical dependency was training us to be codependent—not that we needed any help learning. We did a good job of being codependent all by ourselves."

Many of us began to see that one reason our recovery from addictions wasn't working was that we were being taught to blatantly trust everyone else, but nobody taught us to trust ourselves. The opposite was happening. In the early seventies—the beginning days of the recovery movement, when recovery spread like wildfire from aging male winos to young people, women, children, and the elderly, it was popular to talk about ourselves in degrading ways if we were recovering from chemical dependency. It was common to talk about how sick everything we did was, and about how sick we'd always be. If we had the disease of chemical dependency, we wouldn't have dreamt of saying that we were complete and whole each moment. That would have been heresy, sacrilege, spitting in the face of the principles that saved us—or so we were taught.

If we have alcoholism, we'll have this disease for a lifetime. But we don't have to perpetuate a sick self-image. There's a difference between knowing we'll always be an alcoholic who needs to practice abstinence and calling ourselves *sick, messed up, unhealthy people* all our life. We'll attend support and self-help groups as long as we're alive, but healing doesn't take forever. Each moment, we're as healthy as we need to be, no matter what mistakes we make. The goal of healing from codependency is knowing that we can trust ourselves. Our goal isn't telling ourselves how messed up we are and that we can't be trusted. Each of us is connected to Life. God is connected to us. Some say God speaks to us through intuition. That part of us is like radar or a truth detector. It knows what's true and what's not. It will usually tell us who we can trust, for what, and for how long—if we listen and we're not blocked. That part also knows what we need to do next. It has the ability to compute past, present, future, and the unknown, then calculate the most appropriate decision in ways we couldn't by using only intellect.

The Big Book of Alcoholics Anonymous promises we'll know what to do in situations that used to confound us before we're halfway finished diligently working the Steps. There's no exemption from this promise for people with codependency.

One of the most damaging things that happens to people who lived in abusive situations is that we were lied to. We were taught we couldn't trust ourselves.

Untreated chemical dependency results in incarceration, early death, or insanity. Or it results in long, miserable lives. Recovery is a life-or-death issue. Codependency is equally fatal. Codependency issues either cause us to be among the living dead or choke the life out of us tortuously, slowly. Many of us are so busy looking at the other person, we're not even aware we're dying. Codependents—like addicts—need to work recovery as though our lives depend on it, because they do.

By the time we bottom out from codependency, most of us have lost faith in God. I did. At first I thought my marriage was made in Heaven, and God guided me into it. My marriage did teach me about codependent behaviors, but it taught me the hard way. It wasn't like taking a course at a university. The point of this is, just because we get divorced doesn't mean a relationship isn't successful. We each have the freedom to decide what defines success.

After my spiritual awakening, but while I was still in treatment, I had a slip, meaning I drank again after becoming sober. But by the time I had my slip, recovery principles such as honesty had already affected me so deeply that I refused to lie about my slip, even though telling the truth could mean I'd go to prison. I told the truth anyway. Lying would have put me in another prison. I couldn't handle the guilt. Connecting with God again connected me with a conscience. I admitted to my counselor and the group that the night before (which was Halloween), I'd attended a party on the grounds. Someone had a bottle of whiskey we passed around the circle. When the bottle passed through my hands, I automatically raised it to my lips, and took a drink. Taking that drink was as natural as breathing.

I told the group and my counselor how bad I felt, and how I'd have to start over. I could hardly believe this was me talking. After twelve years of not talking to God, and drinking or using drugs every day, having a conscience was a new experience.

"Did you learn something?" my counselor asked.

I learned drinking isn't fun anymore. Recovery ruined getting high. Associating with people who used was dangerous. When I was around drugs or alcohol, getting stoned or drunk was second nature. "If I don't want to slip," I said, "I shouldn't go where it's slippery."

"If you learned something, it wasn't a mistake," my counselor said. "Your experience was successful. You don't have to start over again," she added. "Keep going from where you're at."

Can we change our perspective on Life? Instead of dividing it into successes and failures, can we see it as a series of learning experiences—courses where we get our BA, master's, and PhD degrees? Can we see codependency and its issues as gateways to spirituality instead of seeing codependency as time wasted being sick? If we change our perspective, then we can trust God, Life, and ourselves again. We'll see there's a good reason everything— including being codependent—happens.

Automatically trusting people is a sign of naïveté and immaturity, not health. It's dangerous. Because we can trust someone one day, doesn't mean we can trust that person tomorrow. People shift and change. Anyone is capable of anything, depending on the situation. Awareness is crucial. We will be guided about who to trust, when, and for what. We'll also be given red flags and warning signals, but we need to pay attention. If we're not certain we can trust someone, get a second or third opinion. Don't trust people blindly—doctors, attorneys, anyone. It's a myth that people are trustworthy, even people in powerful positions. But we can trust God, Life, and ourselves for discernment in the moment we're in now.

When I bottomed out on codependency, I thought God had abandoned me. Later I realized that I had abandoned myself. God couldn't take care of me unless I helped. Who's to say that the marriage was a mistake anyway? Learning about codependency is an important lesson.

When Shane died, I was furious at God. Knowing how real God is made it worse. God has so much power that my son's death could have easily been prevented. God chose not to prevent Shane's death, and now I was supposed to trust God? For what? To destroy my family? I felt like an abuse victim. On the one hand, I depended on God the way a child needs a parent—for my survival. But that meant I was depending on a parent who I felt betrayed me. It was like an instant replay of the worst parts of childhood.

After Shane's death, I also stopped trusting myself. If I had told Shane he couldn't go skiing, he would still be alive. One wrong decision changed the entire course of many people's lives.

I knew God was real. But I didn't trust God, Life, or myself.

I didn't ever regain my faith. Instead, I redefined what faith and trust are. Trust doesn't mean we're going to get what we want. It doesn't mean we're not going to be hurt. Trust doesn't mean we're not going to get sick. Someday, we're all doing to die. Trust means we're willing to live on the edge. It's similar to skydiving. We get to the door of the plane, look down, and there we are—12,500 feet in the air, about to jump out, and hoping a flimsy piece of silk fabric will get us to earth safely.

The odds of being injured or killed in skydiving are less than being injured or killed on the freeway. The difference is, when we skydive we're aware of how vulnerable we are. We lose the *illusion* of safety. In one second, anything could go wrong.

"Do you trust God?" a friend asked one day in the plane on our way to jumping altitude.

I told him I did.

"Then jump," he said.

Many of us lose our naïveté. It's easy to lose faith in Life, God, ourselves. We could wake up tomorrow and by the end of the day, our world could be completely different—changed in ways we don't like. We could lose the person we love most, be betrayed, or victimized. Sometimes we're not certain that Life will take care of us. We hoard everything—food, toilet paper, love, money. Who knows what tomorrow will (or won't) bring? What if God or Life decides to abandon us? We know anything could happen and only God knows what that is. Our eyes are wide open. We know how vulnerable we are.

We don't need to get our trust back. We need to get a new kind of faith. Ordinary faith that says, "If I do good things, good things will happen," isn't enough. We need radical faith instead. Radical faith has its eyes wide open. We're fully aware that anything could happen. We trust God, Life, and ourselves anyway. We know that everything isn't going to be okay; it already is. Life isn't divided into good and bad. It all is what it is. We may never be happy certain events happened, but we can be happy again.

Trust isn't a feeling. It's a choice.

Edge to the door of the plane. Look down. Know how vulnerable we are. Then take a leap of faith.

Get out of the control trap and we'll get some Grace. Remember, Grace is one thing we can't hoard. We only get enough for the moment we're in now.

✎ ACTIVITY

1. **Examine our level of trust.** Rate your level of trust in God, Life, ourselves, and the people we're currently involved with. 0 means no trust; 10 means the most trust possible. Then be specific. What do we trust people for? What does trusting mean to us?

2. **Keep a scrapbook or journal about high and low points.** If we have trust issues, write about the incidents that damaged our trust. Then write about the incidents that proved to us that we can trust Life, God, some people, and ourselves. Write about those moments that caused us to know God is real, that our needs will be met, that we're guided, and not in this alone. In the scrapbook, include pictures or cutouts from magazines—

words, pictures, or stickers that represent how we feel. When we're in a high or low point, work on our scrapbook. Instead of resisting our emotions, let the scrapbook be a safe place to express how we feel.

3. Receive the promises from the Twelve Steps. We're promised intuition and knowing how to handle situations that used to baffle us before we're halfway through working the Twelve Steps. Intuition is that mysterious element; it's a radar that calculates what's happening, what's going to happen, and what we need to do. We deserve the fruits of the promises, but we only get them from working—not thinking about—the Steps.

SECTION THREE

Making a Conscious Connection with Yourself

In Section One, I wrote about these tests and how to use them. Later I wrote about their importance. The tests in this section are designed to help you assess your emotional well-being. Whenever you feel stuck, confused, or want to check in with yourself, take a test—or take them all. Most of the questions double as affirmations. Taking the tests can be enough to get you back on track. There aren't right or wrong answers; the tests are a way to bring awareness of where you're at. One of the biggest challenges we face is staying out of denial. The next is figuring out what's going on with us. These tests will make it easier to assess where you're at. Like the directory at the shopping mall—they'll help you get where you're going.

We began discovering feelings in the sixties and seventies. They'd been around for a while. But they were like the animals on Noah's ark; we hadn't named them yet. And we still didn't know what to do with them once we gave them names. I think we hoped at the other end of the feelings, we'd find a pot of gold. Surprise! All we found was another feeling, then another. There wasn't a pot of gold. We opened Pandora's box when we discovered our emotional selves.

EMOTIONAL HEALTH QUIZ

I. *Emotional Health Assessment*

After reading each paragraph, score yourself from 0 to 10.

0 means no, never, completely disagree;

1 is almost never, rarely;

2 is seldom;

3 is occasionally;

4 is sometimes, but less than half the time;

5 is middle ground;

6 is more "yes" than "no";

7 is fairly often;

8 is usually;

9 is yes, frequently, almost always;

10 is the strongest yes possible, always, absolutely.

When you're done with this section, add your score, then take the next quiz.

1. I'm aware of and present for what I feel. It may take time to understand what I'm feeling, but I can identify and know what to do with or about emotions. _____

2. I'm committed to feeling whatever I need to stay emotionally alive. Surviving—going through the motions or being on automatic pilot—isn't enough. Feelings and experiences are what make life so rich. _____

3. I allow my children to have feelings instead of shielding them from fear, disappointment, or hurt. Learning to deal with feelings is critical to well-being. _____*

* If you don't have children, give yourself ten points for #3.

4. I can care about people without allowing them to control or manipulate me with emotions. ____

5. It's not my job to teach people lessons; it's my job to learn mine. I don't deliberately try to make people feel angry or hurt so they know how I feel when they treat me that way. ____

6. I can be present when people discuss emotions without trying to fix how or what they're feeling. ____

7. I don't spend more time resisting emotions then I do feeling them. Feelings aren't usually a big ordeal. ____

8. I feel emotions before they become unmanageable. ____

9. I'm not an emotional sponge. I can protect myself from other people's feelings and not take them on as mine. ____

10. I can distract myself or ask for help when feelings become too much or more than I can handle alone. ____

Total from Emotional Assessment: ____

Note: Using the Quizzes as Affirmations

Besides statements that don't apply or ones we don't want to affirm, quiz statements can be used as affirmations. Use the ten-point statements in Multiple Choice. Statements to not affirm are marked with one asterisk. Some people say affirmations should contain only positives; others say to negate negatives sometimes. These affirmations do both. They'll work for you if you work them.

Choose a few statements. Read them out loud three times a day for three weeks. The spoken word is a powerful tool for change.

II. *Multiple Choice*

Read each sentence beginning, then circle the letter of the ending that fits for you.

1. **An intense emotional reaction is usually:**
   a) a natural response to trauma.
   b) current emotions *and* repressed emotions triggered from the past.
   c) a drama addict overreacting.
   d) a warning to HALT. (HALT means stopping when we're too Hungry, Angry, Lonely, or Tired.)
   e) a combination of the above.

2. **When we tell people that their behavior hurts us, we can reasonably expect:**
   a) the person will stop behaving that way.
   b) an argument.
   c) they'll tell us what we did that hurts them.
   d) we'll talk about feelings as part of self-care.
   e) more of the above.

3. **The ability to tolerate high levels of emotional pain usually means that:**
   a) we're in excellent emotional shape.
   b) we've lived with much pain and possibly abuse.
   c) we believe we deserve to suffer.
   d) we don't whine or complain.
   e) b, c, or both.

4. **"No pain, no gain" is:**
   a) true for athletes but not accurate regarding feelings.
   b) sometimes but not always true about emotions. Pain can motivate, but it's not the only way to grow.
   c) the best way people learn.

d) a myth passed on by martyrs.

e) true only when someone won't learn another way.

5. **Going back to the past and uncovering repressed emotions is:**

a) how we stay victimized by yesterday.

b) how people avoid today.

c) a waste of time. Let the past go.

d) an unpleasant but important way to overcome most people's biggest barrier to joy.

e) a combination of a, b, and c.

Below are the scores to the multiple-choice questions.

1. 5 for a, b, c, or d ____; 10 for e ____

2. 10 for d ; (0 for anything else)

3. 10 for b, c, or e ____; (0 for anything else)

4. 10 for b ____; (0 for anything else)

5. 10 for d ____; (0 for anything else)

Total from Multiple Choice: ____

III. True or False

Read each statement, then mark it **T** (True) or **F** (False).

1. ____ I can cry when I need to; I can also laugh. The more serious the situation, the more important humor is.

2. ____ I know how to surrender to emotions, then let them go.

3. ____ I know the difference between depression, sadness, and grief. I don't call all sadness "depression." If depression has been an issue, I'm dealing with it, and it doesn't consume me now.

I was at the doctor's office, talking to the receptionist. I didn't know other people could hear. "I know many people take antidepressants. My friends tell me I should go on them because I've felt sad for two months. But I like my feelings. It's pain, but it's MY pain. And I want to feel it if it's there." Suddenly, the people in the room applauded. I realized I hit a nerve. I wasn't the only one missing passions and emotions in the world.

4. ____ I can accept responsibility for my emotions, even when other people contributed to their cause. I allow others to take responsibility for their emotions, too. I allow feelings to be in whomever they're in and people to take responsibility for getting their feelings out.

5. ____ I can safely and comfortably feel and express emotions where I live, work, and socialize now, and in any groups I attend.

6. ____ I could safely and comfortably feel and express emotions as a child. My family encouraged me to express feelings in healthy ways.*

7. ____ I don't medicate feelings with alcohol, food, drugs, sex, work, shopping, or acting out. I don't avoid pain for a long time.

8. ____ I understand the signals when something is up emotionally. I know what my emotional process is.

Give yourself 10 points for each statement marked True.

Total from True or False: _____

* Don't affirm #6 if you marked it false.

Now, add your scores from all three parts of the Emotional Awareness Quiz.

I. Assessment _____
II. Multiple Choice _____
III. True or False _____
TOTAL _____

220–230: You're too good to be true. Either you're a Master, in denial, or you're confused. Spend more time observing yourself with each statement, then take this test again. If you still agree with your score, congratulations!

190–219: You're in excellent emotional shape. You've either worked hard on yourself or come from an emotionally healthy background. You know your feelings as well as anyone can. Being this skilled at dealing with feelings takes grueling work. Good job! Keep it up.

160–189: You'll benefit by doing affirmations, reading the emotions sections of this book, and doing the suggested activities. Depending on where you came from, you may have worked hard get this high score. The good news is: you're emotionally alive.

130–159: Pay attention to feelings. They could be causing problems. You're either in the Codependent Zone or close. Do the emotional affirmations, read this book, and complete the activities in the next section. When you feel, you'll feel better too.

100–129: The light is red—Codependent Zone! Read this book. Do the affirmations and activities. Not dealing with feelings— especially pain—makes codependency hurt. It takes dedication to feel after living through trauma, with addictions, or problems. Feel and you'll get the rewards. Healing begins almost instantly. You'll find balance, freedom, joy, and peace.

0–99: Your emotional life is an emergency. Do *something* to come alive. Read this book. Do the activities. Stop worrying about what others feel. Focus on yourself. Read or reread *Codependent No More* and *The Language of Letting Go.* Consider attending a group. You'll be surprised at how naturally you heal when you jump-start those buried emotions. You've begun an exciting journey. On your mark, get set, feel!

I'm so mad I could . . .
Whenever I feel anger, I feel guilt.
Me? I never get angry.

ANGER QUIZ

I. Anger Assessment

Use the 0 to 10 scoring system, the same as above.

1. I can competently deal with anger. I know when I'm feeling it, and I know feeling it isn't wrong. I can feel it whether it's justified or not, and without feeling guilt. I can express anger without attacking and with love. ＿＿

2. When people appropriately express anger about something I did, I can listen without becoming defensive or feeling attacked. ＿＿

3. I don't tiptoe around angry people. I don't allow people to control me with threats, intimidation, or rage. I don't allow abuse. But I also don't cry "wolf" by calling all anger "abuse." The rules: Don't let anyone hurt me; don't hurt anyone else; don't hurt myself.＿＿***

4. I don't threaten, intimidate, or control people with rage. If I have a problem with anger management, I'll get the help I need. ＿＿***

5. I regularly take a resentment inventory. When I discover resentments, I release them as soon as I can. ＿＿

6. If dealing with anger wasn't role modeled to me effectively as a child, I taught myself. I don't unconsciously repeat self-defeating behaviors. I can choose how to deal with anger now. ＿＿

7. I know the difference between feelings and actions. I can feel anger without acting out. I can want to get even without seeking revenge. ＿＿

8. I want people to be honest if they're angry instead of using denial, the silent treatment, spreading rumors, or getting

even. Because that's how I want people to treat me, that's how I treat them. _____

9. To feel (especially anger), it's important to feel safe. If I'm not in a safe situation, I leave. _____

10. Feeling angry *and* forgiving are both important, but I don't forgive too soon, before I feel anger and see what it wants me to learn. _____

Total from Assessment: _____

***IF YOU'RE BEING ABUSED OR ABUSING SOMEONE, SEEK PROFESSIONAL HELP NOW. YOU'LL FIND ACCESS TO TOLL-FREE HOTLINE NUMBERS AT THE END OF THIS BOOK. CALL 211 FOR RESOURCES IN MOST U.S. AREAS. CALL 911 IF YOU'RE IN IMMEDIATE DANGER.

* One asterisk means don't affirm this if it isn't true, or it's a negative statement.

** Two asterisks mean score another way if this statement doesn't apply.

*** Three asterisks mean *TAKE ACTION NOW!*

II. Multiple Choice

Circle the letter of the ending that fits for you.

1. **When I'm angry:**
   a) I put my hand over my mouth, or count to ten or one hundred if ten isn't enough. When I'm peaceful, I decide what to do. Then I don't do something I regret, and I have more power.
   b) I'm either unaware of it or feel guilty. Later I unconsciously get even or cause a minor or big accident to let the feelings out.

c) I express loudly how I feel before I calm down and forget. That's how I stand up for others and myself.

d) I lose control. There's no telling what I might do.

e) I always have the last word.

2. **If people try to engage me in power plays:**

a) I win.

b) I disengage. It's not fun to play a game nobody wins.

c) I back off, but only because I have so much guilt.

d) I play hard, but not well enough to win.

e) I react, then stop when I realize I'm hurting myself.

3. **If someone angers me and I want revenge, I:**

a) keep asking God to bless the person until I feel peace.

b) stay angry for a while, but eventually make peace.

c) feel guilty for feeling angry *and* wanting revenge.

d) think of the best way to hurt the person I'm mad at, then do it. There's a saying, "I don't get mad, I get even." I do both.

e) may do a combination of a, b, or maybe c. I'm not perfect, but my goal is to release anger, take appropriate actions, then forgive.

4. **When I become angry with someone who is particularly difficult for me to feel angry at, I**

a) write letters I don't send or find other ways to get the anger out.

b) deny what I'm feeling until I explode.

c) see a therapist.

d) have a relationship with the person, but keep the feelings to myself. Eventually I clean house and either forgive or ask if I want the person in my life. One way or another, I learn something, and it works out.

e) may do some or all of the above.

5. **When someone deals with anger inappropriately with me, I:**
   a) set and enforce a boundary. I don't need the drama or abuse.
   b) get a restraining order. When we let someone abuse us once, we're giving permission to be treated that way again.
   c) get scared, then instantly forgive.***
   d) consider the situation and source. If the person is going through a difficult time, I may overlook inappropriate behavior if I'm not being abused. Maybe the person needs a sounding board.
   e) either do a, b, d, or something that includes taking care of myself. Each situation is unique.

Score as indicated below for Multiple Choice.
1. 5 for c ____; 10 for a ____; (0 for anything else)
2. 5 for e ____; 10 for b ____; (0 for anything else)
3. 10 for a, b, or e ____; (0 for anything else)
4. 5 for a ____; 10 for c, d, or e ____; (0 for b)
5. 10 for a, b, d, or e ____; (0 for c)*** and if you're being abused, GET IMMEDIATE HELP

Total from Multiple Choice: ____

III. True or False

Write **T** (True) or **F** (False) before each statement.

1. ____ Until now, the most challenging people to deal with anger with are friends or _____ (fill in the blank).*

---

* Don't affirm True or False statements #1, #3, and #6.

2. _____ It's okay to feel as angry at God as I would at anyone else.

3. _____ My best intimacy occurs when we "kiss and make up."*

4. _____ I release anger as soon as I become aware of it and anything I'm supposed to learn. I don't need resentments for protection; I can set boundaries without staying mad.

5. _____ "An eye for an eye" leaves two people half-blinded. If someone cheats on me, it doesn't help if I have an affair to get even—although I may feel a moment of power. What I do to others, I do to myself. That means if someone hurts me and I get even, I get hurt twice.

6. _____ I don't mind an occasional argument if it doesn't become unmanageable. Arguing helps get out feelings—but only with a consenting adult.*

7. _____ I'd rather be peaceful and effective than angry and right.

8. _____ I can detach and protect myself from negativity or anger that's projected at me.

Give yourself ten points for the following answers to True or False:

1. T or F _____ (This question is for awareness.)
2. T _____
3. F _____
4. T _____
5. T _____
6. T or F _____
7. T _____
8. T _____

Total from True or False: _____

Affirm the Assessment statements (#4 only if it applies) and the correct answers to Multiple Choice.

About #1 in True or False: some people deal with anger effectively except with one person or category of people in their life. If that includes you, give yourself 10 points for honesty. Awareness brings acceptance, which brings peace.

About #6 in True or False: arguing is a personal choice as long as both people agree and there's no abuse. But arguing isn't for everyone. That statement doesn't need affirmation.

#3 in True or False is different from arguing. Anger has little to do with making love. You may want to ask why you need the anger to get "turned on."

> *Anger is like money. It is neither evil nor good—*
> *but the use of it that makes it so.*

Now, add your scores from all three parts of the Anger Quiz.

I. Assessment _____
II. Multiple Choice _____
III. True or False _____
TOTAL _____

> *I have never received Grace*
> *to deal with tomorrow's problems today.*

220–230: You're either a Master, in denial, or responding how you think you should. Look more closely, then take the test again. If your score is still high, congratulations. Anger is a tough one; you could help others learn what you've mastered.

190–219: You're doing great with anger. That's not easy to achieve. You've got something worthwhile to share. You're dealing with anger as well as anyone could.

160–189: Depending on your background, you may have worked hard to get this competent with anger. Do some affirmations. Read about anger and do the activities in the next section. The more comfortable you are with anger, the more peaceful and powerful you'll become.

130–159: You're either in the Codependency Zone or close. Not dealing with anger could be causing problems. Pay attention to anger, whether it's in you or someone else. Read about anger *and* emotions in the next section. Do the activities and affirmations. Many of us weren't told anything about anger except "It's wrong." Many people with codependency issues have a lot of anger, especially those who were abused. We denied anger to survive. It wasn't safe to deal with anger then—but it is now. The time to align with peace and power has arrived.

100–129: You're in the Codependent Zone. Read this book. Do the activities about emotions and anger. Read or reread *Codependent No More* and *The Language of Letting Go*. Get comfortable with anger. It takes a lot of work to deal with anger, but when you do, you're on the road to peace.

0–99: Your anger needs immediate attention. Start dealing with it NOW. Read this book. Do the anger activities. **GET IMMEDIATE HELP IF ABUSE IS INVOLVED.** Look underneath anger for grief, sadness, fear, shame, or guilt. Read or reread *Codependent No More* and *The Language of Letting Go*. You may also want to read books about anger or get anger management training. You'll feel better when anger isn't dominating your life. There are many reasons you're as angry as you are. You'll be a new person when you safely get that anger out and connect with essential power.

FEAR QUIZ

I. Panic, Anxiety, and Fear Assessment

Use the 0 to 10 scoring system here, the same as above.

1. I can competently deal with panic, fear, and anxiety. I understand that fear, panic, and anxiety—including social anxiety—are normal responses to life, even if I don't know what I'm anxious about. ____

2. If I start stressing about having too much to do or what needs to be done, I know how to stop feeling overwhelmed. I relax into Life knowing I'll get everything done I need to do. ____

3. I don't control people to avoid feeling fear about what they're doing or how their behavior may affect me. Fear doesn't cause me to obsess about how things will work out. ____

4. I've been through so much that I'm efficient and level-headed in a legitimate crisis. I put the "negative" parts of my past to good use. ____

5. I surrender to and face universal fears—fear of being alone, money fears, fear of aging, dying, abandonment. I also face fears specific to me. By facing fear, I get out of its grip. ____

6. I can identify when fear is a warning signal or when anxiety is trying to show me I need to pay attention to whatever's going on. ____

7. I don't create unnecessary fear with "what ifs." I don't worry excessively. I avoid anxiety by staying in the moment I'm in now. ____

8. I'm willing to feel uncomfortable to pay the price to grow.

Fear often accompanies doing anything new; I don't let it stop me from doing what I need to do. ____

9. I know the difference between fear, anxiety, panic, worry, a red flag, and a bunch of emotions that are really many repressed feelings from the past. I don't call a big ball of historical emotions an anxiety attack. ____

10. I either understand what I fear or let go until fear reveals what it is. I can calm myself so fear doesn't control me. My fears don't make me try to control other people, myself, and Life. ____

Total from Assessment: ____

II. Multiple Choice

Circle the letter of the ending that describes you.

1. **When I become afraid of failing, I:**
   a) deny it, then usually fail because my work is fear-based.
   b) surrender to and release my fear so I work from peace.
   c) give up, say I don't care, or can't. Then I don't worry about what will happen—I know I'll fail. By sabotaging myself, I gain control.
   d) visualize what I want, let go, and work for the sake of working, not for the outcome. Then, I succeed because I enjoy what I do.
   e) either b, d, or both.

2. **If I become afraid about not having enough money, I:**
   a) hint about my financial problems to people, hoping they'll help.
   b) ask someone for money.
   c) write a check with no money in the bank, and hope I can cover it.

d) pay the basics, give what I can, live under my means, and keep a nest egg. I also say a prayer, like my "God shall supply all my needs." But I don't spend money I don't have.

e) hoard, deprive myself, go without.

3. **If I become afraid about aging, I:**

a) do what I can to stay in good shape and look my best. I take steps to look young without becoming a plastic surgery junkie.

b) give up and let my appearance go completely. What's the use?

c) buy every product I can and regularly schedule plastic surgery.

d) lie about my age.

e) pull the skin on my face back to see what I'd look like with a face-lift, then surrender to my fears and limitations. I focus on the positives that come with aging. I am the age I am.

4. **If I become so fearful I can barely function, I:**

a) pray, meditate, write in a journal, call a friend, and talk about my feelings—do something that calms me. I try to understand the fear, but if I can't, I move forward anyway.

b) call people and beg them to promise me that my fears won't manifest.

c) take Xanax or Valium.

d) call a psychic hotline.

e) cling to someone or go fetal.

5. **If I have so much to do I become anxiety-ridden, I:**

a) scream, feel hyper and so overwhelmed I don't get anything done.

b) remind myself I don't ever have to do more than I can.

c) beg people to help me because I have too much to do.

d) get sick, go to bed, and hope everything will go away.

e) do the work while feeling stressed, then get sick afterwards.

Give yourself the score indicated below for Multiple-Choice answers. For any that don't apply, give yourself ten points.

1. 5 for b ___; 10 for d or e ____; (0 for anything else).
2. 10 for d ____; (0 for anything else).
3. 10 for a or e ____; (0 for anything else).
4. 10 for a ____; (0 for anything else).
5. 10 for b; (0 for anything else).

Total from Multiple Choice: _____

True or False

Mark each statement **T** (True) or **F** (False).

1. ____ I use tools such as prayer and meditation to relax.
2. ____ I don't let past fears control me. Just because something happened a certain way once, doesn't mean it will happen again.
3. ____ Whatever needs to be done can best be done in peace. I deal with anxiety first instead of doing something when I'm afraid.
4. ____ Fear can disguise itself as many things: *I don't want to, I'm not good enough,* or *I don't care.* People cling to people to get security, then call clinging *love.* Sometimes fear keeps people in situations that aren't healthy. Fear can cause people to do many things. I don't let fear control me. If it does, I surrender to it and deal with it as soon as I can.
5. ____ I regularly do something that scares me (or someone else) without taking foolhardy risks. I do this to teach myself courage, to fully live, and so I'm not controlled by fear.

6. ____ I'm in the relationships I'm in and work where I do because I want to be there, not because I'm afraid to leave.

7. ____ I surrender to, and release, fear instead of letting fear turn into control.

8. ____ I'm willing to feel afraid and uncomfortable if that's what it takes to do something new or change.

Score ten points for each True statement.

Total from True or False____

Total all three parts of the Fear Quiz.

I. Assessment ____
II. Multiple Choice ____
III. True or False ____
TOTAL ____

"Do one thing every day that scares you."
—Eleanor Roosevelt

"Do one thing every week that scares somebody else."
—Melody Beattie ... and others

220–230: Are you really this peaceful? Are you a Master or in denial? Look more closely, then take the test again. If you score this high, congratulations.

190–219: You're a peaceful person. You're dealing with fear as well as anyone can—not tempting fate but willing to try something new. And you're willing to feel uncomfortable. You've mastered the key to change. Congratulations! Share what you've learned with others. Contribute to world peace.

160–189: Read about fear and do some activities in the next section. Fear is one of the trickiest feelings there is and the biggest reason for controlling. Work on fear but don't be frightened by your test results. You're not that far away from the top of the charts.

130–159: Fear, anxiety, obsession, worry, and controlling could be problems. You're either in the Codependent Zone or close by it. Pay attention to how much fear is in you, and what it causes you to do or avoid. Read about fear and do some activities in the next section. Also read about emotions, obsession, and controlling. Get more of that fear out of you. Set yourself and others free.

100–129: The light is red. You're in the Codependent Zone. Read this book and do the activities—fear, emotions, obsession, and controlling are priorities. Read or reread *Codependent No More* and *The Language of Letting Go*. Face and release fear, surrender to it, or walk through it. Be still and know that God is God; Life is Life; and it's okay to be you. You'll get the Grace and guidance you need each day. Don't worry about whether it *will be okay*. It already is.

0–99: The fear inside you needs attention *now*. Read this book and do the activities. Also read or reread *Codependent No More* and *The Language of Letting Go*. Learn about codependency, control, obsession, peace, fear, and feelings. Maybe take a martial arts class—something to help you feel more spiritually powerful and peaceful. You'll feel better when fear isn't controlling your life and making you control everyone else.

DRAMA AND MISERY ADDICTION QUIZ

I'm not using "addiction" here the way it applies to heroin, alcohol, or other substances. But we can lose control of our use of drama; it can cause negative consequences for us and others. We can become so numb that we need drama and misery to help us feel alive. Some of us don't think peace, joy, and happiness exist except in movies and books. When you leave the Codependency Zone, peace and joy will become real in real life.

A NOTE TO PEOPLE EXPERIENCING DEEP GRIEF

Please wait until another time to take the drama and misery quiz, a time when your grief isn't so fresh and you're not so raw. Grief will interfere with an accurate score on this test.

If you're uncertain about whether you're grieving (and sometimes we don't know), take the grief and loss quiz. If you think you're in grief, you probably are. Focus on that now. Take gentle, loving care of yourself. Later come back and take the drama and misery quiz. For now, be good to yourself.

I. Need for Drama and Misery Assessment

Score from 0 to 10, the same as above.

1. My life is interesting and peaceful, and I'm present for most moments, not just the high points or fifteen minutes of fame. If something interrupts peace, I deal with it immediately. I've learned that being happy means feeling consistently peaceful, not excited about something "great" that might occur. ____

2. When I'm bored, I find something interesting to do, or a way to become interested in what I'm doing. _____

3. I can feel happy, content, or grateful without waiting for the other shoe to drop or believing it's the "calm before the storm." _____

4. I can detach without becoming numb, cold, or shutting down (unhealthy detachment). I don't let people pull me into their chaos so I feel as miserable as them. _____

5. I go around trouble whenever I can instead of running headfirst into it. _____

6. I don't create the same dramas repeatedly and I won't suffer unnecessarily. Problems are part of life, but I seek positive solutions. I don't need to prove how much suffering I can endure. _____

7. My parents were fairly happy people. They didn't create unnecessary drama or suffer without a reason. _____*

8. I avoid using that breathless "I can't wait to tell you what happened and how horrible it is" voice. I center myself, then talk from a place of peace. _____

9. I don't need the person listening to me talk about a problem to become upset. I don't need to spread misery to be happy. _____

10. In the heat of the moment, problems may look bigger than they are. But I know the difference between inconvenience, solvable problems, serious problems, tragedies, and the end of the world—and the world hasn't ended yet. If I say something is a crisis, it is. _____

Total from Assessment: _____

* #7 above isn't an affirmation.

II. Multiple Choice Quiz

Circle the letter of the ending that describes you.

1. **If people say I'm acting like a drama addict,**
   a) I tell them to take their own inventory instead of taking mine.
   b) I look at what they're saying. If it's true, I deal with it. If it isn't, I consider the source. Sometimes people see in people what they dislike in themselves most.
   c) I either fight with them or call someone else and complain.
   d) I believe whatever people say.
   e) I might do a or b.

2. **When problems appear, I:**
   a) spend more time reacting to having the problem than I do to finding a solution.
   b) believe I deserve whatever bad happens.
   c) feel upset, obsessed, or scared, then realize I'll either get the Grace to live with it or find a solution.
   d) secretly feel grateful for the distraction from boredom.
   e) wonder why bad things happen to me but not to anyone else.

3. **When talking to people socially, I usually talk about:**
   a) whatever the other person wants to discuss.
   b) projects, ideas, ideals—there's no set pattern for my conversations. Each one has a life of its own.
   c) them and myself.
   d) the same things, over and over. My conversations are obsessions.
   e) a, b, or c.

4. **When I call people because I'm upset, and they listen but don't become upset too, I:**

a) appreciate them bringing peace to the situation instead of feeding on my problems.

b) feel rejected. If they cared, I'd get a reaction from them.

c) keep trying to get people as upset as I am until they hang up or engage in my drama. Once I've dumped my misery, I feel fine and go on with my life.

d) keep calling people until I find someone who'll feel as upset as I am.

e) feel guilty for bothering people. Usually I don't call anyone. I suffer alone.

5. **If I'm facing a situation that's potentially tragic, I:**

a) pray, talk to friends, cry, get upset. I'm usually all over the place emotionally, but I do my best to hang in until I know what's going on.

b) wait until I know what reality is until I respond. If the worst happens, there's time to grieve later, when I know what I'm grieving about.

c) am convinced that the worst will happen and ask friends for support.

d) call a psychic, then call my friends and ask what they think will happen. Nothing helps because what I want is for the waiting to end and the tragedy not to happen.

e) might do some of all of the above, depending on how serious the potential problem. Not everything is false drama.

Below are the scores for the answers to the Multiple-Choice questions above. (If any don't apply, give yourself ten points for the score.)

1. 5 for a ____; 10 for b or e ____; (0 for anything else).
2. 10 for c ____; (0 for anything else).
3. 10 for a, b, c, or e ____; (0 for d).

4. 10 for a; (0 for anything else).

5. 10 for any answer: ____; Facing a tragedy is a real problem.

Total from Multiple Choice: ____

III. *True or False*

Write **T** (True) or **F** (False) before each statement.

1. ____ As a child or adult, I became numb. Misery and problems were the only life I knew.*

2. ____ If I call people when I'm upset, I also call them later when the problem resolves. I don't dump my misery on people, then not let them know what happened.

3. ____ I'm not secretly happy when someone says something bad happened. I don't need to feed off people's problems.

4. ____I know my peace and happiness depends on me—not what people are doing, and what I can't control.

5. ____ I'm finding "the Peace that Passes all Understanding" (or it's finding me). To find it, I don't have to accept the big picture. I only need to surrender to each moment and feeling and remember *This too shall pass.*

6. ____ I don't pick fights for drama. If I disagree, it's a legitimate issue and I usually have a peaceful discussion. Sometimes I take a strong stand or speak loudly, but solving problems isn't usually a drama.

7. ____ If someone or something creates constant misery, I either correct or leave the situation, or accept what I can't change. I don't need constant turmoil. I know the value of peace.

* #1 in True or False isn't an affirmation.

8. ____I can enjoy peace without imagining all the terrible things that are going to happen to wreck it. I'm not a "peaceful-phobic."

Score ten points for the following True or False answers (0 for anything else):

1. F ____
2. T ____
3. T ____
4. T ____
5. T ____
6. T ____
7. T ____
8. T ____

Total from True or False____

Add your scores from all three parts of the Drama and Misery Quiz.

I. Assessment _____
II. Multiple Choice _____
III. True or False _____
TOTAL _____

220–230: You're either one in a million or you need to take this test again. Few people score this high—but it's not impossible. Spend more time on each statement. If you know you've integrated these behaviors into your life and they're not just something you *think* you do, congratulations!

190–219: You're someone who knows how to surrender to whatever experiences come your way but you don't create unnecessary problems. You can let go and let God, detach in love, live and let live, but you're human, too. You listen with genuine interest to people. Your responses are helpful. You bring peace to situations. You feel safe with life, so people feel safe with you.

160–189: You could be more peaceful and you probably will—you've already come this far. You'll benefit from working on emotions, trusting life and yourself, and doing the activities in Sections Three and Five. Prayer and meditation will help, too. Scoring high in this section is a by-product of the other self-care we do. Drama addiction is usually one of the last things to go. Be grateful for where you are now. Don't worry. You'll be shown what to do.

130–159: Caution: you're in the yellow zone. You're not in the Codependency Zone but you're not far from it either. Learn to relax. Get some of those old emotions out so it doesn't take as much drama and intensity for you to feel alive. Misery is not your lot, and life is more than something to be endured. You can and will feel better than you do. Do the activities in Sections Three and Five. Practice prayer and meditation. You'll leave drama and misery addiction behind the further you go down the road to peace.

100–129: You're in the Codependent Zone. But it's not the end of the world. Don't focus on the drama and misery; work on the other issues connected to codependency. Then peace and joy will find you. You can have a real life without all that drama. Read this book; do the activities. Read or reread *Codependent No More* and *The Language of Letting Go.* How about getting some support from a group? Keep taking care of yourself and your capacity for peace will grow right along with you.

0–99: I'm not going to tell you your score is an emergency. That would be music to your ears. Relax. Breathe. Millions of us started where you are, taking the first steps on the road to peace. You're about to find out how good it is to be you. You won't need all that drama to feel alive. Read this book. Take your time. Do the activities. Read or reread *Codependent No More* and *The Language of Letting Go*. You could benefit by attending support groups. As the protective walls around you tumble down—the walls you built to survive—you'll become more sensitized. It will take less pain to hurt, and more true problems to rattle you. Peace will become your friend.

GUILT QUIZ

I. Guilt and Shame Assessment

Use the same 0 to 10 scoring system here as in the other assessments.

1. I'm not burdened by excessive amounts of guilt or shame. If someone I love has a problem, I don't believe it's my *fault*. I don't feel guilty that I can't do more, be more, that I'm not different than I am, or somewhere else in my growth. ____

> **"Guilt," she said, "the gift that keeps on giving."**
> **—Anonymous**

2. I'm not ashamed of who I am or where I've been. When I do something wrong, I make amends. I ask for forgiveness from God and the people I hurt (when that won't do more harm than good). Then I accept forgiveness and forgive myself. ____
3. I forgive other people. I won't find forgiveness until I do. But I don't use forgiveness to feed denial, and forgiving doesn't mean I let someone hurt me again. Forgiveness is how I stop being victimized. It connects me with power. ____
4. If I'm doing something that creates guilt, I stop it or reevaluate my standards. If I can't stop, I surrender to my powerlessness. If I'm living up to someone else's standards, I stop pleasing them. I also make sure what I'm feeling isn't an emotion disguised as guilt such as anger, fear, or grief. ____

5. I don't let people control or manipulate me with guilt. I don't use guilt to control myself or them. _____

6. I deal with guilt using: the Twelve Steps, confession, my religion's suggestion, or another helpful ritual. If I feel guilt, I don't deny it. _____

7. I find myself using experiences I've felt guilty about as tools to help others accept themselves. When I tell them what I did, they feel better because they're not alone. Honest sharing is what this journey is about. _____

8. If someone does something inappropriate, then tries to blame me, I don't fall for that trick. I don't accept guilt that isn't mine. _____

9. I remove any ceilings or limitations I created because of guilt, shame, something someone told me, or something I told myself. Whether the ceiling is on money, work, relationships, love, health, or growth, I surrender to the limitation. Then I set myself free to go as high and far as I can. _____

10. I don't have to hide who I am, what I've done, or what I'm doing. I also don't have to disclose personal details to anyone I don't trust. _____

Total from Assessment: _____

II. Multiple Choice

Circle the letter of the ending that most accurately describes you.

1. **If an interaction with someone leaves me feeling crazy or confused, I:**
   a) blame myself. The problem must be me. It couldn't be the other person.
   b) ask someone what I should do.

c) tell the other person to take their insanity somewhere else.

d) go along with the other person, even knowing the situation doesn't feel right. Later, I get mad when I realize I was manipulated.

e) back off, sort out what happened, then look for the lesson. Usually when something feels crazy, it is. Sometimes it's time to walk away, but some situations can be resolved.

2. **If I make a mistake or do something wrong, I:**
   a) take responsibility and make amends as soon as I can.
   b) get embarrassed and get myself in deeper. I eventually admit making a mistake, but it's difficult. I have so much guilt that I'm afraid if I admit my mistake, I'll lose the little self-esteem I have instead of remembering it's the other way around.
   c) act like nothing happened.
   d) call everyone I know, and then get a team on my side. Sometimes I even lie and say I told my therapist what happened and he or she agrees that I'm right. How can I lose an argument when my therapist is on my side?
   e) might do a, b, or c, but ultimately I clear the air and make appropriate amends.

3. **If I know someone is lying, but I can't prove it and the other person won't admit it, I:**
   a) believe the other person. I have too much guilt to trust myself.
   b) stick to what I know is true. If I slightly suspect something, that's different. But I don't need proof when I know the truth deep inside.
   c) start obsessing and try to catch the other person red-handed.

d) let go and wait for guidance. Unless believing a lie could physically harm me, I wait until I have proof and know what to do about it.

e) might do any of the above.

4. **If someone does something I absolutely can't forgive—or if I've done something I can't forgive myself for, I:**

a) try not to think about it or let it bother me too much.

b) work harder to forgive. I use affirmations, prayer—whatever it takes for as long as it takes. I know how important forgiveness is. I work until I get it right.

c) accept the situation as it is—that I can't or won't forgive. I don't resist it. Acceptance at least brings some peace.

d) turn it over to my Higher Power. If it's ever time, forgiveness will happen.

e) do some or any of the above.

5. **If someone and I both hurt each other, I:**

a) make amends—if the other person apologizes first.

b) forget about what the other person did and take responsibility for myself.

c) feel justified for a while, then clean my side of the street. When I do, I'm the one who gets the power and peace.

d) decide who behaved the worst. If it's me, I make amends first. If it's the other person, I wait before I say sorry. If all I did was react to someone's bad behavior, then the responsibility for making amends isn't mine.

e) apologize. I make amends even when I don't do anything wrong. I feel guilty *all* the time.

Below are the scores for the Multiple-Choice statements. Give yourself 10 points for any that don't apply to you.

1. 10 for e ____; 5 for b, c, or d ____; (0 for a).
2. 5 for b ____; 10 for a or e ____; (0 for anything else).

3. 5 for c; 10 for b, d, or e _____; (0 for a).

4. 10 for any answer. If you checked a, someone hurt you deeply. Be gentle with yourself.

5. 10 for b or c _____; 5 for d _____; (0 for anything else).

Total from Multiple choice: _____

III. *True or False*

Write **T** (True) or **F** (False) before each statement.

1. _____ I'm willing to feel that twinge of guilt called *afterburn* that often accompanies saying no or setting boundaries. I know I don't have to change my boundaries because I feel guilty when I tell people something they don't want to hear. That guilt twang that comes with setting boundaries will soon disappear.

2. _____ I'm aware of the different faces and forms of guilt. I know the difference between guilt from violating my standards; illegitimate guilt from not living up to other people's expectations; other people's guilt that I pick up (for instance, when an abuse victim feels ashamed instead of letting the perpetrator have the guilt for abusing); guilt that's a stage of grief (such as *I could have prevented it, if only I had or hadn't done what I did);* and other feelings disguised as guilt—anger, fear, or hurt. No matter what kind of guilt is in me, it's my job to get it out.

3. _____ When something "bad" happens, I know God isn't punishing me.

4. _____ I lived or now live in a fundamentalist environment with strict rules for right and wrong, and no room for error or freedom to be who I am. This fundamentalist system

* #4 isn't an affirmation.

"I can honestly say I don't have much guilt. I've worked hard on myself. When guilt comes up, I surrender to it. I let it be there or flow through me, instead of resisting. I look at what it's trying to show me. Is there something I'm supposed to see? Guilt is such a paralyzing emotion; I release it as soon as I can."

—Anonymous

may be at work, home, church, school, an organization—even a recovery group. It uses guilt and strict rules instead of encouraging people to trust themselves. Self-esteem is gained by following rules and lost by making mistakes. This system produces guilt, takes the joy out of life, and stops me from trusting who I am.*

5. ____ I don't apologize for everything I say, do, think, or feel. I don't constantly feel like a bad child doing something wrong. I'm comfortable being who I am. I have the right to make mistakes, learn from them, forgive myself, and let them become part of my life plan. Often when I think I'm off track, I'm right where I'm supposed to be.

6. ____ If I was abused, I know the abuse isn't my fault. I don't continue victimizing myself by believing I deserve what happened. I give the shame back to the abuser. I refuse to accept it as mine. **

7. ____ I'm not carrying any dark secrets that I haven't shared with anyone—no dark stains on my soul. We're each accountable for our behavior. But no matter what I've done, I'm forgivable. I can be and am forgiven.

8. ____ If I believe lies or get manipulated or used, I don't feel guilty. I take responsibility for myself by getting out of the

** If #6 doesn't apply, give yourself 10 points.

situation when I realize what happened. There are people in the world with less than honorable motives. I can bump into them without blaming myself.

Score ten points for the following answers to True or False.

1. T _____
2. T _____
3. T _____
4. F _____
5. T _____
6. T _____
7. T _____
8. T _____

Total from True or False_____

Add the scores from all three parts of the Guilt and Shame Quiz.

I. Assessment _____
II. Multiple Choice _____
III. True or False _____
TOTAL _____

220–230: Other than Masters, the only people I've met this guiltless don't have a conscience. Are you really this guilt-free or do you feel so guilty you think you have to score that highly to have any self-esteem? Are you willing to take these tests again? Spend more time observing yourself with each behavior. If you still score so highly, teach someone else how to become that guilt-free.

190–219: Congratulations! You're human. You make mistakes, then learn lessons that turn into experiences you use to help others. Most of the time, you enjoy being you. Nobody has to tell you to smell the roses; you're aware of the beauty in the world. Being this guilt- and shame-free doesn't come easy. You either worked hard to release guilt, come from a loving family, or didn't (or don't) get into much trouble. You might struggle sometimes, but so what? You're doing a great job.

160–189: You'll feel pounds lighter when you let go of more guilt. You deserve to appreciate yourself more than you do. If you're an abuse victim, you've worked hard to become this shame-free. The tragedy of abuse isn't only the original incident. It's that we stay victims by blaming ourselves for what happened. Read about guilt in the next section; do some affirmations and exercises. Accepting forgiveness—forgiving ourselves—can be difficult. But I don't have to tell you this. You're learning it yourself.

130–159: You're in the yellow zone. Caution! Guilt and shame could be running your life. Read about emotions and guilt in the next section; do the affirmations and activities. You're not living in Codependency Zone, but you're not far from it either. Guilt is paralyzing. Start and keep moving. Make any necessary amends, then see how much fun life is.

100–129: Ouch! You're in the Codependent Zone. This much guilt hurts. Do you spend a lot of time saying "sorry"? Or do you feel so defensive you can't admit mistakes? That much guilt destroys self-esteem. It makes self-love almost impossible. Commit to getting rid of guilt. Read this book. Read or reread Codependent No More and The Language of Letting Go. Do the affirmations and exercises about guilt and victimization. You'll connect with power and see what a gifted, beautiful person you have been and are.

0–99: Oops! Your biggest mistake is carrying this much guilt. You may have some legitimate guilt, but you've got some that isn't yours. Read this book. Do as many affirmations and activities as you can. Read or reread *Codependent No More* and *The Language of Letting Go.* How about getting some professional help or attending a group? The Twelve Steps have a great formula for letting go of guilt. Have you lost a lot? Are you from a fundamentalist environment? Do you have shame from things you've done in the past? (If the answer to the last question is yes, you're not alone. Many of us do. There's a way to undo it.) You'd be surprised at how badly some people feel about something they did that has grown unrealistically out of proportion, and how they let this thing unnecessarily wreck their lives. "The Promises" in the *Big Book of Alcoholics Anonymous* say if we work the Steps, we won't regret our pasts. Well, members of other Twelve-Step programs such as Al-Anon get these rewards, too. Take steps to get rid of guilt. You'll have more capacity for fun and service when you're not spending so much time feeling badly about who you are. You've lived with guilt so long you may not know there's another way to feel, but there is. A new world is waiting for you.

GRIEF AND LOSS QUIZ

I. Grief Assessment

Score the statements from 0 to 10, the same as in the assessments above.

1. I grieve any childhood losses—what I didn't get, what I had then lost—and how they affect me as an adult. I have a healing attitude toward the past. It can all work out for good. _____

2. If I didn't get something important as a child—like love or security—it doesn't mean I didn't deserve it then or don't deserve it now. I don't incorrectly make sense of loss by believing it's my fault. _____

3. I'm not currently facing a significant loss—death, divorce, chemical dependency (in a loved one or myself), abuse, separation from family, illness, betrayal, and loss of a relationship, home, job. _____

4. I'm committed to feeling grief instead of avoiding it or denying what I feel. I also know no matter how much I hurt, it's not okay to hurt anyone else or myself. _____

5. If I'm obsessing about a loss, or trying to control something because losing it will hurt, I'm gentle with myself. I understand that obsessing and controlling can be more than codependency; they can be stages of grief. _____

6. If someone breaks my heart, I allow it to heal instead of refusing to ever be hurt or love again. _____

7. I know how to grieve or I'm learning. I don't enjoy loss, but I'm not afraid of grief either. I don't have to live up to anyone's expectations about how long grief takes. I decide what's an important loss. As long as I don't hurt anyone else, how I grieve is my business. _____

8. Many codependent behaviors are stages of grief. If I get frozen in a stage of grief or codependent behavior, I get unstuck by surrendering to the behavior and the feelings underneath it. Then almost naturally, the behavior changes. ____

9. I prefer to know and face the truth, even when it hurts. I also know denial is a shock absorber, not something that's "wrong." I can go through grief without judging the process. ____

10. I eventually accept the changes life brings as my life plan and destiny. ____

Total from Assessment: ____

II. Multiple Choice

Circle the letter of the ending that best describes you.

1. **If someone is obsessing and hurting from grief, I:**
   a) listen and help as much as I comfortably can. I can practice compassion and still have limits.
   b) tell the person to get off the pity pot.
   c) suggest the person get professional help or attend a Twelve-Step group.
   d) avoid the person. I don't know what to say to grieving people.
   e) might do any, some, or none of the above. Each situation is different.

2. **If I'm on the verge of crying, I:**
   a) ask the doctor for antidepressants.
   b) successfully hold back the tears.
   c) cry, no matter where I am or what I'm doing.
   d) wait until I'm alone then cry—but only if I can't help it. I hate shedding tears.

e) either do a, c, d, or a combination. There isn't *one* way I handle situations.

3. **If I'm going through deep grief, I:**
   a) go easy on myself. I may cocoon, feel angry, avoid irritating people, get crazy, feel mad at God, take a vacation, or get professional help. I surrender to each moment. If I take medication, it's only with supervision. Grief is an important transition—not wasted time to be endured. Grief will teach me what it wants me to learn.
   b) keep going. That's life.
   c) don't notice it. I've had so much loss that I think sadness is how people feel.
   d) consider it a free pass to drink, act out, use drugs, or hurt people that still have what I lost.
   e) may do a, try to do b, and hope for the Grace not to do d. There isn't one way I grieve.

4. **When I'm going through grief, my friends:**
   a) don't understand unless they've had the same loss.
   b) are the worst people to be around.
   c) are the best for support.
   d) avoid me until I'm better.
   e) do the best they can with what they know.

5. **If I'm grieving or facing a big loss, the first person I turn to is:**
   a) God.
   b) not God. I'm too angry. God could have prevented the loss. Luckily, God doesn't give up on me. Someone with a similar loss comes along and welcomes me to the "grief club" I just unwillingly joined.
   c) a parent, mentor, friend, adult child, sponsor, or spouse.
   d) nobody. I keep my pain to myself.
   e) anyone who's willing to listen.

Below are the scores to the Multiple-Choice Quiz above. For any that don't apply, give yourself 10 points.

1. 5 for c ____; 10 for a or e ____; (0 for anything else).
2. 10 for c, d, or e ____; (0 for anything else).
3. 10 for a or e ____; (0 for anything else).
4. 10 for any answer. Respect who you're comfortable with.
5. 10 for any answer. The choice about who to turn to first when you're grieving is yours. Don't let anyone—even me— tell you you're grieving wrong.

Total from Multiple Choice: ____

III. True or False

1. ____ If I had the power to change something big about my life, I know exactly what it would be.*
2. ____ I haven't experienced a major change (even desirable) in the past year, but not because I'm stuck.*
3. ____ I'm experiencing a "rite of passage" such as graduating, getting married, having children, retiring, getting sober, becoming a grandparent, having a child move away from home, moving, taking care of a parent, aging changes, or any of many life stages.*
4. ____ I grieve instead of immediately replacing my loss with something or someone similar.
5. ____ Sometimes I secretly desire to be done with life. I wouldn't kill myself, but part of me has given up. I believe in a better life after death. This one sucks. I've worked hard to be good, but I still get one loss after another. Each is harder. People have it worse than I do, but I've had more than my share of trouble.*
6. ____ I don't pride myself on my ability to endure suffering,

but I understand the importance of surrendering to and feeling old and current grief and trauma.

7. ____ I'm trapped! For reasons that aren't justifications, I can't make the changes I want. My life is filled with doing things I don't like. I'm waiting for some far-off time for things to get better.

8. ____ I've been through deep grief. I don't believe "what doesn't kill us makes us stronger." I'm not a martyr. But I'm more peaceful than many people who haven't been through as much loss. My losses haven't made me bitter. They've made me compassionate and turned me into who I am.*

Give yourself ten points for the following answers to True or False. This Quiz is to help measure your grief more than for affirmations. Many answers are statements to help you see something you otherwise might not notice. Sometimes we don't know we're grieving; we think it's "just how life is." That may be, but we'll be more peaceful if we let ourselves grieve.

Score 10 points for the following True or False answers.

1. F ____
2. T ____
3. F ____
4. T ____
5. F ____
6. F ____
7. F ____
8. T or F ____

Total from True or False____

* True or False statements #1, #2, #3, #5, and #7, aren't affirmations. Only use #8 if it applies to you.

Add your scores from all three parts of the Guilt and Shame Quiz.

I. Assessment _____
II. Multiple Choice _____
III. True or False _____
TOTAL _____

220–230: The Grief Quiz is about understanding how much change—desirable or not—is going on so you know how to best take care of yourself. Is your life that free of change and loss? Do you need to look deeper? You're either living under a lucky star or in denial. If you take the test again and still score the same, you're likely not in grief. Focus on another issue because this one doesn't hurt.

190–219: Unless you know otherwise, this score indicates that you're not going through any significant grief, loss, or change. If you are, you're coming out the other end. It also looks like you've dealt with past losses. Maybe you could be of service to others and focus on another issue where you need work.

160–189: This score indicates some grief or change. It may not be overwhelming, but give yourself time to accept whatever's taking place. Talk to safe friends who understand. Maybe you could be of service to others just beginning to go through what you've experienced. Helping others will help your heart heal, too. You may be more of a Master than someone who scores higher. You know what it feels like to lose someone or something you love. You know what it feels like to be turned upside down and live in pain and the unknown. You will be guided. You are led. You have much to offer—not later, but *now*. Read this book. Do the emotional activities and affirmations (but not the Drama and Misery Test). Read or reread *Codependent No More*, *The Language of Letting Go*, and *The Grief Club*. Also, read about the other scores except the higher ones in this test. Something in each may apply to you.

130–159: You're in the yellow zone. This indicates grief. If you don't let yourself feel your grief feelings, grief could turn into habitual codependency. Read the next score up and do what's recommended there for healing, and the scores underneath. Stay aware. Feel what you feel—whether it's nothing, numb, rage, sad, fear. Watch for others who appear in your path to help you. Watch for others you can help. Like the song says, may the circle not be broken. It's the circle that will help your heart and the world heal from loss. It's the circle of real love.

100–129: Ouch! You either hurt or you're too numb to feel it. Make a commitment to life and grief. You may also benefit from reading the next two score zones higher. Something from each may apply to you. Read this book; do the emotional affirmations and activities (except for Drama and Misery). Also, read or reread *Codependent No More*, *The Language of Letting Go*, and *The Grief Club*. The Masters at grief are people who score low. You know what it feels like to have a broken heart. You know just because you love someone doesn't mean you get to have that person in your life. Life isn't fair. Cry when you need to; feel rage when you feel that. But don't hurt anyone else or yourself—and don't let anyone hurt you. You didn't cause the loss, even if your grief lies and says that you did (or unless you're in jail because you're truly guilty of breaking the law). No matter what happened, let life shape you into the sensitive, compassionate person you are and will become.

0–99: You're in a lot of pain, whether you feel it or not. You may want to read the next three or four scores up. Be gentle. Don't expect too much from yourself. Take each moment as it comes. Sometimes when we grieve, we believe we're being punished and deserve to lose what we lost. We may believe we deserve to be abused. The opposite is true. You need extra love. Let this journey take you where you're going. Give yourself the time you need. Healing your pain is a priority. Read this book. Do any activities that appeal to you. Also read or reread *Codependent No More, The Language of Letting Go,* and *The Grief Club.* Maybe get professional help or attend a group. You'll get all the help you need to take care of yourself. Although you didn't ask for this, you can come out the other end a Master—someone who will help heal our world.

SECTION FOUR

Catch and Release: It's Only a Feeling

1 • Opening Pandora's Box

THE COLOR WHEEL

We discovered feelings in the sixties. They'd been around a long time, but they were like the animals on Noah's Ark: except for a few who hadn't been named yet. (Later many of us discovered they also come in pairs.) Then the importance of emotions started becoming clear. Emotions motivate behavior. If people feel angry, they scream, hit, and kill. If they feel sad, people may cry, stay in bed, or even commit suicide. Feelings can make people do all sorts of good or crazy things—from falling in love, to being generous, to feeling resentful and getting even. Either we deal with feelings or feelings control us. Or we medicate feelings and become addicted.

I didn't like feelings from the first one I felt. I didn't know what they were, but I knew I didn't feel good. I thought I was the only one who felt pain from being alive. *Something's wrong with me. Other people are happy,* I thought. But even housewives were taking Valium to relax and "mother's little helpers" (amphetamines) to deal with life. All over the world, men and women welcome anything that eases the pain of living. They've been chewing coca leaves, drinking wine, and staying stoned in opium dens for years.

223

When we began naming emotions, we started with four basic feelings: angry, sad, happy, afraid. At first, women thought men had different primary feelings: hungry, has to go to the bathroom, sexually aroused, and tired. Later, we discovered men have the same feelings as women. What men lacked was permission to feel—except for anger. Anger was macho, okay. Eventually the four basic feelings expanded. Now the feelings color wheel has hundreds of emotional shades and hues. But acknowledging emotions created a problem: What were we supposed to do with the little buggers now that we knew they were here?

After Pandora's Box has been opened and the bad in it has escaped, all that's left is hope. It takes more than that with feelings. We need to know—not hope—that what we're feeling right now is perfect, important, but not concrete. Each emotion will come and go in its own time. Let's see if we can learn to speed our emotional seasons up.

Coming to Consciousness

Learning how to deal with feelings became an evolutionary process. The Baby Boomers were becoming adults. We had a strong sense of mission: we wanted to change the world. Consciousness had been around before—hidden in the pyramids of Egypt, buried with Atlantis, mumble-jumbled by Babylon. Whenever we got too smart for our britches, something came along to let us know there was a Power Greater than Us. We wanted to know why we're here, what our purpose is. We wanted to be more than roles. We wanted equal rights. We wanted to know what makes us tick, why we do what we do. People were seeking Truth. We were coming to consciousness. Or maybe consciousness sought us.

Many credible therapies and theories surfaced when we tried to figure out this feelings dilemma. Albert Ellis founded Rational

Emotive Therapy (RET). He said that what we think creates how we feel. RET has validity, but if all we do to create emotions is think, then all we have to do to deal with feelings is simple: think something else. But thinking them away isn't always effective. It's similar to *What came first: the chicken or the egg?* It doesn't matter what comes first because once the egg is laid, it's here. The same is true about emotions.

Feelings have a life of their own.

Therapeutic communities developed a group therapy called The Game. In it, group members shouted anything to the person in the hot seat—lies, jabs, or mean, hurtful truths. The goal was to break through the barrier people created that prevented them from feeling emotions. We wanted to get them screaming, crying, feeling anything—we didn't care what it was as long as they felt something. We wanted people to have an emotional breakthrough. Crack that shell open and something magical happens. A hardened criminal turns into a loving human being. Sometimes this happens after dealing with one repressed emotion. Growth occurs. But we can't run around screaming at everyone to shatter the walls they've built around themselves. We still didn't know how to deal with feelings in a way that works.

Many people turned to talk therapy. They talked about emotions. And talked and talked and talked. Some people reclined on a therapist's couch, paid money, and talked about their lives and feelings for years.

Transactional Analysis devised permissions therapy. It tells people that they *can* feel. This is an empowering technique. It helped me. Permissions therapy is the underlying structure in *Codependent No More.* Giving people permission to feel gives us a key that unlocks ourselves and who we are. It also counteracts the "don't feel" rule, the chains that kept us locked up.

The more we learned about feelings, the more important we

learned they were. Blocked feelings became identified as *the* barrier to joy, functional behavior, opening our hearts, and later even physical health.

We realized that many people in chemical dependency recovery had been medicating emotions. Before the sixties, *The Big Book of Alcoholics Anonymous* identified two problematic feelings: resentment and fear. In recovery, we were taught to constantly ask ourselves and others two questions:

1. What happened?
2. How do we feel about it?

It was suggested that we stay current with feelings and avoid guilt. *Guilt kills,* we were warned. That meant, if recovering people lie and create guilt, they'll drink to cover that horrid emotion. Then they'll become mentally ill, die, or go to jail.

Recovering people were also told to discuss emotions with any people involved with that emotion. If we felt sad about something someone did, we went to the person and explained how what they did made us feel. Oops! Correction. People don't make us feel. Carefully guard our words. Make certain we take full responsibility for how we feel. It was our feeling and we needed to "own it," even though someone's behavior helps us feel that feeling. "If I could make you feel, then I could make you rich," recovering people told one another. "I can't do either. Whatever is happening, you're doing to yourself."

We presumed that if we told people how we felt about what they were doing and these people cared about us, they'd stop doing whatever they did that we were responding to with anger, hurt, and fear. That usually doesn't work. Expecting people to change their behavior so we won't have feelings comes dangerously close to manipulation and control.

After years of people reclining on therapists' couches and many annoying hours of people droning on and on about how they felt, we had an "aha" moment. Talking about feelings doesn't get feelings out. The opposite occurs. Talking, dwelling on, and thinking about feelings often makes feelings grow bigger and feel worse. The bigger an emotion feels, the easier it is to fall into what feels like a bottomless emotional pit. Anger especially escalates by talking about it. The more people talk about anger, the more enraged they become. Talk isn't enough to make feelings disappear.

Louise Hay's book *You Can Heal Your Life* revolutionized how we saw feelings and ourselves. Emotions aren't connected only to thought; mind, body, emotions, and spirit are all connected to each other. We're one with ourselves, whole or holistic beings. Repressed feelings—emotions we don't get out of ourselves—make themselves at home in our body's organs. Anger likes to live in the liver. Grief prefers the lungs. Feelings don't create psychosomatic or fake illness; unfelt feelings literally can make us sick. *You Can Heal Your Life* validated what inner child and family of origin work discovered: Whether we repress them, obsess about them, resist them, ignore them, or talk ad nauseam about them—feelings stay in us wreaking havoc until we get them out.

"Dealing with feelings" means getting feelings out of us.

We weren't certain how to do this, but we were open to any ideas people had and we worked hard. The more we felt, the harder we worked. The harder we worked, the more feelings we uncovered. We wrote in our journals, went to therapy, attended feelings groups, and continued talking about feelings. People in Twelve-Step groups did Fourth and Fifth Steps. Many of us used holistic approaches, hoping that would help. We put crystals on our chakras. We had "rebirthing experiences." We did family of origin work. We bought whatever therapy trend promised to help us get feelings out—from weekend workshops to aromatherapy to wearing copper pyramids on our heads. Listening to the song "The Rose," we'd focus on all the love we didn't get when we were children. We'd cry together, go through boxes of tissues. Some people yelled until they were hoarse in primal scream therapy. If it promised to get our feelings out, count us in! We wanted to get this feelings things over with so we could get on with our lives. We wanted the Great Emotional Cure.

We hoped at the other end of the feelings, we'd find a pot of gold. Surprise! All we found was another feeling. Then another. It was endless. There wasn't a pot of gold. There wasn't an emotional cure. That's when we got it: As long as we were alive and not repressing, we'd be feeling something. Some days, we might have five or ten feelings. Even if we repressed emotions, we'd still be feeling; we'd just be denying or avoiding the inevitable. We opened Pandora's Box. We discovered our emotional selves. We could use whatever technique we wanted, but no matter what we did it would be one feeling after another for the rest of our lives.

Some people reacted to this discovery with cynicism, others dread. We were tired. We didn't want to deal with feelings forever.

We came full circle.

Antidepressants flooded the market. "No worries," the pharmaceutical companies said. "These drugs aren't addicting like 'mother's little helpers' were. People won't get high. Antidepressants and antianxiety pills won't change how you feel."

Ninety percent of the people I know who began taking antidepressants *for a little while* or to get through a bad spell, have now been on them for a decade or more and intend to take them the rest of their lives. "I feel happy, happy, happy now," one woman said. (Until that particular pill would stop working and she'd have to switch medications.) She didn't like her boyfriend and hated her job, but when she took her happy pills, she could tolerate anything—no matter how awful it felt. Frequently, people who take antidepressants lose interest in sex. "It's worth it," one man said. "I couldn't find a relationship anyway. That's one reason I was depressed."

Things aren't bad or good—it's the use or misuse of them that makes them so. But in spite of what the pharmaceutical companies say, antidepressants tend to eliminate legitimate emotions. If people on medication feel feelings, they're surface ones—irritation, annoyance, bitterness. Many people on antidepressants lose their passion. That's what makes their sex drive disappear—not that passion is limited to sex. Numbness has become the predominant popular cultural emotion—along with anger and fear. Even people in the arts are taking antianxiety performance drugs. Reviewers are commenting on the lack of passion that's turning previously stirring live symphony performances of Bach and Beethoven into the symphonic equivalent of Muzak. Do twenty million people or more really have clinical depression? What's the problem? Why are they depressed? What made them chemically imbalanced in the first place? The criteria for getting antidepressants is simple: go to any doctor and ask. You'll walk out with a prescription that day.

Many therapists make it a condition that clients have to take antidepressants or they won't work with them. It makes their work easier if feelings don't get in the way. But how can we experience true growth and transformation if we don't get to the underlying feeling motivating our behavior? Many prisoners are automatically put on antidepressants. Jails in some counties have contracts with doctors so that any prisoners who need to be medicated can be put on medication immediately (an issue that comes up on the board of directors of a diversionary program I serve on). It's not just one city or state that medicates prisoners. From my current work in corrections, it is common knowledge that many prisons use antidepressants and antianxiety drugs widely among the population. It makes prisoners easier to house—especially since prisons have gone nonsmoking. The population is easier to control.

Many people in chemical dependency treatment are immediately and automatically placed on antidepressants, too. I talk to one person after another who gets out of treatment with bottles of new medication. It makes facilitating feelings groups easier if people don't feel. They can talk from their heads instead of their hearts.

I was at the reception desk paying my bill at my holistic therapist's office. We don't do talk therapy; it's a process of looking at whatever emotion is up, and seeing if there's any past emotions connected. We also look to see if the feeling is motivating any behavior or is attached to an inaccurate belief system. (Now we know that emotions create beliefs.) For instance, if I'm feeling abandoned, I might believe I'm not loved by God. That belief gets ingrained in me, affecting how I live. So I want to release the emotion and the inaccurate belief, then let Life teach me—through a series of experiences—something new, healthier, more enlightened, for instance, that I'm loved by God. But it's not an intellectual process. It's discovery, and we integrate it. It gets into our cells and changes how we behave, interact with people, live life. If we let Life trigger emotions, growth happens naturally, organically. That day, I went in to talk about the experience that happened when I went to my high school and saw the picture of me as a teenager and all those thick, mucky feelings started coming out—feelings from my ancient childhood past.

People had been bugging me to go on antidepressants since it happened because I'd felt miserable for months. They were on antidepressants and it bothered them that I wanted to feel my feelings. I explained to the receptionist I didn't want to take antidepressants. I didn't take them after Shane died. Why would I take them now? "It might be pain, but it's my pain, and I want to feel it!" I said. I must have been talking louder than I thought because the other patients in the waiting room applauded my monologue when I stopped talking.

Hurray! I thought. *I'm not the only one who wants emotional color back in Life.* Numbness is contagious. So where do our feelings come from? How do we get them out of us so our lungs don't wheeze and our liver doesn't explode, and the feelings don't control us? What's the trick?

The Secret to Feelings

Gestalt therapy, one of the first approaches to emotions that emerged, came about the same time as transactional analysis and RET. Heavily influenced by Buddhism, Gestalt therapy was developed and written about by Frederick and Fritz Perls. Their approach to dealing with feelings is: Feel them. Get into the emotion. Grovel in it. Become one with it. Feel our way through it. Then it will leave by itself. That's all it wants us to do—acknowledge its presence fully and completely. At first it was like the pioneers crossing the United States before we had roads: feeling each feeling took a long time. Then we became more fluent with feelings. We learned to do it faster and faster—like flying in a jet instead of traveling in a covered wagon.

Here are a few ideas that make feeling emotions easier.

The way to get feelings out is to catch and release. When we used to go fishing, we pulled every fish we caught out of the water and took it home even if we weren't going to eat it. Then we realized fish were living creatures. We shouldn't kill them unless we intended to eat them. It wasted Life. We developed a new way to fish called "catch and release." We caught the fish, tagged it to prove the big one didn't get away, then we set the fish free. That's all we need to do with feelings. We can deal with a feeling in less than a minute (although many take longer), once we learn the trick. We release the feeling and old belief, and Life teaches us something new. Then along comes another emotion, another belief, and a new lesson. It's a natural, organic process called spiritual and emotional growth. We don't control the process. Life grows us.

Resistance, judging feelings as positive or negative, and talking about feelings endlessly will often turn emotions into a bigger ordeal than necessary. I spent ten years grieving the loss of my son. But grief isn't *one* feeling. It's thousands of emotions—one after another along with many lessons about life, living, and death. The process for feeling any emotion of the hundreds that exist is almost exactly the same. We're aware and quiet long enough to identify and feel the emotion. We connect with the original emotional energy. Let the emotion be what it is. Sink into it. Don't resist, push, or try to force it. Don't pretend or act as if. Give in. Surrender. Honor, acknowledge it, whatever words we want to use. We connect with the feeling. We completely feel it. It has to be a perfect fit—like trying on the right pair of jeans.

Resistance to and judgments about emotions can make them unpleasant and hurt more. The more skilled we become at surrendering to the feeling—the quicker we tag the fish and get it back into the water—the easier feeling emotions becomes. Nonresistance helps neutralize pain. The second we stop caring what feeling is in us, the problems from feeling the feeling are eliminated. Whether it's anger, confusion, hatred, or fear, we pull that fish in and tag it. It's ours. We become one with the feeling. Then we breathe it out. Let it swim away into the ocean to wherever felt feelings go.

Judging emotions as positive or negative, good or bad, also makes feeling them more complicated. We judge some emotions as "bad, negative" feelings. Then we call others "good, positive" feelings. But the truth is, they're all the same. They're feelings. There isn't any difference between feeling sad and happy—except the judgment we make in our minds. The second we stop judging the emotions, surrender to whatever it is, then breathe it out, it's gone. It doesn't matter what the feeling is. Think of the most brilliant symphonies ever created. It's the range of moods that make them so stunning—the deep, moody emotions compared to the light trilling. There's as much difference between angry and excited as there is between purple and green. They're both colors.

Different, but the same. We might have personal preferences, but they're all feelings on the color wheel.

The one exception to this is sometimes feelings we call premonitions, or warning feelings. Those may stay with us, like a flashing yellow light, until we see the caution signal flashing.

We need feelings in the world. They help us create great music, books, paintings, and stories. They make everything we do better, because we're emotionally alive. They help guide us. They tell us when we hate the situation we're in or whether or not we love what we're doing and who we're with. They put life in what we do; they show us what interests us. They're the color, passion, and spice of life.

I can't teach you how to catch and release, but you can learn it. You probably won't be able to do a feeling in thirty seconds in the beginning, any more than you could tag a fish that quickly the first time you went fishing. But you can get better and faster each time. Don't make it a contest. Take as much time as you need to connect with and feel each feeling. We're not going to blow through all feelings quickly, but some we can. The most innocuous activities can help bring up and release an emotion—watching movies, laughing, exercising. Our intuition will guide us into doing what we need to trigger emotions. We'll get an idea. If we don't ignore it, we'll do the next thing, feel, learn our lesson, and grow. Obvious activities can trigger emotions: attending family reunions, the death of someone we love, losing a job, or getting a promotion or raise. Events trigger emotions, and so do people's actions.

Contrary to what we were first taught, we don't have to tell everyone each feeling we have, even if it's connected to them. The person was the trigger; the emotion belongs to us. We need to make one person aware of what we're feeling: ourselves. How do we know when we have to talk to a person about a feeling? After we release the emotion, we'll be clear. We'll know what to do. We'll naturally do it. We'll trust ourselves. We won't have to think about

it. When we stop trying to figure out life and intellectualize everything, when we begin to feel and release our feelings, we start to
live organically. Naturally. We do the next thing. We're not living
emotionally driven lives or being controlled by our feelings. We're
living from our center. There are times we need to talk to a person
about a feeling. But do it after we've released the emotion. We'll be
more powerful. People mistakenly think the way to express anger
is scream, holler, or argue when we're angry. All that does is cause
a fight or allow anger to control us. It weakens us. The most powerful expressions of anger are after we've released it. The most effective person in a crisis is the person not acting out of fear. Catch
and release is the secret to mastering emotions. We feel each emotion by becoming one with it for a moment. We let it have its way
with us. Then we breathe it out—like stale air. Then we ask what
we're supposed to learn—if anything—from the emotion we felt.
Or we don't have to ask—Life will show us. Learning the lesson
will occur naturally, by itself.

Sometimes we feel more than one emotion at once: a current
feeling and similar past emotions. We can usually tell when this
happens because our reaction will be more intense than the situation calls for. If something happens and we overreact, it's usually
because we're feeling the current emotion along with an emotion
(or four) that are similar that we have repressed and have kept living inside us for years. How do we deal with those situations? Catch
and release. Intense emotional growth occurs when this happens.
Usually our lessons are like courses: We'll have an introduction,
then beginning lessons. We'll get into the heart of the course, have
pop quizzes and tests. Then we'll finish the class. Emotions will be
part of the entire process, but so will letting go of old, limiting
beliefs, and letting Life teach us new, healthier ones so we can become more enlightened or "lighter" as we go through Life.

I've also found that feelings often come in layers of threes, such as fear, shame, and guilt. Or anger, sadness, and fear. It can be any combination of emotions. But our lessons are leading us to the same place—our Oneness with God, Life, others, and ourselves.

Catch and release is the basic process for all the feelings talked about in Section Three—and any emotions not included in the tests. There isn't one feeling that can't be handled using this technique other than an occasional premonition. But catch and release takes practice. I've been working on it for years. We'll each get the help, teacher, triggers, and support we need when the time is right, if we're open and willing to learn. It doesn't matter where we live or how much money we have. The process will find us. The important idea is the same as when we're fishing: we have to get the hook in the fish's mouth. With emotions, we have to completely surrender to and connect with the way the feeling feels. Don't be scared. It's only a feeling—emotional energy. It won't hurt that much, especially if you don't resist and judge.

Remember, I'm your travel guide. I've walked this path. If I can do it, you can too. Keep it simple. Feel whatever we feel.

ACTIVITIES

1. **Understand our resistance.** What's our biggest barrier to feelings? A family prohibition? Afraid if we start crying, we'll never stop? Too busy? Do we think we're stronger if we don't give in to emotions, if we maintain emotional control? Vulnerability and surrender are strength. If we don't know why we resist emotions, make discovering the answer to the question a written goal.

2. **Best and worst.** What's our favorite feeling? I don't mean the one we most like to feel; I mean the one we most commonly feel, our first reaction to most situations. Some people respond

to almost everything with anger, some with guilt, some fear. What's your most common emotional response? What's the most difficult feeling for you to feel? If you don't know the answers to either question, write the questions as goals in your journal. Life will show us what we need to know.

2 · Dealing with Feelings

Anger is the hardest feeling for me. I turn it inside out. Then it comes out as guilt. Some people do it the other way around: they feel angry when they feel guilty. Some emotions are like coats we can wear with either side out. I'm more comfortable feeling guilty than I am being angry. I was trained that anger is wrong. I have to give myself permission to feel anger, otherwise I'll go right past it and bury it inside myself.

Anger is a difficult feeling for many people. It's not safe to express anger if we're around someone who's drinking or an abusive person. Often, family members may not know how angry they are until the chaos from addiction stops.

When I went to treatment, a family member came to visit. She said the same things to me she'd said for years: I was a liar and a horrible person, manipulating everyone. I had already had my spiritual awakening and was truly sober and working my program. We had a meeting with my counselor. I listened while this person raved on and on about how I couldn't be trusted and I might as well leave treatment now, go live with her. I'm not blaming; this person had lived for years with my active addiction. That couldn't have been a picnic—it would have driven anyone nuts. But as I listened, I felt something shaking loose inside. The truth was, I'd been furious at this person for years. But whenever I even started to feel angry, I went directly to guilt. I'd tell myself I was horrible, a bad person. Then I'd push the anger deeper inside. Because I wasn't medicating emotions now, I couldn't do what I'd done in the past. Suddenly, I started to explode. Sheer unadulterated rage came pouring out of me. I've never roared so loudly in my life. I couldn't stop myself. The dam unplugged. I yelled so long and loudly the walls in the building rattled. I frightened my counselor and myself. That's an example of a current event triggering a current and past emotions where a feeling looks like an overreaction. It isn't an overreaction; it's current and past emotions bursting out, all at once. Most emotional releases aren't that intense but many can be interesting catch and releases.

It was the greatest, most transformative emotional release I've ever had. I felt like overcooked spaghetti for days.

If we've been emotionally blocked for a while, our emotions might start coming out on their own. Watch for hints, clues. We'll begin to become aware of our process. Sometimes we'll feel tired, lethargic. Sometimes we'll feel exasperated. Or we'll feel tense, confused. Feelings don't go away. They stay in us until they come out and we'll know when they do (come out). There are better, safer ways to deal with anger than the way I did, but that was the first feeling I'd felt in years. I was off to a good start.

Sometimes talking or writing in a journal helps us connect with buried feelings. Many activities can help shake feelings loose. While we're writing, we might begin to feel the emotion. We'll get clues, or start to loosen the emotion so it can come out.

It's much better and safer to release anger first, then decide if and how to handle it with any people involved. We'll be aligned with our power. We'll be guided. If we suspect we have anger at someone, ask for it to be shown to us. If we've spent five years numb, not feeling, deadened, we may feel angry for months or a year about all we've endured. I've learned a trick for dealing with feelings I've repressed for a while: I'm ready to put my hand over my mouth so I don't say something I regret. I'm too volatile. Find a safe place to express our anger. If we yell, holler, and blow a gasket while we're driving, roll the windows down in the car. We don't want all that energy pounding around us while we drive.

Anger can be an indicator that we need to set a boundary. Ask our feelings what they're trying to show us. The most ironic thing about anger is that usually the very thing we're working so hard to repress is exactly what Life wants us to feel and express.

1. How angry are we really? When society first began dealing with feelings, we used the charts with the faces. We started out with four faces: one smiled, one frowned, one looked terrified, one cried. Now there are hundreds of faces for emotion. The problem with using the face charts is that many of us have been in denial so long, we'll look at the faces and point to the smiling one. "I feel like that," we say. We may think we do. Emotions will surface on their own because they want to release. If we follow our instincts, doing the most inconsequential activities can be exactly what we need to trigger the next feeling. If we haven't been consciously feeling emotions, we can bet we have some going on. Unless the feeling is tiny—like an emotional hiccup or burp—it's probably current and past emotions together. That happens frequently. Most of us have repressed much more than we realize. If we need help or a jumpstart, we can go to therapy or a feelings group. If we're confident in our emotional skills, we can journal by ourselves. It will probably take more than talk or writing therapy to release the emotions, but by talking or writing, we'll get hints about what we feel. Don't censor. See what comes out.

2. More or less anger. I'm not going to tell everyone they need to get angrier. Anger management has become a social problem. Some people need to feel angrier than they do; others need to stop getting so mad. I had an incident where I bought a new refrigerator. The store delivered it, plugged it in. It didn't work. I told the deliverymen to take it back. They wouldn't; they said their job was done. I called the store. The store clerk said, "You bought it. It's your problem. You've got a warranty. Call the manufacturer." I was livid. This was a new refrigerator. It hadn't worked from the moment it was delivered. There was no way I was going to spend a month getting it fixed. I wanted the new one to work. I told this to the young man, only raising my voice slightly. "I don't have to take this kind of abuse," he said. I was shocked. My God. I didn't help create that kind of inappropriate boundary-setting by writing *Codependent No More*, had I? That's not what I meant at all by telling people not to allow themselves to be abused. Whenever people express anger at us, it doesn't mean they're being abusive. I know some women who refuse to let anyone talk—even in a calm tone—about how angry they feel about them. Some people call any expression of anger or dissatisfaction, or saying no, "abuse." We need thicker skin than that.

Some people need to become angrier, some are too angry. Recovery means learning different behaviors for each of us even though we'll have many common patterns and traits. There's a difference between appropriate expression of anger and verbal abuse. Name-calling, intimidation, threats—that's abuse. Degrading, disrespectful talk is abuse. If you're not sure you're going to properly express anger, put your hand over your mouth. Walk away. Feel your feelings. Then decide what to do and say. I hung up the phone, drove to the store, then asked to talk to the supervisor. Within two hours, I had a new refrigerator in my kitchen—one that worked. Dealing with our anger first is far more effective than dealing with someone when we're in the midst of the emotion. Angry or hostile communication usually doesn't work.

3. **When is it time to let it go?** We need to fully feel and release anger before we forgive, otherwise it's denial. But if we've felt the feeling, it may be time to take the next step. The only cure for being angry at someone is to feel the anger completely, then ask God to

bless the person—even if we're asking fifty times daily—until we mean it. It's time to forgive. Is it time to make peace with someone? Sometimes, it's not a person we need to forgive—it's Life, God, or ourselves.

3 • Fear

The reason I chose fear as an emotion to address in this book is that fear is the underlying emotion motivating manipulation and control.

Fear is cold. It holds us back. It takes the joy out of life. We're afraid the other shoe will drop. Well, if we're listening to somebody take his shoes off and we hear only one shoe hit the floor, another shoe will be dropping or else the person will be sleeping with one shoe on. Is there a reason to be afraid? If you're with an alcoholic not in recovery, there's no reason to fear that person might drink. Plan on it until he or she goes to treatment.

The best thing I did for myself is jump out of a plane. I didn't do it because I was brave. I did it because I was filled with so much fear I wanted to push through some of it, blow the rust out of the pipes. Jumping out of an airplane truly helped me connect with fear. One man was able to go off antianxiety medication after making one skydive. I'm not suggesting anyone skydive. That's as personal a decision as who to marry is. But how afraid are we? Are we so filled with fear we can barely function? Are we afraid of Life? Is there something we're afraid of losing? Are we afraid of losing control? You can't lose something you don't have. People talk about universal fears—fear of death, abandonment, other common fears. Other people—and Elisabeth Kübler-Ross is one—say there are only two legitimate fears: fear of sudden loud noises and fear of heights.

The same process of connecting with emotions helps with fear. But there are also some steps we can take to calm ourselves: meditate, pray, learn breathing exercises. One of the most therapeutic activities to make ourselves stop worrying is to *make* ourselves worry and feel afraid instead of fighting the feeling. If we're anxious and afraid, stop what we're doing. Then sit still and make ourselves feel afraid, worried, panicky, or anxious for fifteen minutes. We may find that the harder we try to stop being afraid, we can't. But as soon as we try to make ourselves feel fearful, we can't feel afraid. The harder we try to feel something, the less we can. It's a therapeutic technique based on Viktor Frankl's Logotherapy and an excellent way to break through resistance. This technique can be used with anxiety, worry, obsession—any of fear's relatives.

One day I went to my acupuncturist. He always asks, "How are you feeling?" I tell him—unless I'm happy. Then I say, "I'm actually completely happy and peaceful, but I'm afraid to say it. I'll jinx it if I do." I'd seen the pattern. Whenever I told him I was happy, I'd be wallowing in emotional muck by the end of the day. Talking about happiness made the feeling go away. We were talking about this when a light went on for him. He finally understood the emotional cycle.

"Stop being afraid of saying you're happy. After you accept being happy and say that's how you feel, maybe you will go home and the happiness will leave and you'll feel angry. Or confused. Or a problem will come up. So what? It's the yin-yang circle. Everything in life is constantly changing—including our emotions. What goes up, comes down. The circle is constantly moving."

From that moment on, I stopped feeling afraid to say when I felt happy. So what if the other shoe dropped or the wheel of life turned? Whatever happens next, happens.

We can count on change. Everything comes to pass, including feelings: the pleasant ones and the miserable ones. Perfect moments don't last. Enjoy them while they're there; then surrender to and enjoy the next emotion and moment, too. Surrender to whatever we're feeling now. That's what true happiness is.

1. Do something scary. We don't have to let fear control us, unless we want to. Eleanor Roosevelt said, "Do one thing every day that scares you." I say, "Do one thing every week that scares somebody else." Let fear become our friend. When unpleasant moments happen, they're out of our hands anyway. We never see them coming and if we did, we couldn't stop them. When we're in true crisis, we're cool, calm, collected. We're at our best. We're probably much better at handling stress and troubles than people who come from quieter, calmer backgrounds. It's been proven that people from troubled situations have a much greater ability to handle stress, uncertainty, and crisis than people from sheltered lifestyles. Let our past work for us. Don't let fear have the upper hand.

2. Know yourself. Earlier, I said if I had to express this entire book in two words, I could: Know yourself. What are we afraid of? Something known? The unknown? Is our fear trying to show us something? Fear can attract the thing we fear. Don't forget—we're protected. We're in God's hands. We may have felt alone, but we're not. If fear is a problem, we don't have to suffer. Meditate, pray, breathe. Then take another deep breath. Now, one more. We can learn to relax and quickly release fear.

4 • Company Doesn't Love Misery

Some of us have been trained to be drama addicts; we've lived with so much crisis and loss we've been numb all our lives. It takes a nuclear explosion or an earthquake for us to feel anything. Drama is like air to us; it's the only thing that makes us feel alive. Drama or misery addiction isn't a feeling; it's an attitude, a state of being and needing.

I used to believe in the power of negative thinking. If I expected the worst, I'd never be disappointed. We can't feel any lower if we're living on the bottom. Now I enjoy not having any expectations at all. Life will take us where we're going. We're protected. We don't need to worry about where we're going. Our job is to surrender to each feeling and the moment we're in now.

Do we know any drama addicts who want to pull us into their crises? It's easy to pick them out, the healthier we become. They'll call screaming and raving. When we pin them down, it's about a speck of dust. The best way to deal with them is ask: Exactly what is the problem? Speak clearly to drama and misery addicts. Tell them they can go down that road if they want, but we're not going with them. Drama and Misery Addiction isn't something we can apply the catch and release formula to, but it belongs with feelings. We'll be less dramatic and miserable the more skilled we become at awakening feeling, and releasing our emotions.

Work at changing our underlying belief that we deserve to suffer. Change it to: We deserve to live in peace.

1. Identify drama and misery addicts. Do you have friends or family who are drama addicts? Are you living in misery? The best thing to do is to be aware. Are you creating drama? Listen for the tone in our voice, the sheer excitement we feel when we have a problem or misery to share, the hyperactivity going on in our behavior. Are we calling someone, trying to drag them into feeling miserable? Why? Instead of creating an earthquake, become the epicenter of peace. When we come alive emotionally, we won't need drama to survive.

2. Give the problems to our Higher Power. List the problems—real or imaginary—in our life on a daily basis. The problems can be big or small. Are feelings bothering you? Worried about some-one? Mad? Something going wrong? Feeling overwhelmed? Bill day and we feel lousy because we never think we'll have enough money even though we somehow do? Now go over the list. Mark which problems are real and which are self-created dramas. Then give ourselves fifteen minutes to worry about all these problems. Feel as anxious and upset as we can, and don't stop until we feel as miserable as we can. I mean, really get into it with ourselves. Misery likes company, so have a party and invite ourselves. Then, after we've worried ourselves sick, officially hand the list of problems to God. Put it in our special place, wherever that is—our God Box, a holy space, a file in our computer. We've done our part—we've worried, gotten upset, and felt miserable. Now, turn our will and Life over to the care of God and go about our day.

3. Rate our progress. If drama addiction is a problem, take the test in Section Three and become aware of our progress twice yearly. Are we improving? Are we refusing to get in someone's car and take the trip to Drama Land? Have we stopped trying to get people to feel miserable with us? Have we stopped creating false problems? Do we feel emotionally alive? Do we spend more time feeling peaceful than we do feeling upset? When we're so peaceful we know we don't need to take this test any more, we'll know we've outgrown our need for drama. That's when we've moved out of the Codependent Zone.

5 · Guilt

Have you ever felt so guilty about who you are that you wanted to go to bed and curl up in the fetal position and hide from God? Have you ever felt so awful about something you've done you feel positive you're unforgiveable? Have you ever punished yourself by not allowing yourself to enjoy success? I have. No doubt. Guilt is the worst feeling there is.

Guilt is slightly different from the other feelings. That's why it's in its own section. One reason it's different is that most feelings have a distinct, recognizable energy. Anger is raging, seething— from frustration to outrage. Fear is cold, icy, clammy. Sadness? So easy to recognize. Some of us cry; some don't shed tears, but we know when our heart aches. Unless we're absolutely numb from denial, emotions have a recognizable emotional sound to them. *Except for guilt.* That devious trickster doesn't vibrate or move at all. Sometimes it paralyzes us so much we can't move. Or it may come out as anger. It can scare us. It tells us if we acknowledge its presence, then we'll be the horrible person we're afraid we are.

This is the irony of guilt. There are two kinds of people in the world: people who feel guilty and people who don't. Often the people who should feel guilty, don't. They don't have a conscience! If they do, it's not connected. Then we have the people drenched in guilt. They are usually the kindest, most loving people we'll meet. We can see and feel the goodness in them. We'd trust them with our lives. We look at them and cannot figure out why they can't forgive themselves. Then we look in the mirror and realize we haven't forgiven ourselves for the same things we've been able to forgive others for doing.

Feelings aren't logical or rational. Guilt is the least rational of them all. There are several kinds of guilt. Let's see which kinds we have.

Legitimate Guilt

If we're doing something that's creating guilt, don't expect to stop feeling guilty until we stop doing it. If we're guilt-prone people, we're not going to get by with it. We won't allow it. Who are we kidding? Look more closely. Are we really violating our standards?

Maybe we're learning compassion—learning not to be so judgmental with other people so we can stop judging ourselves. Maybe the lesson is that we're only human and we don't need to be perfect.

The only cure for legitimate guilt is to make amends. Either apologize, make a living amends, or both. A living amends is where we change our behavior, instead of only saying sorry with words. For instance, we tell people we're sorry we didn't pay them back the money we owed them when we said we would, then we begin making payments on time.

Finish making amends by asking for forgiveness. This can be done by ourselves. My favorite forgiveness prayer is by Howard Wills, a healer and friend: *Please help me forgive them, help them forgive me, and help us all forgive ourselves. Please God. Thank you God.* © *Howard Wills.* Say this prayer as often as needed, even if that means fifty times weekly. Twelve-Step programs and religions have rituals to help us release guilt. We can do all the Steps and rituals in the world, but they won't work until we accept forgiveness, forgive others, and forgive ourselves.

Illegitimate Guilt

Illegitimate guilt is confusing. We may be creating it in ourselves by telling ourselves we should we doing something else, or we haven't done enough in a situation. Some of us have lacked self-appreciation so long that we habitually feel guilty about everything. It's our favorite feeling, the first response we have to most situations. Or guilt could be anger turned inside out. This guilt can sometimes be let go by using the "catch and release" method. Sometimes we get so tangled in our heads we can't tell if it's legitimate guilt or not. Ask for clarification from our Higher Power.

We have every right to be here and to be who we are. If we can't shake our illegitimate guilt, try writing what we feel guilty about.

If we can't figure out what we feel guilty about, it's likely the guilt isn't real. Whenever we're in front of a mirror, look directly into our eyes. Say aloud: "I forgive you," even if we don't know what we did wrong.

Then, ask ourselves if there's someone we haven't forgiven. Sometimes we can't forgive ourselves until we forgive someone else. Do unto others as we want done unto us isn't a suggestion; it's a law about how the universe works. If we're judging others, we won't stop judging ourselves until we stop judging them.

Grief Guilt

It took me a long time to learn about this guilt; nobody told me. I learned it the hard way. I began to notice it in every single person who lost something: Guilt is a stage of grief. It's not real guilt, but it feels legitimate. Whenever we lose something or someone, we blame ourselves. If only we had done more—better, differently—we wouldn't have lost what we did. We'll ask ourselves a million times what we could have done to prevent what happened. Usually, we'll come up with several ideas. Then we torture ourselves with them. I'm not talking about looking at our part in problems or taking responsibility for our behavior. I'm talking about holding ourselves responsible for destiny, Acts of God, and God's will. We're not God. Stop doing His job. We are not the Powers that Be—Thank God.

Grief guilt feels relentless and overwhelming. It's also confusing: We can't forgive ourselves because we haven't done anything wrong—it's a stage of grief. Yet we feel such an underlying sense of responsibility. If we could look at this as a stage of grief and not a feeling—the way unloading the dishwasher is part of doing dishes—it would help. We don't have to take it seriously when it tries to bat us around and make us feel more miserable and grief-stricken than we already feel. We can also allow it to be there, instead of trying to intellectualize or resist it. Grief isn't an intellectual experience. People will tell us we're silly, of course we didn't do it—but that doesn't help. We can't make guilt go away with words, especially this kind of guilt.

We'll whisper, constantly, in this voice to ourselves, saying, *If only I'd done this, or not done that.* We'll tell ourselves horrible things about what we should have and could have done to prevent the loss. It happened. Nothing on this planet happens that is not ordained by God. Stop taking responsibility for God's job. Take responsibility for our job and stop blaming ourselves (or others) for the way the world is unfolding. We're not in charge.

A Stay of Execution

Guilt has many awful side effects. It stops us from succeeding the way we could. We tell ourselves we don't deserve success. Guilt keeps us from feeling peace. Guilt puts a ceiling on us. Sometimes we get sick and don't believe we deserve to get well. If we did, we wouldn't have gotten sick, right? Wrong! We limit ourselves to how much we'll allow ourselves to receive from God, other people, Life, and ourselves. Nobody can put anything in our hands if we won't unclench our fist to receive. Probably the worst thing about guilt, though, is that guilty people punish themselves. We don't even wait for God or Life to dole out our just reward. We're judge, jury, and executioner. We're good at it, too. Some grieving people allow themselves to become abused because they have so much guilt over what they think they did. We punish ourselves by not allowing ourselves to enjoy the little or big pleasures in Life. We suffer. That's what we tell ourselves we deserve. Guilt's a liar!

Stay the execution. The news just arrived: You've been given a reprieve. Let ourselves be fallible human beings the rest of our lives. We can even be a little bad once in a while! We don't have to be saints. We don't wear a halo. We don't have to be this perfect person we tell ourselves we need to be. Perfection is how we torture ourselves. Guilt keeps us from enjoying the gifts of this world—including peace and ourselves. This biggest gift we've been given is life in an abundant universe. We're even allowed to ask for what we want. By reading this segment, know that we have officially been pardoned, let off the hook. For the rest of our lives, we get to be human beings. Furthermore, we do not have to do our best all the time. Sometimes just do what we do.

1. Let ourselves be blessed. Remove the limits of self-hate. We talked about boundaries being the limits of love. If guilt is a problem, then we've put the ceilings, or limits of self-hatred, on ourselves. What do we want that we tell ourselves we don't deserve and can't have? What's that thing we've been wanting, but we tell ourselves we don't deserve? Have you ever really looked at people? They're human. So are we. Why don't we see how much fun we can have and how many blessings we can open ourselves up to for the rest of our lives?

2. Work, work, work. Guilt can be the hardest feeling to release. We may have to work on it and be aware of it much of the time. We may have to constantly give ourselves permission to: take time off, buy ourselves a treat, or relax and watch a movie. We may have to stop and consciously let after-burn—that stinging bite of guilt—pass through us each time we're good to ourselves. Are we ready to be done with guilt? That's all God's been waiting for so He could give us the dreams and desires of our heart. Write a list of everything we'd like to do and everything we'd have if we weren't guilty and really believed we deserved it and there wasn't anything wrong with us asking. Go for the pot of gold. Then put this list in our special place. Give it to God. Give our guilt to God, too. We may have to pull out all the stops. Say the forgiveness prayer. Look in our eyes in the mirror and tell ourselves we're forgiven. Work hard on this one—because we're worth it. Can you imagine what it would be like to live life completely, one hundred percent guilt-free, feeling deserving of all God's blessings? It's possible—for you and me.

3. Forgive others. The only way we can be forgiven is if we've forgiven everyone else. If we haven't, we'll block forgiveness for ourselves. If we haven't forgiven our ancestors, parents, enemies, or friends, we won't forgive ourselves. It violates a law of the universe. Is there someone we haven't forgiven? Whose name passes through our mind and tweaks our resentment? Who can't we think of with peace in our heart? If we truly want to be guilt-free, we have to give forgiveness away to everyone to get it for ourselves. Make a list of all the people (including yourself, God, and Life), that you haven't forgiven. Then go to work at: 1) feeling and releasing all emotions about the names on the list and 2) forgiving every name on that list until we're one hundred percent resentment-free.

4. Be of service. Many people with codependency issues confuse being of service with being codependent. We can be of service without losing ourselves and crossing into the Codependent Zone. We need to be of service to be healthy, to love ourselves, and mostly, to be free from guilt.

6 · The Way to the Heart

One of my biggest leaps or changes in thinking since writing *Codependent No More* is understanding what a huge part grief plays in codependent behaviors. The obsessing, guilt, fear, control—all those are behaviors we do when we're grieving. These behaviors aren't sick. They're normal responses to losing our marriage, seeing our child addicted, taking care of a loved one who's dying. I addressed loss and grief in my other writings about codependency, but grief plays a bigger part in what we label codependent behaviors than I once believed.

The problem with codependent behaviors is that we haven't allowed ourselves to grieve what we lost. We need to know the difference between sadness, depression, and grief. Are we facing a loss right now? Have we lost so much, but we've been too busy to give ourselves time to grieve because we've had to take care of everybody?

I devoted an entire book to grief, *The Grief Club: The Secret to Getting Through All Kinds of Change.* I'm not trying to sell books. I came close to death several times after Shane died. One thing that strengthened my will to live was my decision not to abandon Nichole. But the other factor that influenced me is wanting to make Shane's death count. Readers would write to me, telling me how my writing helped them and how happy they were now. Here I was, drowning in an ocean of grief, couldn't even help myself. It was hard to care about life again. But I didn't want to leave a quitter. Losing Shane was too important not to count. I was watching a movie one evening. In it, each of the characters had experienced one major loss. I watched thinking: *I've lost everything all of them have lost put together, plus more. And those people lost a lot.*

The *Grief Club* covers all kinds of losses—growing up in an alcoholic family, being abused by a spouse, losing someone to suicide, being abused as a child, being placed for adoption, having a serious illness. It includes doing hospice care for a dying spouse, gambling losses, dealing with Alzheimer's disease, Debtors Anonymous, and many more losses. Each chapter is an independent story. There are activities at the end. I put my best into that book. It's dedicated to us—you and me—and everyone and everything we lost. I wanted to make those losses count. I wanted to turn them into healing. If you even suspect unresolved grief is a problem, do yourself a favor. Read that book. Give your heart a chance to heal.

Coming Alive

Feelings are the colors of life. Whether it's pain, joy, deep sorrow, or tears of joy—each feeling is important. We don't have to tell the world what we're feeling. We don't use our feelings to control other people, or tell them what they're doing makes us sad, so they need to stop doing it to us so we don't feel. Our emotional self is the key that unlocks our hearts. By opening our hearts, we will find out who we are, and we'll find joy and peace—not just our peace, but the peace that passes all understanding, the peace of our Higher Power.

Color life vibrantly. Extend our emotional color palette. Go beyond agitation and irritation. Stretch. Reach for all the feelings we can experience. Feelings won't hurt us. They'll bring us back to life, wake us up. Feelings will make us the whole, complete person we already are.

✐ ACTIVITY

Use the list of feelings below for an emotion jump-start. When or if we're not certain what we feel, review the list. What catches our eye? What could it be that we're feeling? Or work the other way. Choose an emotion that appeals to us, then write in our journal about it until we find that feeling or another one—then catch and release it. Also, add any other feelings to the list as you become aware of them.

Abandoned	Bored	Confident	Disappointed
Abused	Boring	Conflicted	Disapproved of
Abusive	Bossy	Confused	Disapproving
Afraid	Brave	Connected	Disbelieving
Agitated	Broken by Life	Constricted	Disconnected
Agonizing	Brokenhearted	Contaminated	Diseased
Aimless	Burdened	Content	Disempowered
Alone	Burdensome	Controlled	Dishonest
Angry	Calm	Controlling	Disliked
Annoyed	Cared for	Crazed	Disrespected
Anxious	Caught	Crazy	Dissatisfied
Appreciative	Centered	Creative	Distracted
Argumentative	Certain	Crippled	Distraught
Arrogant	Challenged	Critical	Distrustful
Ashamed	Charming	Cruel	Dominant
Astonished	Cheated	Curious	Dominated
Aware	Childish	Cynical	Doomed
Awe	Childlike	Deadened	Drained
Babied	Clear	Deceived	Dying Inside
Balanced	Clever	Deceptive	Eager
Bankrupt	Clingy	Defensive	Embarrassed
Beaten	Cloudy-Thinking	Dependent	Empowered
Belittled	Comfortable	Depleted	Endangered
Belonging	Committed	Depressed	Energized
Betrayed ↙	Compassionate	Deprived	Engaged
Bitter	Competent	Deserving	Enlightened
Blackmailed	Competitive	Desiring	Enmeshed
Blamed	Complacent	Despairing	Enraged
Blaming	Complete	Desperate	Entangled
Blessed	Concerned	Despised	Envious
Blocked	Condemned	Detached Coldly	Evil
Boastful	Condemning	Detached in Love	Excited
Bonded	Condescending	Devastated	Exhausted

Expectant	Hopeful	Invigorated	Naïve
Failure	Hopeless	Irresistible	Narcissistic
Fearful	Horrified	Irresponsible	Needed
Fearful of Aban-	Humble	Irritable	Needy
donment	Humbled	Irritated	Numb
Fiercely Inde-	Humiliated	Isolated	Nurtured
pendent	Hungry	Jealous	Nurturing
Flexible	Hurt	Joyful	Obligated
Foolish	Ignored	Judged	Obsessed
Forgetful	Imbalanced	Judgmental	Offended
Forgiven	Impatient	Knowledgeable	Off-track
Forgiving	Imposed Upon	Lacking	Open
Free-Spirited	Imposing	Late	Optimistic
Friendless	Impressed	Lazy	Orphaned
Friendly	Impressionable	Lethargic	Out-of-Sync
Frigid	Impressive	Lifeless	Outraged
Frozen	Improper	Lonely	Outspoken
Fulfilled	Inadequate	Lost	Over Caring
Funny	Incapable	Loved	Over Involved
Furious	Incompetent	Lucky	Overly Concerned
Giggly	Incomplete	Lusting	Overly Optimistic
Gracious	Indebted	Lynched	Overly Respon-
Grateful	Indignant	Manic	sible
Grieving	Infatuated	Manipulated	Overly Sensitive
Guided	Inferior	Manipulative	Overpowered
Guilty	Innocent	Martyred	Overtalkative
Happy	Insane	Maternal	Overweight
Hated	Inspired	Mean	Overwhelmed
Hatred	Insulted	Miffed	Overworked
Helpless	Interested	Miserable	Pampered
Hoarding	Interesting	Misled	Panicky
Holy	Intolerant	Mistreated	Paralyzed
Homicidal	Intuitive	Misunderstood	Paranoid

Passionate	Right	Supported	Unsocial
Passionless	Rigid	Surprised	Unsupported
Paternal	Robbed	Surrendered	Untouchable
Patient	Sad	Tense	Untrusting
Peaceful	Safe	Terrified	Unwanted
Perceptive	Scared	Tired	Unwilling
Perfectionistic	Self-Absorbed	Tolerant	Unworthy
Phony	Self-Loathing	Tortured	Upended
Powerful	Sensitive	Touched by God	Uptight
Powerless	Sensual	Tranquil	Used
Present	Separate	Trapped	Useful
Proper	Serene	Traumatized	Useless
Protected	Sexual	Tricked	Vengeful
Protective	Shameful	Trusting	Victimized
Psychic	Shocked	Ugly	Victorious
Punished	Sick	Unappreciated	Violated
Purposeless	Sickened	Unattractive	Wary
Questioning	Silenced	Uncertain	Wasteful
Receptive	Silly	Uncomfortable	Weakened
Regretful	Sincere	Uncommunicative	Welcomed
Rejected	Singled Out	Unconcerned	Whole
Relaxed	Sneaky	Undecided	Willing
Remorseful	Sorrowful	Undeserving	Wise
Repelled	Spacey	Unemployable	Withdrawn
Repressed	Speechless	Unforgiveable	Worn
Repulsed	Starving	Unforgiven	Worried
Resentful	Stressed	Unforgiving	Worthless
Resigned	Struggling	Unfulfilled	Wrong
Resistant	Stupid	Unjustly Accused	Wronged
Responsible	Successful	Unlovable	Yearning
Restless	Suffering	Unloved	
Restrained	Suicidal	Unlucky	
Revengeful	Superior	Unskilled	

SECTION FIVE

Troubleshooting Guide

1 • What to Do When

An ideal life is lived by responding spontaneously to each situation. We trust our inner guidance; we stay open to the challenges and opportunities in each moment. Although there aren't any rules, some solutions may work much of the time in certain situations. Below are some suggestions for what to do when we encounter common problems. See if these suggestions work. If they don't, try something else. Much of life is trial and error, or the process of elimination. What follows are Rules of Thumb to spark inner guidance about what to do when the following situations occur.

We Don't Know Whether to Stay or Leave

What do we do when we don't know whether to stay or leave? If we've left, how do we know if we've made the right decision?

"I agonized from the day I married my husband to the day I filed for divorce about whether the marriage was going to work," one woman said. "After we finally separated, I agonized for years about whether I'd made the right decision. Now I realize I could have saved myself years of torture by trusting what I wanted, where

I was, and how I felt. The agony I felt after leaving wasn't inde-
cision; it was guilt about violating my religious beliefs about
divorce."

Whether to stay, leave, or reconcile is a common dilemma. If
we're being abused, the answer is clear: leave now. Don't tell the
abuser we're leaving. Don't say where we're going because it could
get us injured or killed. Make a safe, hasty, unannounced departure. That answer is one of the few rules to follow.

The situations that can create years of pain are those in which
we're not being abused but we're consistently miserable. We can't
decide if the relationship is over—if we should leave or stay together for the children.

"My ex-husband would have been perfectly content to spend
the rest of his life making me miserable," said one divorced woman.
*Women are usually more open to change and ending relationships;
men usually want to avoid change at any cost. They'll stay in a relationship eternally, even when it isn't working.*

Don't waste our energy agonizing about staying or leaving.
When it's time to end the relationship, we'll know it. The relationship will be dead; it won't have a pulse. If we don't feel that way yet,
the relationship is living. Stop torturing ourselves. This is the rule
of thumb when we don't know if we should stay or leave: *If we're
not clear about leaving, the relationship isn't over.* Stop resisting. Be
in it. Take care of ourselves where we are.

Sometimes when we worry if the relationship will work, or if
the person will leave us, we're projecting our own desire for the
relationship to end onto the other person. But we're not ready to
admit it. It's okay to be uncomfortable. It's okay to be undecided.
When it's time to end a relationship, it often happens so naturally
it happens almost by itself. Before we can say *it's over,* someone is
on his or her way out the door.

Something's Wrong But We Don't Know What

What do we do when we feel like something's wrong but we're not sure what the problem is? Many things can be going on.

1. Maybe something isn't wrong. Maybe we're sensing a change coming, but we don't know what it is. What we're feeling is a premonition that something is right around the corner. But if it's around the corner, we can't see it yet so we might as well stop trying and wait until Life shows us what it is. One rule of thumb for what to do when something's wrong and we don't know what it is: *Make a conscious decision to wait and see.* A premonition that something's coming doesn't mean something bad is going to happen. It helps to stop judging Life's events as good and bad. All that does is make ourselves feel scared. We walk around with a sense of impending doom. It's out of our hands. Let go of our need to control. Step gracefully into the unknown.

2. Sometimes when we don't know what the problem is, it's because we're in denial. Maybe we've gone numb. We're unaware and we've stopped feeling our emotions. What's happened is, we lost conscious contact with ourselves and Life. A good solution for this is the Gratitude Exercise. Each morning, get up and write ten things happening that we like, dislike, or that evoke a neutral reaction. The rule of thumb here is: *Sharpen our awareness skills.* Soon we'll have a breakthrough. The fog will lift. We'll see what the problem is.

3. Another possibility is that we're being lied to, manipulated, or misled. *If someone is lying to us, we're not in the Codependent Zone; the other person is behaving inappropriately. Don't blame ourselves.* It isn't our fault if someone is skillfully lying to us. That person is likely going out of his or her way to deceive us. We don't

want to run around playing detective. Ask God to turn on the
Light. Ask for help, clarity, guidance. The rule of thumb here is:
Ask for the courage to see and accept the Truth, even if it hurts.

4. Another possibility when we feel like something's wrong is
that it may be something as simple and harmless as we're having a
few off days. Most of us have them. It's a normal part of being
alive. We feel a sense of impending doom. Things don't feel right.
But our response may be blown way out of proportion. It may be
nothing at all. The rule of thumb here is: *This too shall pass.* At least
one-third of the time when I'm convinced disaster is around the
corner, there isn't any problem. Write the question: "What's happening that's making me feel like there's a problem?" Make getting
the question answered a written goal. You'll either settle down or
be shown what the problem is.

We Know We Should End the Relationship,
But We Keep Going Back

What do we do when we absolutely, positively know we want out
of a relationship, but we keep going back?

This can be extremely painful. It can be more painful when it
happens and we resist. Vacillation is a normal part of endings. Resisting vacillation is similar to the Chinese finger-cuff trick. The
harder we try to get out, the more stuck in it we get. Stop trying to
force our way out. Practice nonresistance. So we decided to end it,
said never again, don't call anymore. He or she called. Before we
knew what happened, we went back once more. Now, we're back to
square one trying to convince the person we mean it this time;
we're really done. To complicate things, we've taught the other person that if he or she pushes, our boundaries collapse. It's not the
end of the world.

Become aware. Watch ourselves. Sometimes it's the tiniest behavior that keeps us going back against our better judgment.

"I tried for three years to end a relationship. It wasn't meeting my needs. It wasn't what I wanted. But whenever he called to see me, there I was—despite what I said—seeing him again," one woman said. "Sometimes I'd watch Caller ID and not answer the phone. I'd stare at it, paralyzed, like it was going to jump up and grab me. I wasn't taking his calls but I wasn't free yet—not if I couldn't talk to him and say what I meant.

"One day when we were talking on the phone, I realized that in the beginning of the relationship, I'd been extremely manipulative. I kept acting like I didn't want anything, like it was a casual relationship. The fact was, I did want something. I wanted a commitment. I wanted marriage. I wanted a real relationship. I hadn't been honest—authentic—from the start. Everything I did was designed to control him, pull him in. The problem was, by the time I did pull him in, I realized I didn't like him. That's the trouble with manipulation. We're so busy being dishonest we don't even know if we want what we're trying so hard to get. I couldn't be honest with him now because I didn't know how. I'd never been myself with him; I'd been who I thought he wanted me to be."

This woman stopped resisting. If she got pulled back in, she accepted it. She didn't torture herself or call herself a failure. By observing herself and not resisting what she did or didn't do, she became clearer and stronger each time he called. "It wasn't long before I began being who I was with him," she said. "I started speaking my truth. At first it was in little bits and pieces. Then, gradually I became more of who I really was with him. By the time the relationship really ended, I was absolutely honest with him about who I was, what I wanted, and how I felt. I learned the most important part of the lesson long after I thought the relationship was over. The reason I kept getting pulled back in was because the relationship wasn't over yet. When it was, I stopped going back."

Often we learn the best when we don't know we're learning. When I worked as a newspaper reporter or even now when I interview people, I often get the best quotes when the person I'm interviewing thinks the interview is over and I'm on my way out the door. The person is more relaxed. He or she feels free to be honest. The heart of the story comes out. The same idea applies to any situation where we think we're stuck. The rule of thumb when we keep getting pulled back into something—a relationship, job, or situation—after we think it's over is: *Sometimes we learn the most important part of the lesson after we think class has ended. Stay present. Class isn't over until it's finished!*

We Fall Out of Grace

What do we do when we've been feeling peaceful, then suddenly the Grace stops and we feel controlled, controlling, tense, uncomfortable, and overwhelmed?

We're not always going to feel at peace, in Grace, and led—even when we're taking care of ourselves the best that we can. Sometimes, we revert to control mode. We're scared, feeling like we have too much to do. We try to do five things at once, start running around in circles, and don't get anything done. Then our pile increases from five to six things and we feel more overwhelmed. The rule of thumb when we have more to do than we can do is: *We never have to do anything we don't get the power and ability to do. We don't have to do what we can't.*

Another rule of thumb when we're running around in circles trying to get five things done is an old recovery saying: *First things first.* Break our list of to-dos down by priority, then take it one thing at a time. Instead of trying to do five things at once, focus totally on one thing, whatever needs to be done first. When we complete that, move on to the next.

In some circumstances, we've been pushing ourselves too hard. The reason we're not accomplishing anything and we're feeling tense and controlling is because we're exhausted, worn out, and tired. Instead of working harder, we need to rest. The third rule of thumb for this situation is: *Do the opposite of what we think. Instead of pushing ourselves harder when we're exhausted and overworked, take a break. Don't return to our work until we're rested.* We can often accomplish in minutes what we couldn't do for hours while we were tired. Fill up our tanks.

Other times, our perfectionism kicks in. We tell ourselves we have to have everything done perfectly, all at once. We don't. Know what's on our to-do list. Know what needs to be done and when. If we absolutely can't do it, then we can't. Don't hide, make excuses, or lie. The last time this happened to me, I felt overwhelmed with guilt for being late. Then I found out the other person wasn't waiting for me; he was behind, too. The timing worked perfectly for both of us. The problem wasn't that I was late or behind schedule; I wasn't trusting Life.

What can make us feel most tense and uncomfortable is when we think we have to control things and we don't. Controlling doesn't feel comfortable, especially when we've had a taste of living in Grace. The final rule of thumb for when we feel overwhelmed and like we have to control everything and everyone, is: *Surrender our need to control and be perfect. Settle for excellence instead.*

Our Friends Say We're Crazy, But We're Doing What We Need to Do

What do we do when we're listening to friends and people we trust who are suggesting we need to be doing something, but our hearts lead us down another path? Are we being stubborn, not listening to the warning signs, living by self-will?

Sometimes our answer and guidance comes from people, from what they suggest. Most of us have heard the saying, "If everyone says it waddles and quacks, it's probably a duck." On the other hand, it's all most people can do to figure out what they need to be doing. How can they possibly know what's right for us? God alone knows our heart. Being healthy means listening to and trusting our own hearts—not being controlled by well-meaning friends. Maybe we're learning a lesson they haven't yet learned. Maybe they don't see the situation clearly. It's our lives and what we do is our call.

You're the one who will be living with your choices. "I couldn't live with myself if I abandoned him now," a woman said when everyone was nagging her to leave her relationship. It wasn't an ideal situation, but she wasn't being abused. She wasn't complaining or acting like a victim. She made a conscious choice that what she was doing was what she wanted and needed to do to be comfortable with herself. That's a great definition of health!

This is the rule of thumb for when friends tell us to do something different from what we're choosing to do: *Don't turn our lives and wills over to the care of anyone else other than our Higher Power.*

We Don't Have Funds for Therapy or Treatment

What do we do when we're convinced that the help we need for our growth is out of our reach?

If going to a particular treatment center is something we'd like to do, put it on our goal list, then surrender. Whenever I've needed the most help, I've had the least money. This is the rule of thumb for when we can't afford a particular treatment center or therapist: *If we're sincere and honest about changing and humbly ask for help, we might not get the help we want but we'll get the help we need.*

Examine our motives. Do we need to do this, or is it something we've talked ourselves into believing we have to have? Do we believe someone has a magic wand they can wave and fix us? Nobody does. If that's what we're looking for, save our money and time. People can help, but the point of change is within us. It doesn't come from a particular person or place. We can get where we are.

Sometimes we want to go to a treatment facility or therapist because we're being led and that door is going to open. Other times, it's ego. We want the best and nothing else will do. Have we tried anything else? Have we let go of our need to control the shape and form our help comes in, and accept the assistance we're sent?

We Need to Set a Boundary with Our Best Friend

What do we do when we need to set a boundary with a friend and we know the situation will explode and we may lose this friend forever—or for many years?

A woman wrote to me, explaining how all her life she'd heard that romance can come and go, but friendships are forever. But the problem she encountered was that the closer the friendship is, the more difficult it is to set boundaries. She was dreading setting a boundary she knew she had to set because she knew she'd lose this friend. She wanted to know what to do. All I could do was validate her experience. Friendships can be forever but they can also be the most difficult place to speak our truth.

Some friendships are one-way streets. Often if we do set a boundary, we gain our power but lose our friend. Many friendships are as unbalanced as romantic relationships: one person has the power. The other person centers his or her life around what the friend with the power wants.

In romantic relationships, most people expect to have arguments. Friendships often have different rules. When it comes to setting boundaries, friends can be the worst. Even bringing up a small issue in a friendship can start an argument that spirals out of control. In some friendships, we may feel blackmailed: We either shut our mouth, accept the situation as is, or we lose our friend. We could say that person isn't really our friend. But few of us want to lose someone who's been in our life for twenty or thirty years. On the other hand, we don't want to not be able to take care of ourselves.

There isn't a rule of thumb for this situation. It's difficult, sticky, delicate. The only rule of thumb to remember is this: *When we don't set the boundaries we need to set, we often lose the relationship anyway because we feel blackmailed, unhappy, and trapped. It's not comfortable to be anywhere we can't be who we are and speak our truth.*

One thing we can do that helps is to learn to graciously and smoothly set boundaries. That may not get our point across if what needs to be said is, "You're stuck in the victim role, draining my energy, not taking care of yourself, and it's been going on for years. You're taking advantage of our friendship. I love you. But it's too much for me right now." It's similar to when we confront people who owe us money. Someone is going to be uncomfortable—the person owing us money, or us. We can bite our lip, hold back our words, get peace at any price. We can be the one who feels uncomfortable. Or we can speak our truth and let our friend feel awkward and uncomfortable instead. Move slowly, cautiously. Clear our emotions first. Use our gentle, loving voice. Speaking softly and not coming from an angry, emotional base may not change things. But it might!

How would we feel if our friend set a boundary with us, confronted us on a behavior, or did what we're considering doing with him or her? How would we want him or her to handle it? Sometimes the only rule to follow is the Golden Rule: *Do unto others as we'd like to have done unto us.*

Before confronting a friend, ask some questions. Is our friend always this way or is he or she going through a hard time? Is the person in deep grief or loss? People in deep grief can be a lot of work. But how would we want our friend to treat us if we were grieving? This is a complicated situation. Move slowly. We'll find a path through the mess.

God Is Late

What do we do when God is late?

We work and try so hard sometimes to do and get things right. We find the line between healthy and the Codependent Zone. We're loving others but loving ourselves. Most of all, we're doing our part and patiently waiting, but God is late. There are times when it really looks and feels like God is the one not doing His part.

I don't have a pat answer. I try to be understanding. It's a big world with a lot of universes in it. God has a lot of work, a lot of people asking and waiting for help. I know that there are many people hurting a lot worse than me. I wait my turn in line. Then there's that concept I've learned: living in the mystery. That means, trusting what we don't know instead of trusting what we know and understand. It means having the courage to walk into the unknown. The rule of thumb for this one is: *Take one or two steps more. Right around the bend is when we'll see the Light. God isn't late. We're early. Don't be impatient. Instead, be present for the moment we're in now.*

We Feel Unsupported

Feeling unsupported is one of the classic codependent beliefs, one that many of us have carried around for years. If we want anything done, we need to do it ourselves. We can't depend on anyone; if we do—he or she will let us down. People tell us to trust our Higher Power, but we'd like someone or something we can see, feel, touch to be there for us. We've taken care of so many people. Just once, we want someone to care for and support us.

The first activity in this book is to look in the mirror and tell ourselves that Life is on our side. Let's end this handbook on a similar note. Here's the rule of thumb for when we feel alone: *All these years we've felt like we've been doing it by ourselves, we've been supported by God, people, and Life.* It's easy to see what we didn't get. Practice seeing what we did get, who's there for us, and what we have. We don't have to control anything—including ourselves. A Force bigger than us has been supporting us all along. That support will be there for us. Our only part is to lean into it and trust.

2 • How to Find Help for Almost Everything

Help has never been so easy and so close. For free referrals to almost any kind of help or answer you need—from cancer support groups to help when you don't have enough money—dial 211. Funded by the United Way, the 211 referral number is now in all fifty states and some parts of Canada. A sign of true power is when we're able to admit we need help, and then ask for it.

Go ahead. Show yourself how strong you are. Ask for the help you need, and then act on it when you get it. Not all resources may be right for you. Trying something three times is a rule of thumb when it comes to help—unless you clearly know the first time that this person or resource is wrong for you. Don't talk yourself out of calling resources or referrals by saying, "I asked for help before and they turned me down." After my divorce from the father of my children, I went to the local welfare agency and asked if they could help me. I didn't have medical insurance. The children and I often didn't have enough food. I was in that uncomfortable place between making too much to get any financial assistance and not making enough to live on (and I was living modestly). They turned me down. Somehow we struggled through.

There were many times I thought I should stop writing and get a job as a waitress. I wouldn't be with the children as much, but I'd make more money waiting tables, and I wouldn't have the financial stress. Now, after trying for five years, I finally received a contract to write a book about codependency along with one-third of a $500 advance. Something told me to go back to the Welfare Department and ask for help again. I almost didn't go. But there was no way I could take care of two young children, write for the local newspaper, and write a book in three months. It was physically impossible. I went back to the welfare department with my book contract in hand, and asked for a little help—just for a short time. To my surprise, the woman working the desk said yes. I worked twelve-hour days, seven days a week. At supper time, I'd hear a knock on the door to my cement-walled, windowless office—a four-by-six-foot cubicle in the basement by the washer and dryer. On the floor outside my office would be a bowl of chicken noodle soup and a hot dog. The children had fixed supper for me again. We were in this together—a team.

I finished the book. We had the biggest celebration we'd had in years. We went to Burger King and we each got to have three things: a burger, fries, and a beverage. We had a picnic on the living room floor. We did it! Together, as a family, we climbed the mountain of this book and made it to the top. Less than two years later I was able to pay back the welfare department every penny they had given me. We had five great years until Shane died, shortly after his twelfth birthday.

I'll never forget what it feels like to not have enough—or to barely have enough. I'd also trade everything for one more minute with Shane. Ask for help. Say thank you when you get it. But the most important—the only—thing that matters is the love we give and receive.

Learn to love and take care of yourself. You'll learn to love others better. Being healthy doesn't mean being so tough we don't care, or so hard-hearted nobody can hurt us again. The path we're on might start with not giving so much or so compulsively but living and loving with an open heart—even when that means paying the price of saying goodbye too soon—is where this journey leads. Don't stop until you're there.